# The Global Architect

*The Global Architect* explores the increasing significance of globalisation processes on urban change, architectural practice, and the built environment. In what is primarily a critical sociological overview of the current global architectural industry, Donald McNeill covers the 'star system' of international architects who combine celebrity and hypermobility; the top firms, whose offices are currently undergoing a major global expansion; and the role of advanced information technology in expanding the geographical scope of the industry. The book looks at some of the world's most famous architects and most powerful firms, and its empirical coverage ranges from North America and Europe to the Middle East to East Asia.

**Donald McNeill** is Associate Professor at the Urban Research Centre, University of Western Sydney, Australia. He received his Ph.D. in City Planning from the University of Wales, and is the author of two books: *Urban Change and the European Left* (Routledge, 1999) and *New Europe: Imagined Spaces* (Arnold, 2004).

D1347871

# The Global Architect

Firms, fame and urban form

**Donald McNeill**

Routledge
Taylor & Francis Group

NEW YORK AND LONDON

First published 2009
by Routledge
270 Madison Ave, New York, NY 10016

Simultaneously published in the UK
by Routledge
2 Park Square, Milton Park, Abingdon, Oxon OX14 4RN

*Routledge is an imprint of the Taylor & Francis Group, an informa business*

© 2009 Taylor & Francis

Typeset in Perpetua by Wearset Ltd, Boldon, Tyne and Wear
Printed and bound in the United States of America on acid-free paper by
Edwards Brothers, Inc.

*Library of Congress Cataloging in Publication Data*
McNeill, Donald, 1969–
The global architect: firms, fame and urban form/Donald McNeill. – 1st ed.
p. cm.
Includes bibliographical references.
1. Architecture and globalisation. 2. Architectural practice. 3. Architecture
and society–History–20th century. 4. Architecture and
society–History–21st century. I. Title.
NA2543.G46M38 2008          720.1'03–dc22 2007052146

ISBN10: 0-415-95640-4 (hbk)
ISBN10: 0-415-95641-2 (pbk)
ISBN10: 0-203-89474-X (ebk)

ISBN13: 978-0-415-95640-6 (hbk)
ISBN13: 978-0-415-95641-3 (pbk)
ISBN13: 978-0-203-89474-3 (ebk)

# Contents

# Figures

All photos are by Kim McNamara, used with permission.

# Acknowledgements

This book has been a few years in the making, and there are a number of people and institutions to thank. I came to write it as an outsider to architecture as both profession and academic discipline, having become interested in the topic while writing my doctorate on urban politics in Barcelona, followed by a short visit to Bilbao to examine the new Guggenheim art gallery. I was interested in how politicians and urbanists in such cities were using architecture to at least partially reinvent their identities, and my initial focus was on how these projects were conceived and structured by the local state. Exposure to the Bilbao Guggenheim led me, inevitably, to look beyond the Basque city and ponder how its fame exploded, creating the much-talked-about 'Bilbao effect'. Its chief architect, Frank Gehry, has seen his reputation rise incrementally to the extent that he featured in cartoon form on *The Simpsons*. The work on Bilbao survives in this book, updated to form Chapter 4.

The other chapters have unfolded unevenly around it. Chapter 3 could not have emerged in the shape that it did without the advice of Kim McNamara, who introduced me to celebrity theory. My understanding of non-Western issues concerning skyscrapers, a key theme in Chapter 6, was significantly shaped by Tim Bunnell and the geographers at the National University of Singapore. Chapters 1 and 2 were strongly influenced by the thirty or so interviews I conducted with architects and, in two cases, their publicists in London, Sydney, New York, Melbourne, Hong Kong, San Francisco and Singapore, each of whom took time from their busy schedules to sit down and talk through their firm's operations with me. In some occasions I have quoted them directly, but the collective knowledge of these individuals, combined with a reading of the trade press, provided me with a privileged schooling in key issues concerning architectural firms and their geographical strategies. And they have left me with far more material than could possibly fit into this book. Many thanks are thus due to Keith Brewis, James Calder, Robert Cioppa, Ralph Courtenay, John Denton, Richard Doone, Peter Drucker, Roger Duffy, Francis Gretes, Keith Griffiths, Ivan Harbour, Richard Hassell, Ralph Heisel, Tan Kok Hiang, Ken McBryde, Nadja Leonard, Zak McKown,

Patrick MacLeamy, Stuart McLarty, Mark Middleton, Brad Perkins, Lee Polisano, Richard Saxon, Gene Schnair, Sam Spata, Ken Shuttleworth, Chuck Siconolfi, Stephanie Smith, Nick Terry, David Tregoning, Raphael Viñoly and Andrew Whalley.

As noted, I have published some of the material used here elsewhere, though I have trimmed, expanded, restructured and updated it where appropriate. A few sections in Chapters 2 and 3 have been cut and reframed from D. McNeill (2005), 'In search of the global architect: the case of Norman Foster (and Partners)', *International Journal of Urban and Regional Research* 29 (3): 501–15. Some of the sections in Chapters 2 and 4 on 126 Phillip Street and Aurora Place, Sydney first appeared in 2007 as 'Office buildings and the signature architect: Piano and Foster in Sydney', *Environment and Planning A.* 39: 487–501. A version of Chapter 4 was published as 'McGuggenisation: globalisation and national identity in the Basque country', *Political Geography* (2001) 19: 473–94. A small section in Chapter 5 on AMO/OMA's rebranding of the European Union was published as 'Performing European space?', *European Urban and Regional Studies* 13 (1): 83–7, in 2006. Chapter 6 was partially derived from 'Skyscraper Geography', *Progress in Human Geography* 29 (1): 41–55. Sections of Chapter 7 appeared in 2006, published as 'Globalisation and the ethics of architectural design', *City* 10 (1): 49–58.

Thanks to my friends and colleagues at the Urban Research Centre, University of Western Sydney, and the Department of Geography, King's College London, for their interest in this project and collegial support. For funding, I would like to acknowledge the assistance of the British Academy and the Nuffield Foundation for grants that allowed me the geographical scope to carry out the interviews. Particular thanks go to Stephanie Smith of innovarchi for her feedback on Chapter 2; and to Susan Fainstein and Kenneth Frampton for introducing me to some key people in New York, and in London to Leslie Sklair and Conor Moloney for their collegial interest in these themes. At Routledge, I am grateful to Dave McBryde for commissioning this book, and to Steve Rutter for his enthusiasm, patience and guidance in the later stages of publication. Many thanks also go to Sharon Zukin and the anonymous reviewers of both the proposal and the draft manuscript for their supportive comments. Anne Horowitz and Beatrice Schraa provided invaluable editorial support and guidance.

Above all, thanks to Kim for her love and support, and to Carol, Sue and Kevin, and Mia, Mikaela, Robert and Robyn for everything.

# Introduction

Architects have always been avid travellers. In 1665, Bernini was invited to Paris by Louis XIV to work on the Louvre, his fame travelling before him, in one of the earliest examples of an architectural star system (Filler 2007: xvi). In 1754, the Scottish neo-classical architect Robert Adam made a tour of the most famous buildings and sites of antiquity of France, Italy and Dalmatia, combining 'the attributes of student, well-to-do traveler, explorer, collector, and scientific observer' (Ockman 2005: 161). In 1929, Le Corbusier visited South America, his return voyage enlivened by a meeting with Josephine Baker; he would even impersonate the dancer at an on-board costume ball (Bacon 2001). In the 1940s, the advent of Nazism drove some of the leading proponents of the Bauhaus – Gropius, Breuer, Mies van der Rohe – into exile in America, where they would help to redefine commercial architecture. American design and construction firms have been operating internationally for over a century, driven partly by US foreign policy initiatives, but partly too by an early export-consciousness on the part of construction firms (Cody 2003). And over several centuries, colonial adventurism has seen the systematic, state-aided export of architects, engineers and building systems, leaving behind a fascinating set of architectural trails around the world (see, for example, Cohen 1995; King 2004; Nasr and Volait 2003).

This book describes the rapid intensification of these travels, to a point where overseas work is a routine aspect of contemporary architectural practice. The territorial boundaries that had kept most architects tied to a small set of national markets no longer make much sense for design firms capable of operating in the dynamic economies of the Gulf and China. This is a moment in which architectural studios have suddenly been flooded with graduates of unprecedented technological literacy, able to manipulate the shape, structure and function of a building without recourse to pencil or model. The geopolitical fixities of the Cold War softened up to create new markets in East and Central Europe, and 747s take architects with home offices in places rarely associated with global renown, and drop them in equally unlikely locations (Genoa to New Caledonia, Melbourne to Wiltshire, Venice Beach to Bilbao, Rotterdam to Seattle, Basle to

Beijing), wired up with a battery of Blackberries, virtual white-boards and high-speed laptops.

What might a global architecture be? For some, it reflects the logic of the free market, or transnational capitalism. In this context, we might understand architecture as a range of 'spatial products' (Easterling 2005: 3) which plug territories into global economies. These are, in the words of Keller Easterling, the 'Teflon formats of neoliberal enterprise', such as 'resorts, information technology campuses, retail chains, golf courses, ports, and other enclave formations' (2005: 1). Here, global architecture equates with cultural homogenisation, leaving a rash of seemingly identical airports, office towers and new town developments scattered across Germany, Thailand and Australia. For others, it has meant the sprinkling of iconic, or would-be iconic, structures in capital cities and regional centres, be they museums, parliament buildings or universities. These strikingly formed buildings – and the Sydney Opera House was perhaps a watershed moment for architecture in a media age – are consumed and registered as the backdrop to television car adverts, casually registered from the front of a postcard, or not least, consciously visited in an ever-growing circuit of international tourism.

In the chapters that follow, I discuss the globalisation of architecture within a set of perspectives emerging from human geography and sociology, located in a

*Figure I.1* Sydney Opera House.

range of processes which are shaping the way in which architecture as a profession, as an art form, as a business, is being conducted. These perspectives include the economic geography of architectural firms within global capitalism; the evolution of architectural practice from the auteur to the multinational full service firm; the sociological literature on presence, distance and proximity; the nature of place identity and the built environment, as understood by cities; and buildings as 'condensation sites' of broader political and cultural narratives. There are a number of important discussions of these areas, which have helped shape the ideas in this book, including critical accounts of architectural practice within wider social processes (Frampton 2005; Harvey 1994; Imrie 2003; Knox 1987; Sklair 2005; Zukin 1991). However, the most significant works for my purposes are those that delve deep within the architectural profession, such as the work by Cuff (1992) or the contributions gathered by Saunders (1996). The importance of a 'heteronomous' as opposed to 'autonomous' approach to understanding architecture, giving agency to the client, the public, the media, the politician and the building professions in the development of architectural product, has been brilliantly developed by Magali Larson in *Behind the Postmodern Façade* (1993), an important starting point for this work.

This perspective highlights the fact that architectural practice is driven and structured by powerful forces that have little to do with architecture itself. The usefulness of seeking out the 'heteronomy' of architectural design in a global context is theoretically elaborated by Kris Olds in his book *Globalization and Urban Change* (2001):

> While the rhetoric and discourses associated with the profession [of architecture] hark back to the day (idealized of course) of independent artistry, architects today are *dependent* upon numerous other processes, institutions, and actors to enable them to engage in work . . . [A]rchitectural professionals who provide services to prestigious clients, must be aware of their situated position with respect to relational networks, institutions, and key material outlets (i.e. texts) for their ideas. This is because they often attempt to implement a myriad of internal (professional) and external (societal) goals during the processes of formulating the images that they hope to see inscribed in the landscape.
>
> (Olds 2001: 141–2)

So, while the architects and images travel fairly easily, their scope of operation remains fixed within local regulatory systems, financial cycles, socially acceptable aesthetic discourses and vernacular design histories, and political decision-making processes. To be successful, architects must know how to run a business. They need to successfully partner or interact with other built environment professionals, be they urban planners, quantity surveyors, project managers or structural engineers. And they need to communicate effectively with clients, those who actually pay for and commission buildings, who are as a group highly diverse, including politicians on government building committees, corporate Chief Executive Officers, property fund managers, civil servants and so on. When designing abroad, they will need to take into account cross-cultural differences and protocol. So, we can surmise that architectural practice is embedded within a range of practices of varying complexity and spatiality, covering corporate structure and practice, financial cycles, expert knowledge systems, corporeal travel and cultural trust, political expediency and culturally relative aesthetic conceptions (Olds 2001).

My starting point is to consider the architectural *firm*, a fundamental unit in the geographical organisation of the production process. Thus Chapter 1 seeks to map out the new geographies of architecture as understood as a business practice, and explores how markets are understood and constructed by architects. I consider how many firms are developing innovative modes of business organisation through joint ventures and strategic alliances, and how firm size is an important determinant of architectural output. The firms covered in this chapter include Skidmore, Owings & Merrill, perhaps the epitome of the architectural 'megapractice', but also Aedas, a branded firm that evolved from the merger of two medium-sized practices with very different regional markets, and Foster and Partners, who have developed into one of the most significant firms currently operating around the world.

A key issue here is how firms organise themselves to meet the challenges of *regularly* building in distant cities. Many architecture firms possess a certain aura, ethos, way of working, reputation or hierarchy that may be challenged by designing internationally, either due to concessions to joint working, or through firm expansion. So Chapter 2 explores the techniques used by firms to increase their ability to operate at a distance. The improvement in air travel has expanded the latitude of lead architects to travel almost without limit; intranet, email and increasing band-widths have very recently offered greater scope in linking head design studios with site offices; outsourcing has opened up the possibilities of twenty-four-hour working. I illustrate this through a case study of an office tower, Sydney's Aurora Place, which was designed at distance by Genoa-based Renzo Piano Building Workshop working in partnership with locally based architectural teams. Strategic decisions have to be taken on how the principal design studio, or studios, are operated, and where the key designers are located. I continue the discussion of Foster and Partners by exploring how they have expanded their scope to meet client demand and new market opportunities, while maintaining the leadership of charismatic name 'designers'. I also examine the importance of face to face communication in the successful operation of an international firm, and describe the annual MIPIM property fair, held in Cannes, which provides ample opportunity for commercially-minded architects to mingle with politicians, property developers and investors.

In Chapter 3 my focus turns more explicitly to the nature of the architectural star system. It begins by discussing the rise of Daniel Libeskind as a media-savvy 'starchitect', who has used a variety of forms of publicity to project his design significance to a variety of publics. The chapter then focuses on the nature of 'brand' and 'signature', and again uses Norman Foster as a central case study. The chapter discusses the role of a design leader as a source of inspiration, but focuses in particular on the search for a unified, consumable style (a brand), as balanced with an innovative, unpredictable 'signature' (alluding to roots in artistic creativity). It suggests that peer esteem combined with broader public recognition are fundamental to the creation of the celebrity architect, and I highlight the importance of travel – both to the building, and of images of the building – to their professional success. It then evaluates the ability of an architect's signature to add value to the building that they have designed.

In Chapter 4, I turn to one of the most celebrated iconic buildings in recent times – the Bilbao Guggenheim. My intention here is to deepen the understanding of the nature of the client relationship by exploring the situation of the museum within Basque geopolitics and culture. With cities riven by de-industrialisation and governments unwilling or unable to raise taxes to bail them out, urban managers such as mayors, chief executives or head planners have come to treat the city as a corporation seeking to gain a market 'niche' in competition with other entrepreneurial city rivals. I then move on to explore the 'Bilbao effect', which has been attributed to the commissioning of signature architects – Hadid, Piano, Meier, Koolhaas, Gehry, Foster, Calatrava, among others – to rebrand, reposition, or otherwise publicise the cities of advanced capitalism through boldly expressive showpiece museums, libraries, concert halls, railway stations and convention centres.

Embedded within the discourse of global architecture lies the deep contradictions of pursuing autonomous aesthetic projects, and satisfying (or promoting) capitalism as a cultural and organisational form. Rem Koolhaas has been one of the most original thinkers on the nature of contemporary architectural practice, and Chapter 5 critically considers some of his key interventions. His firm, the Office for Metropolitan Architecture (OMA), and their fledgling brand consultancy AMO, have sought to interrogate the scope of architectural practice under conditions of globalisation. Along with many other projects, AMO has worked on a rebrand of a commercial enterprise (Prada) and a public entity (the European Union) and has developed a powerful and innovative publishing strategy for the firm. Working through a reflexive position on the challenges facing the architect, Koolhaas – despite seeming to revel all too frequently in provocation and sloganeering – also displays an astonishing ability and willingness to expose the messiness of contemporary urbanism.

Chapter 6 highlights the ongoing contradiction faced by designers who are often asked to produce standardised design solutions, as opposed to those who are asked to produce 'difference' through an iconic design. By focusing on the 'geography' of the skyscraper, the chapter considers the embrace of height as an indicator of national virility in the so-called 'tall building race'. Tall building technology has been an important US manufacturing export for much of the twentieth century (Cody 2003). Companies such as New York's Milliken Brothers prefigured contemporary debates in the first decades of the twentieth century with their establishment of branch offices in cities as diverse as London, Cape Town, Mexico City, Honolulu and Sydney to serve different regional markets. I suggest that skyscrapers be understood 'relationally' in terms of their role as connecting agents in colonial and post-colonial economies, and I discuss the role of expressive buildings in the context of the Gulf. I then consider the role of contextualist skyscraper design, where Western architects seize on local or vernacular motifs as they seek to avoid charges of homogenisation.

In Chapter 7 I discuss how architects are challenged by important ethical issues within a capitalist economy. As Blau has argued:

> Unable to secure a monopolistic control over building, architecture is extremely vulnerable to economic fluctuations. The vulnerability is the source of continual controversy over what professional firms can and cannot do to keep a foothold in the market without jeopardizing professional ethics and integrity.
>
> (Blau 1987: 12)

The autonomy sought by designers is compromised by any number of things: beautifully designed airports only add to global warming; well-meaning monuments can take on stark new symbolism under repressive regimes; the place-making rhetoric of architect-masterplanners can be cannily manipulated by developers to seek zoning changes, greater building volume, and planning approvals. I discuss a number of case studies where leading architects have undertaken controversial commissions – Chinese State Television, airport design and major urban redevelopment schemes – which require careful ethical consideration.

# 1 The globalisation of architectural practice

There can never have been a moment when quite so much high-visibility architecture has been designed by so few people. Sometimes it seems as if there are just thirty architects in the world ... Taken together, they make up the group that provides the names that come up again and again when another sadly deluded city finds itself labouring under the mistaken impression that it is going to trump the Bilbao Guggenheim with an art gallery that looks like a train crash, or a flying saucer, or a hotel in the form of a twenty-storey-high meteorite. You see them in New York and in Tokyo, and they are, with just two exceptions, all men; they are on the plane to Guadalajara and Seattle, in Amsterdam, and all over Barcelona of course.

(Sudjic 2005b: 296)

Often seen as 'boutique' or 'signature' architects, the likes of Renzo Piano, Daniel Libeskind or Cesar Pelli are noted for having a small number of high-profile projects in sensitive, often city-centre, sites. These architects – with a strong visual code that travels easily – are often commissioned by governments and public sector bodies for this very reason. Nonetheless, the vast majority of globalising architectural practices are engaged in volume building, running multiple commissions in different countries concurrently. For these firms, the challenge faced is that of growth and expansion into new markets. For them, mergers and strategic alliances are rational business practices, allowing them to gain competitive edge by their size and internal efficiency, delivering buildings to clients on time and to budget.

The key point considered in this chapter is that firms have to consider how they organise themselves both geographically (in terms of territory), and sectorally (in terms of expertise at particular types of work). Firms often refer to this as a matrix. As such, reaching a global client base is not as simple as opening branch studios located in key cities in regional markets. It also involves being aware of – and logistically able to – compete in sectors with a strong overall growth worldwide, which is particularly important when looking for repeat business from particular clients. The challenge for firms is to work out how best to organise themselves to be proximate to clients while having the reach to operate in several geographical markets simultaneously. The globalisation of property markets and, as a consequence, the increasingly competitive nature of the architectural profession has seen the emergence of major practices from a number of different countries, but has also offered opportunities for relatively small practices with global ambitions.

This chapter identifies some of the key issues surrounding the growing significance of globalising processes for architectural design. I begin by discussing the locational geography of globalised architectural practice, charting the nature of architectural markets, both geographical and sectoral. I discuss some of the challenges involved in designing in China, one of the key geographical markets for Western firms. Second, I consider the nature of the architectural firm, and the specific nature of architecture as a business activity. I consider the importance of size, exploring the 'boutique' firm, typically small in size, with a small number of projects at any one time, with growth horizons deliberately limited to retain a close correlation between the input of its founding partners and the design process. Three firm case studies follow which are indispensable to any discussion of globalisation and architectural practice. One is Skidmore, Owings & Merrill (SOM), seen as being an exemplar of the globally operative 'megapractice'. Another is Aedas, probably the most self-consciously 'constructed' global firm, who have rolled out a global practice on the basis of a clearly defined, deliberately executed business model. The third is Foster and Partners, who have the distinction of being a megapractice that has been built around the figure of one charismatic designer. Taken together, I argue that an understanding of architecture as a process requires a consideration of the organisation of the firm, and of the business of architecture.

## Architectural practice and the race for new markets

Who are the global architects? One of the best attempts to identify these firms was first instituted by the now defunct magazine *World Architecture*, subsequently published as the World Architecture 200, then 100 by *Building Design* magazine. The surveys provide architecture's equivalent to the Fortune 500 ranking of firms. While not independently audited (firms voluntarily return surveys sent out by the magazine), the tables give a broad-brush view of the major firms operating worldwide. The 'headline' table is a basic listing of the world's firms according to their size (measured in terms of employees, with a ballpark figure of annual fee income). Large firms will have in excess of three hundred registered architects working for them at any one time. In addition, the tables are disaggregated and reconstituted in two basic ways: into regional markets, and into market sector. However, a key point to consider is that each of these regional and sectoral markets deliver substantially different fees. While the top-ranking firm in Africa,

Boogertman and Partners from South Africa, earned $9.8 million in 2005, the leading North American market player, Gensler, achieved $212 million in that year. And while the fairly specialised – and largely state-funded – criminal justice sector delivered the DLR Group $20 million in fees in 2005, commercial building would yield $151 million to Gensler.

The survey ranks firms across sixteen sectors: urban design, hotels, transport, health care, sports stadiums, government buildings, residential, retail, education, leisure, defence, masterplanning, cultural, industrial, criminal justice and business design. Of the top-placed firms in the World Architecture 100, the vast majority will have specialist teams working in many of these sectors. Most of these firms have originated in, and remain controlled from, the US. Firms such as Skidmore, Owings & Merrill, RTKL, Hellmuth Obata Kassabaum, Gensler and Perkins and Will have gradually built up a reputation for strong, solid and reputable project delivery in the commercial sector. Along with other major players, such as Nikken Sekkei, the giant Japanese firm, and the UK-based Building Design Partnership, these practices have tended to operate a branch office strategy, a necklace of regionally based subsidiaries which compete in specific regional or sectoral markets (Knox and Taylor 2005).

There are nine regional markets listed: Central and South America, Central and Eastern Europe, Pacific Rim, Central Asia, Western Europe, Australasia, Middle East, North America and Africa. These markets are unlikely to have entirely congruent economic cycles, and the past two decades have seen regional economies rise and fall. Design firms have had to decide their expansion strategies accordingly. For example, the East Asian currency crisis of 1997 constricted a number of large emerging economies, particularly Thailand, the Philippines and South Korea, which had initially offered lucrative commissions for overseas designers. The deregulation of British financial markets, followed by European financial integration, opened up the European marketplace in the early 1990s, with firms such as Kohn Pedersen Fox, Hellmuth Obata Kassabaum and Skidmore, Owings & Merrill opening design studios in London. The Middle East, and particularly the United Arab Emirates, have proven to be important markets in recent years, which in turn has driven demand for architectural services.

A word of caution is required, however. Most major firms – even those who work abroad – rely substantially on work in domestic markets. It is a striking fact that the architectural world is still noticeably regionalised, and may continue to be so. Many of the firms considered here, however, are interested in designing abroad either as a means of diversifying their client base (to help ride out localised recessions), or as a means of seizing repeat business as existing clients globalise, or as a result of having a particular sectoral expertise that can only be fulfilled by doing similar work when and where it arises around the world, or because the challenge of building in a foreign context is professionally and personally satisfying.

It should come as no surprise that one of the key markets for architects over the last decade has been that of China. Ever since the Chinese Communist Party's dramatic policy shift in 1978, which opened up opportunities for capitalist business practices and land relations, the country has undergone a drastic process of urbanisation (Olds 2001). China's rapid economic growth has offered many opportunities for Western firms to gain work, whether from France, Germany, the Netherlands, the UK or the US. This has a number of dimensions. First, Shanghai's early emergence as a major economic powerhouse in the mid-1990s generated a raft of new architectural commissions, from conservation-minded approaches in the heritage quarter of Xintiandi, to the development of a new office centre at Lujiazui with a number of prestige skyscraper office buildings. Second, Beijing has become an important centre for signature architects, from Herzog and de Meuron, designers of the Beijing Olympic Stadium, to Paul Andreu (of the National Theatre), to Rem Koolhaas' OMA, who are designing the Chinese State Television headquarters. Third, the explosive building boom in the Pearl River Delta (roughly speaking, the triangle between Hong Kong, Zhuhai, and Guangzhou) that followed its assignation of Special Economic Zone status under the Open Door Policy, offered some openings for foreign architects. Fourth, major cities in the rest of China, such as Chongqing, Changsha and Tianjin, are growing rapidly, creating their own demands for new airports, new towns and shopping malls.

Gaining work in China provides a challenge to these Western firms (see Bielefeld and Rusch 2006; Nussaume and Mosiniak 2005). For example, Gene Schnair of SOM has pointed out the difficulties of retaining control of design quality:

> Many Western firms end their involvement after the schematic design phase and then hand the project over to the local professionals, whose interpretations often miss the original designer's intent. SOM insists on extending its role one step further, preparing architectural design development documentation, which takes the design to a preliminary level of construction documents.
>
> (2004: 24)

For Nikolaus Goetz (2006), a partner in the German firm Von Gerkan, Marg and Partners (gmp), there are a number of obstacles to be met:

> We are constantly confronted in China with a 'legal jungle' that is not easy to comprehend fully. This problem can only be solved if we, as German planners, enter into a planning partnership at the earliest possible moment. But ... this model raises the risk that the Chinese partner, after working with the Western architecture practice for a time, will persuade the client that it is possible to go on planning and building without the foreign partner.

Ultimately, he will say, he has managed to learn enough from his experienced Western partner already.

(Goetz 2006: 134)

There are further problems. These include complications over liability insurance, where the foreign firm – if commissioned as master planners – is responsible for the work of the local partner. Then there are the cultural challenges: 'Europeans often act more emotionally, while the Chinese usually hide their emotions behind different behaviour. Here I am thinking of the Chinese smile, for example, which by no means always means agreement. Acknowledging this and being aware of it can avoid a lot of disappointment' (Goetz 2006: 135). As gmp also found, there are differing client expectations over the architect's role:

> one of our Chinese clients expected gmp to find appropriate arguments to double the area of a building volume that had been restricted to 100,000 square metres. Green areas needed in terms of urban development were to be built on, or fixed building heights exceeded by 40 to 50 metres.
>
> (Goetz 2006: 136)

For Gene Schnair of SOM, the prevalence of design competitions means that 'the flashiest design usually wins, sometimes at the expense of functionality, durability, and the larger urban design issues' (Schnair 2004: 24).

However, while the Chinese market was red-hot for foreign architects from the mid-1990s, most predict that this will not last for much longer. As Luna (2006: 33) notes, 'The majority of non-Chinese firms presently engaged in the country will continue to play an important but ultimately transitional role in the transfer of technology'. In their place, Chinese-owned firms will initially grow their domestic market share, and seek opportunities abroad, initially in the Southeast Asian and Indian markets. Already, there are a number of Chinese architects that may feature in a future Chinese star system: Rocco Yim (Rocco Design), Ma Qingyun (Mada S.P.A.M.), Gary Chang (Edge Design Institute) and Ai WeiWei (Fake Design). Along with these boutique firms, the huge state-run design institutes will presumably evolve into fully commercial operations (Xue 2006). The high-profile commission to design a new headquarters for Chinese State Television in Beijing (discussed in Chapter 7) paired Rem Koolhaas' OMA with the East China Architectural Design Institute (ECADI):

> For the whole duration of the year 2003, ECADI sent a total of 20 designers, including architects and structural and MEP engineers to Rotterdam to participate in the design, but also to share many everyday routines with the members of OMA. During schematic design and preliminary design, many ideas were exchanged – ECADI was learning about the design philosophy

and practice of OMA while providing insight into Chinese codes and building practices and allowing the scheme to develop smoothly towards its implementation. During the construction drawing stage, OMA also sent several architects to Beijing to join the design team of ECADI to continue the cooperative aim and spirit.

(Li Yao 2005)

In turn, we can expect an increasing sophistication on the part of Chinese clients, reflected in a greater willingness to commission Chinese architects for major projects. Clients such as Zhang Xin, of the property developers SOHO China, have nurtured indigenous architects as well as commissioning foreign designers, for the increasingly important high-end residential market (Wu 2004; Xue 2006). In addition, private practices are complementing the monolithic, state-led design institutes which have dominated major construction projects. These architects are increasingly trained abroad, and are returning with an altered sensibility about the nature of Chinese design. For example, as Levinson (2004) notes, these new private practices are strongly branded: practice names include Standard Architecture, Original Design Studio, X-Urban, United Design Studio, Atelier 100s+1. However, 'unlike their counterparts in the East Village or East London, where such practices often generate little but paper projects, private practitioners in China are benefiting from an abundance of opportunities to build' (p. 76). It appears likely that in a decade or so, we will see the consolidation of a generation of multilingual, highly creative Chinese architects who will contribute to the development of new paradigms in architectural design. Until that point, the Chinese construction market in major cities – and not just Shanghai and Beijing – will continue to see major foreign firms (usually invited by competition) working on both large public commissions, and commercial construction.

There is one further point to consider in terms of regional markets, which is the choice of city for the location of a firm's studio. In Southeast Asia, for example, many firms find that Singapore and Hong Kong have a convenient business climate (in everything from taxation policy through to convenience for air travel through to use of English) as well as being excellent geographical bases for reaching a range of national markets, such as Indonesia, Malaysia, India or China. Small firms such as Singapore-based Woha Design or Forum Architects are thus able to expand their geographical reach despite the relatively small number of domestic opportunities. In the context of the US, East Coast studios are seen as key in order to have a presence in European markets, while a West Coast office has an easier relationship with Asia. As I discuss below, firms have adopted a wide range of strategies in terms of relating to their client base, having a strategic hold in particular markets, and achieving design goals.

## Working with clients

> With the deregulation of financial markets (especially international lending), the growth and geographical expansion of pension fund investing, the emergence of new mechanisms to link real estate financing more closely to broader capital markets (securitization), the lowering of barriers to foreign investment in land, and the development of vastly improved information databases on property markets, global real-estate strategies are now being pursued with vigour.
>
> (Olds 2001: 23)

It may be a simplistic point, but without clients, architects would have little to do except design and speculate on paper. And there can be little doubt that the key driver of overseas expansion by architectural firms is the corresponding growth strategies of transnational corporations. Whether working directly for a property development consortium, or servicing public clients such as governments and their associated agencies, architectural practice is absolutely central to the property development process. The product that architects sell, then, is strongly determined by the economic constraints and space demands made by the client. As Nick Terry of Building Design Partnership (BDP) notes:

> Design innovation is a key thing, but it's not at the simplistic level of just a visual image, that's important obviously, but – this is where sector expertise tends to come in – you can get two or three architects to design an urban regeneration scheme based on retail, let's say, and the layperson, or the client who hasn't done it before, probably won't be able to tell much difference between them. They'll see different architectural treatments, different forms and massing, and detail, but the key driver is something called the retail diagram, or economic diagram. Because if the economic diagram is flawed, then no matter how good the architecture is around it, the scheme will fail. It'll fail in urban terms, it'll fail in economic terms. We tend to work out the economic diagram at the same time as working on the visual diagram, and we try to merge the two.
>
> (personal interview)

A strong service firm will provide more than just design solutions, but will also provide knowledge of local regulatory contexts, cultural norms, and economic costs. This has parallels in most professional service sectors. As Beaverstock *et al.* (1999) note in the context of law firms, 'the global client requires a global law firm with the capacity to provide a service which combines both international expertise and experience with local knowledge and cultural sensitivity' (p. 1860). Architects' clients want to know how far relative land costs in diverse markets will affect the design solution, and localised office worker cultures in terms of how differing forms of design might be received by occupiers.[1]

To provide such services architectural firms face the challenge of reconciling rapid expansion with the risk of compromising design quality. Many firms concentrate design leadership in their head office, following a looser, project-by-project structure where local representative architects are hired. Establishing branch offices requires building relationships with clients in particular geographical locations, who may in turn introduce the architects to other key business contacts. A contrasting example is offered by Melbourne-based firm, Denton Corker Marshall, which after a period of overseas expansion began to cut back on its office network as it became more successful and gained 'name' recognition:

> We have over the last two years closed quite a few of the offices in the sense that we've gone through a reverse rationalisation. . . . We didn't have a name so we had to run offices and become part of the scene. We had to hire locally registered architects, we had to chase potential developers and look for work locally, so we actually went through this phase of opening offices in HK, KL, Singapore, Jakarta and then ten or twelve years later we opened in London and then Warsaw. But in the last ten years we've found that we don't need to have all of those offices, we've found we can get work in all sorts of places without having the offices.
>
> (John Denton, Denton Corker Marshall, personal interview 2004)

The overseas expansion of firms is usually demand-led, with many design firms owing their presence in new markets to the globalisation strategies of clients. HOK, otherwise known as Hellmuth Obata Kassabaum, are a good example. Beginning as a regional firm in St Louis, with a strong presence in mid-Western US markets, the firm gradually expanded throughout the US in the early 1970s, through a mixture of acquisitions of existing firms and new start-ups. By the late 1990s, HOK had offices around the world. As Jerry Sincoff, the firm's president and CEO during the 1990s, commented:

> With a few notable exceptions, we've expanded when our clients have given us project opportunities. We knew we wanted a Berlin office, and we chose Berlin after considering a number of options. Similarly, we opened an office in Mexico because we wanted to be there. But most of our offices have opened with a specific client opportunity. And then we've gone on from there to develop other clients and projects to make the office work and grow.
>
> (Sincoff 1998: 4)

As well as opening branch offices, the firm's European wing established strategic alliances among firms with footholds in different regional markets. For example, in 2001 HOK announced the formation of the HOK European network, encompassing the medium-sized firms Arte Charpentier (Paris), Altiplan (Brussels), Estudio Lamela (Madrid) and Novotny Mahner (Frankfurt), in response to a demand by globally operative clients such as Cisco Systems to have a local presence in key regional European capitals (Delargy 2001). The firm retains its corporate group – of marketing, finance, HR and legal – in its St Louis office.

This was a similar story with Kohn Pedersen Fox (KPF), who moved into London in the mid-1980s. For Robert Cioppa, major property developers such as the Canadian firm Olympia & York were fundamental in offering them opportunities in overseas markets, in this case London:

> The UK focus came first, in the early to mid 1980s. Basically that was due to a couple of reasons. One, we were able to secure a commission in London for Goldman Sachs, and at the same time in 1986 we had an exhibit of our work at the RIBA headquarters in London, and it became clear at that point that London and Europe was a very strong market. We then succeeded in winning a competition in Frankfurt, and then Canary Wharf [in London] started. Prior to that we had work with Ware Travelstead who initiated that project. So we started to get a centre of gravity. Once the Olympia and York projects started going forward it became clear there was a need to be here [in London]. There were obviously certain tax and VAT reasons, and to service the projects well, but also it seemed like a logical move at this point, given the amount of work we had. So there was a group that came over here to work on projects initially. . . . The strategy at the time [was based on] a universal notion that London would become a financial centre, as it was bridging the time zones between Asia and the United States, and that there would be a significant shift in financial institutions to London. So we serviced financial clients but there were also the developers coming here under the same premise, so it became a service-oriented move. The complexion of the office has changed since then, it's now much of a European/UK practice than it is for servicing US corporations.
>
> (Robert Cioppa, partner, Kohn Pedersen Fox)[2]

Thus firms have a strong understanding of future growth markets, and pay attention to providing what the specific market wants. For most architectural firms, the trigger for designing abroad comes through either an external invitation from a client, or through a design competition. Repeat business is another important avenue, where a large corporation that is expanding overseas will use design firms that they know and trust, often from domestic markets. Many of these corporations will have global property or estates strategies, and facilities managers who will play a large part in commissioning favoured architectural firms to undertake their design projects as they switch their operations transnationally. To take advantage of geographical differences in factors of production, and to facilitate the rapid switching of resources between countries, many firms require flexible office space, both in terms of its internal layout, and in terms of being able to sell on or profitably rent offices should the corporation relocate.

Grimshaw Architects, with offices in London, New York and Melbourne, followed a slightly different model, and provide a good example of a non-American company that has begun to successfully challenge in foreign markets. Under the leadership of Nicholas Grimshaw, the firm developed a high profile for elegantly engineered high-tech structures, particularly London's Eurostar rail terminal at Waterloo, and Cornwall's Eden Project, a huge biome for housing plants from around the world. Their expansion into the US and Australia were based upon significant one-off commissions, the Danforth Plant Science Center in St Louis, and Spencer Street Station in Melbourne. Both allowed for the establishment of design studios in New York and Melbourne, and both were undertaken in partnership with other practices, HOK and Daryl Jackson respectively. However, it is worth noting that in the case of Danforth, this was done with HOK as technical architects; in the Melbourne case, which was a large publicly funded infrastructure project, the firm formed a joint venture with the well-established Melbourne firm, Daryl Jackson. Joint venture companies are where 'the design architect and the collaborating architect form a separate business for their joint firms, which has its own contract with the client, its own accounting setup, plus highly detailed stipulations of the services provided by each party' (Stephens 2006: 102). These partnerships allowed the firm to establish a presence that could generate further commissions, enabling the critical mass of architects to enter design competitions, and so on.

Regardless of which model is adopted, to service globally operative clients, architectural firms are also reliant upon many other producer service groups to function effectively. One driver of the globalisation of architecture has been the parallel expansion of engineering firms (Rimmer 1991), property development companies (Olds 2001) and financial and business service firms that have 'brought' their favoured design companies into new markets. As evidence of the importance of this, the World Architecture 200 survey also asks architects to rate their favoured service engineers, cost consultants, structural engineers, project managers and building contractors. This corresponds with a demand-side and supply-side dynamic to service sector growth, where activities in other sectors create a demand for architectural services, while shifts in *ability* to provide services – ICT improvements, design software innovation, increasingly flexible air travel – are increasing the scope of design firms to supply those services (Bryson *et al.* 2003). So, as with other professional service firms in advertising, law or accountancy, firms have to adopt a management model and firm structure that will allow them to compete both geographically and sectorally. To do so successfully requires a careful understanding of one's market, but also of one's firm.

## The business of architecture

> If I were the head of a school and could have a revolution in the schools, I would teach economics and social realism and how society really works. Then I would teach, as some firms do, like KPF, how to get the job and keep it. KPF actually convinced clients to leave Philip Johnson for them. They found out that Philip Johnson had a $20m building and they said, 'you think you've got the best? We can do better than Philip'. They took the job right away from him. Now that is competitive, capitalist training and it ought to be part of the way ethics is taught in schools – when is it stealing jobs, when is it legitimate, when should you wait until an architect is fired etc. All these are ethical and difficult issues that are not addressed.
>
> (Charles Jencks, in Chance 2001a: 16)

Architectural firms are often cited as an example of advanced business services. Along with industries such as management consultancy, accountancy, law, IT and advertising, they could be seen to be 'facilitating the development of large trans-national firms that can operate effectively in more and more locations around the globe' (Jones 2005: 180). Such industries share a tendency to cluster in global cities, close to the likely clients for their services. For example, Rotterdam has acted as a hub of Dutch architecture which has become very competitive in the world market (Kloosterman and Stegmeijer 2005).

Most major architectural firms are seeking to provide a full service to clients, who are able to get master-planning, engineering, concept design, interiors planning, project management and quantity surveying services carried out by a single firm, with perceived advantages in terms of communication. Others have been characterised as 'strong idea' firms who provide a powerful concept, a highly skilled resolution of costs with expressive, relatively original design, and who will tend to work in collaboration. This has implications for how the firms are theorised. For example, in *Architects and Firms* (1987), Judith Blau reports on survey research conducted with 152 Manhattan-based architectural firms in the 1970s. She raised a long-standing perception among some commentators that divided architects between those with 'conviction', with its attendant dangers of insularity and form-obsession, and those who see architecture as a business, where architects have 'abdicated their own artistic convictions and independence to elite demands and commercial interests' (Blau 1987: 14). She continues that 'neither point of view is correct: architects have neither succumbed to art for art's sake nor is their economic dependence on clients matched by an ideological identification with them' (pp. 14–15). Indeed, architects are increasingly happy to make the point that being competitive in various regional and sectoral markets is fundamental to their continued existence (albeit not couching it in the aggressive language of domination and market 'penetration' that one might find in other sectors). And there are others who make it clear that even as they undertook less-than-inspiring designs for corporate clients, they would see such activities as sub-sidising the creative process, allowing them to work on intellectually challenging, interesting projects in loss-making competitions.

Thus it should be clear that the motivations of architectural firms cannot be defined by market-driven rationality alone. There are many reasons for this, but I see two as being fundamental. First, in terms of profitability, the private nature of many firms (where share ownership is held tightly by a self-selected group of partners) means that growth strategy is not driven by public shareholders. As a result, the economic parameters set by each firm differ markedly. Age is a defin-ing factor in architectural success, much more so than in other professions, as Eugene Kohn recognises:

> I tell students architecture can be very frustrating. I once gave the keynote speech at the University of Pennsylvania to the graduating class of architects, artists and planners. I said that architecture is like running a marathon, not a sprint. I used investment banking and law as examples of shorter races. If you are interested in making a lot of money and being successful quickly, you might want to try investment banking, where you can be enormously successful by age 35 to 45, and then depart. You can start out in law or investment banking at salaries of $100,000 to $150,000. A graduating architect with a Masters degree is lucky to make $35,000 to $50,000. But what makes it exciting to be an architect is that at ages 60, 70, 80, or 90, you can still be effective.
>
> (Kohn 2004: 29)

Many retiring partners rely on succession to guarantee future retirement income, and in such cases incremental expansion of fee income is seen as being the prior-ity. The desire to ensure succession is an important part of any practice, and is often a delicate process (Knutt 2001; Hay 2004; Pogrebin 2006; Dunlap 1999; Kamin 1997). Nor is expansion a necessary goal: retaining a small but compact design studio is held to be the key to fulfilling creativity – the firm is large enough to take on major projects, but small enough for design principals to guarantee quality control and attention to detail.

Second, firms can be separated into those that seek to work through economies of scale, by reproducing tried and tested design formulae, and firms that value the opportunity to experiment in new fields or sectors. Zaha Hadid and Patrik Schumacher, whose practice is among the leading avant-garde firms in world architecture, recognise this precisely:

> The avant-garde segment has quite a bit more space to maneuver than the mainstream commercial segment. This is because our work is considered to be a kind of multiplier. Economically our buildings operate as investments

into a marketing agenda – city branding, for instance – with a value that might at times considerably exceed the budget allocated to the project itself. Although we have budgets to work within, our projects are usually not measured in terms of industry standards of cost-effectiveness. They are paid for by funds that have been extracted from the cycle of profit-driven invest-ment – either as public tax money or as sponsorship money administered by a cultural institution's board of trustees. Obviously such funds too are indi-rectly contributing to an overall business rationale. But as designers we can enjoy and utilize the relative distance from concerns of immediate profitabil-ity to further our experimental agenda. We understand that this position is peculiar to a rarefied segment of the profession.

(Harvard Design Magazine 2004: 50)

Those firms which have grown beyond this scale will often use commercial com-missions to subsidise competition entries and research into new technologies or building materials, where possible. They are also able to attract young graduate architects willing to spend long hours without significant remuneration. This invisible economy is well-known but rarely documented – the young architects are able to work closely with designers whose work has inspired them, either to build up personal CVs or, in the process, working with like-minded designers who may become future partners in newly-established firms as their career choices unfold.

A further point of clarification about architectural firms is required. Speaking about corporations generally, O'Neill and Gibson-Graham (1999) have drawn attention to the importance of a 'decentred and "disorganized" representation of the enterprise' (p. 11), as an 'unpredictable site of multiple and contradictory processes' (p. 12). Identifying the centredness of the architectural firm involves a curious paradox. On the one hand, large firms are often treated as monolithic, where little is revealed beyond their corporate identity. Thus SOM, HOK, BDP and KPF are often represented as archetypal 'faceless' firms, without an identifi-able individual design leader. On the other, 'boutique' firms can be excessively personalised by the media and public, where the design leader is attributed with the entire creative output of the practice. This can be particularly problematic when the identities of skilled design architects are subsumed beneath the firm's figurehead (McNeill 2005).

Many architects have preferred to separate the culture of the business world from the art of design. However, the existence of journals such as *Marketer*, the newsletter of the Society of Marketing Professionals, or books such as *The Business of Architecture* (Inside the Minds 2004), which gather together homilies from leading partners in some of the major practices in US architecture, such as KPF, Callison, Gensler and HKS, illustrates the importance of business practice, and in particular marketing. Consider the following interview in *Marketer*:

SALLY HANDLEY: Many architects are disdainful of marketing.

GENE KOHN: Don't believe it. They may be disdainful publicly, or they may be disdainful about making a phone call or making contacts, but I have to tell you the best architects out there are terrific marketers. They just don't use the word marketing. I was the first architect to say selling is OK. The famous architects, Meier, Stern, Gehry ... are all great marketers. They use pressure. They make phone calls, they visit, and they entertain. I understand from people who have been to Renzo Piano's office in Genoa that his office is up a great hillside. He serves beautiful lunches, shows the view of the city, the scenery ... what is that? That's marketing. He's not doing that just to be nice. He wants to get the job.

(*Marketer* 2002: 5)

Eugene Kohn is blunt in his recognition of the need for architectural firms to market themselves. His business acumen is partially responsible for the emergence of Kohn Pedersen Fox as one of the world's leading commercial design practices. Kohn himself lectures on the Advanced Management Development Program in Real Estate at the Harvard Graduate School of Design, and argues that this program fulfils the need for architects to be able to exercise leadership skills and negotiate with government, clients and boards (*Real Estate Weekly* 2002).

Kohn's point is that reputation is built among key individuals in the building procurement process, among those involved in searching, interviewing and then commissioning buildings. There are a number of professional groups which have influence in this process, such as development executives, chief executive officers, quantity surveyors, facilities managers, structural engineers and so on. The reputations of these firms are filtered through a number of channels: through the trade press, through word of mouth, through performance in design competitions, through excellence in particular sectors of construction (e.g. hospitals, office buildings, museums) through to the key 'bottom line' indicators of completing to budget and on time.

An important role in the architecture firm is thus that of the public relations or media officer. In *Is it All About Image?*, Laura Illoniemi (2004: 25–9) sets out five reasons for the importance of PR in major firms: first, there is a need to bridge the technical detail of a project with a more popular news story that will be of interest to a wide audience; second, PRs can 'place' stories in major newspapers through the cultivation of critics and news editors; third, they can similarly downplay or hide projects that may not fit with the firm's desired image; fourth, they can broker a neutral message between practice and client at the sometimes tense final stages of a project; fifth, they provide professional media management which may be required in large, high profile projects. Thus in the crucial brokering of a project, whether it be between architect and client, or architect, client and public, the design artefact and development process is something that is highly mediated.

Dealing with the media is thus a fundamental part of running a successful international practice. However, as Roberts (2003: 31) has argued, 'The global manager is born out of a huge anxiety about vulnerability'. And there is considerable room for anxiety within globalising architectural firms, many of whom increasingly face challenges both from competitors inside the profession, but also from outside, in the form of large, multi-sector services firms, such as Andersen Consulting or Capita Symonds. This is the competitive climate within which major commercial architectural firms have to operate.

## Joint ventures and alliances

It is difficult to identify precisely what makes for a 'boutique' architectural firm, and the term itself may not be entirely appropriate. However, many architects note that once a practice goes above approximately forty to fifty fee-earning architects, its ambience changes. This can be for a number of reasons, but may include: outgrowing the physical limitations of the existing design studio; the appointment of new senior design architects from outside the firm; an increase in overheads and financial commitments; and an incremental rise in project commissions, which beyond a certain point will make it impossible for a firm's lead designer to have a clear input in every project.

Nonetheless, small practices are viable when working in partnership with larger firms of 'production architects', who may either be a development group's in-house architectural team, or may be a separate firm which specialises in large-scale project work, but which lacks a reputation for design leadership. For example, Tsao and McKown, a small New York-based firm, were commissioned to design Singapore's huge mixed-use skyscraper complex, Suntec City; Renzo Piano Building Workshop regularly designs major projects around the world, including the New York Times building in New York, in partnership with Fox and Fowle; the leading commercial firm Kohn Pedersen Fox worked with Yoshio Taniguchi on the redesign of New York's Museum of Modern Art, on the basis that it may give them increased edge in winning museum commissions, increasingly dominated by European or Asian-based firms. Smaller, younger firms agree to partner with established boutique firms to raise their own profile (Stephens 2006).

The competition for Ground Zero gave the idea of team-working momentum. Three of the submissions came from quickly assembled teams of 'boutique' architects. THINK brought together Frederic Schwartz, Rafael Viñoly and Shigeru Ban; United Architects comprised UN Studio, Foreign Office Architects and Greg Lynn; and Steven Holl, Richard Meier and Peter Eisenman and Charles Gwathmey, four of the best-known individual architects in the US, presented a jointly conceived project. Even SOM would partner with firms such as Sanaa and Field Operations (Yang 2004). The reasons for doing so reflected the complexity of the commission, such large-footprint, masterplanned projects, may require urban planning, urban design, engineering and transport specialists, creative design approaches associated with fashion and avant-gardism, as well as commercial building experts.

This division of responsibilities can cause tensions, for a number of reasons. First, there can be difficulties in establishing the credit due for a particular building. For example, in the case of the de Young Museum project in San Francisco, Herzog and de Meuron were referred as the 'primary design architect', with Fong & Chan acting as 'principal architect' (Stephens 2006: 102). The latter took a larger share of the fee, justified by their responsibility for any legal issues arising from the completed building (Stephens 2006: 100). This distinction can become problematic given that the general, non-trade media are reluctant to complicate stories by discussing more than one individual designer. In the case of the Seattle Public Library, the official listing was OMA/LMN; the latter, a Seattle-based firm, engaged in a joint venture with OMA. However, in the majority of the press coverage, authorship was accredited almost exclusively to Rem Koolhaas. Second, as the landscape architect Diana Balmori has argued, collaborations often come about in a rushed response to RFPs (Requests for Proposals), where commissions for major jobs result in the rapid assembly of a group of design studios which aim to present the appropriate collaborative mix to win over a competition design jury (Yang 2004).

## The megapractice: Skidmore, Owings & Merrill

First established in 1936 by Nat Owings and Louis Skidmore in Chicago, SOM – as it is widely known – expanded rapidly in response to a number of lucrative commissions in post-Depression Chicago and New York. Their then unusual decision to add a civil engineer, John Merrill, to their partnership in 1939 set the firm's course as a multi-service operation capable of constructing major projects. With a number of large commissions for the Chicago World's Fair and US military facilities, SOM was able to expand rapidly in a variety of building types. Through the successive emergence of new generations of key architects, notably Gordon Bunshaft and Bruce Graham, and engineers, such as Fazlur Khan, the firm would become best-known for corporate office buildings, developed from the firm's three key offices in New York, Chicago and San Francisco. SOM were generally seen as at the top of the profession in terms of commercial architecture, developing a series of highly-regarded towers 'united by a uniformly high standard of programmatic conception, materials, and detailing' (Filler 1990: 31). Following Gordon Bunshaft's breakthrough with Lever House in mid-town Manhattan, major landmarks included the John Hancock Center in Chicago (1965–70), and the Sears Tower (1970–3) in the same city, both heralded as significant advances in skyscraper form, particularly in terms of the reconciliation of style and structure (Adams 2007; Bush-Brown 1984; Drexler 1974).

However, despite their prolific output in a wide range of sectors from commercial offices to airports in both the US and further afield, SOM would find themselves in financial difficulties in the late 1980s, reflecting profound changes in the key sector that they had hitherto relied on, the commercial office market. This domestic challenge coincided with the deep property recession of the late 1980s and early 1990s, and saw the firm lay off several hundred employees (McKee 1996: 231). Gross receipts dropped from $157 million in 1989 to $67 million in 1993, with employee numbers dropping from 1,500 to 557. Furthermore, SOM's reputation as designers of the total building, from interiors through to structural engineering, was also challenged (Ockman 1995). Innovation in structural engineering allowed most tall buildings to be constructed without an architectural firm's involvement, leaving design firms competing on the basis of façade design and silhouette. As Martin Filler notes:

> By the early eighties the older belief in corporate discretion quickly began to disappear. Emboldened by the laissez-faire atmosphere created by Reaganomics and the most spectacular stock market prosperity since the twenties – as well as a pervasive endorsement of the flagrant display of wealth exhibited in all aspects of consumer behavior – the major corporate clients of the big architectural firms called for and responded to designs in which assertive forms and showy materials mimicked a hollow grandiosity and unbridled crassness reminiscent of the Gilded Age.
>
> (1990: 25)

Increasingly, buildings were being constructed by speculative developers seeking designs that would mark out their buildings. As a result, the firm's uncompromisingly modernist designs saw it lose its competitive position to newcomers such as Kohn Pedersen Fox, who embraced the postmodern turn in office design (Filler 1990). The firm's shift from the austerity of the post-Miesian International Style to a commercial brand of postmodernism met with negative critical notice. Structures such as One Worldwide Plaza (1989) in New York, or San Francisco's 345 California Center (1986), were cited as examples of over-built or insensitive developments.

Yet by the mid-1990s, the firm was reporting a rebound to $117 million in revenues, and a staff of 800, with nearly half of its workload being overseas (McKee 1996). Indeed, in the early 1990s, 90 per cent of SOM Chicago's work was reported to be outside the US, compared with 50 per cent in the mid-1980s (Kamin 1994). For these reasons, SOM began to establish itself in numerous regional markets overseas, particularly in the field of commercial office design.

In 1999 it appointed Ken Brown, an ex-vice president of General Electric, as the first non-architectural CEO of a major design firm. Brown's departure from the firm only nineteen months later fuelled the perception that business leadership and architectural practice do not easily mix. Ultimately, it appeared that Brown grew frustrated with the embedded power of SOM's (then) twenty-seven partners, reflecting the fact that 'the CEO's has always been an awkward role, of power and helplessness, of presence and absence. He makes decisions, but delegates most of their implementation. He knows things, but mostly what others, with superior knowledge of their respective areas, tell him' (Haigh 2004: 18). And in many ways, this is because of the juggernaut power of the corporation itself: 'designed to tick over, and structured not to depend on any individual genius. Ironically, this is not because it is an environment of impersonal control, but because it is a sum of human strivings' (Haigh 2004: 91–2).

Nonetheless, it has been suggested that his time at the helm was significant for SOM in at least five ways. First, he argued that SOM allowed clients a longer period of fees payment than in most industries. Second, he established a 'risk committee', as a means of ensuring that commissions were fully evaluated in terms of staff resources, legal responsibility, and financial risk. This included a more systematic examination of competition entries, previously often seen as being left to the purview of individual partners. Third, he sought to distribute the geography-specialism matrix more efficiently, where clients from a particular sector – such as aviation or health – might be directed to the appropriate design office in a more systematic manner. Fourth, he reformed the internal organisational processes such as human resources, accounting, and information technology. Fifth, he moved SOM into earlier points on the 'value chain', where – as with competitors such as HOK – the firm intervenes in the development process at an early stage, such as advising developers on the optimal building configuration on a particular site to maximise profit (Fairs 2000; Ward 2001).

Certainly, the justification for having a non-architectural CEO was reflective of the complexity of SOM's organisational structure. The firm has three key design offices: New York, San Francisco and Chicago. Each of these offices has oversight of the smaller outposts (Washington DC and Los Angeles by New York, London by Chicago, Shanghai by San Francisco). The governance structure of the firm consists of twenty-seven partners, with two governance committees which are elected by the partners: the Executive Committee, and the Evaluation and Compensation Committee, both of which contain one representative from each of the three main design offices. The first considers strategy, the second the share of ownership or salary that each partner is due over a two-year cycle.[3] This structure is important, given the firm's notoriety for inter-firm rivalries, and even 'turf wars' (Nance 2006). As Chuck Bassett, a key partner in the San Francisco office between 1955 and 1981, has confirmed, SOM's clients have sometimes short-listed two different offices within SOM, or have switched between offices for subsequent commissions (Art Institute of Chicago 1989a: 90).

Such stories highlight the importance of the three key design studios within the firm. However, the firm's structure is also partly dictated by the partnerships within each office, where each partner has many of the characteristics of an individual firm, with their own set of budgets, jobs, and teams. The issue of succession is another sensitive issue, particularly in terms of the financial settlements due to retiring partners (Kamin 1997). In 2006, one of SOM's best-known designers, Adrian Smith, left the firm amid whispers of a power struggle over future design ideologies (Pridmore 2007). Yet even within each office, the firm's output is diverse. While SOM New York is often characterised as being associated with the high-rise commercial office building (associated with David Childs, particularly – see Figure 1.1) other partners in that office have developed strong

*Figure 1.1* SOM/David Childs: Columbus Circle, New York.

reputations in the fields of urban design (in the case of Marilyn Taylor), or schools (in the case of Roger Duffy). Much of the rationale for these turf battles, however, includes the need to ensure career advancement paths for younger architects. There are suggestions that the current period will mark out a significant generational shift in the firm's trajectory (Nance 2006), as seen in the launch of its 'public' design review process, *SOM Journal*.

The contemporary partners have had to battle with the stereotype of SOM as a faceless architectural firm, designs emerging from behind an impenetrable office block, fashioned from a standardised template, controlled by a monolithic design committee (Sorkin 1994). All was not seen to be well with design quality and innovation even within the firm. At around the same time as Ken Brown's reforms to the SOM organisational structure, a similarly far-reaching reform of SOM's design process was taking place. The decentralised structure of the firm meant that there was little formal review of design quality standards firmwide. In an effort to address this, a group of partners pushed forward a bold scheme that aimed at raising standards through a form of public critique. In late 2000, an external auditing panel of five members (including an engineer, an architect, an artist, an academic and an architectural critic), surveyed fifty projects from the firm's total output in its seven offices (see Bernstein 2002). The published results included transcripts of the jury's deliberations, which are not always flattering. The success of the scheme has seen the periodical production of *SOM Journal* (Wang 2001, 2003, 2004; Ghirardo 2006). This provides an interesting counterpoint to the self-published monographs of many architectural firms.

So how does SOM compare with the boutique firm? Certainly, smaller firms can suffer from the frustration of having to compete directly with major firms. Alejandro Zaera-Polo, of the increasingly renowned Foreign Office Architects, sees SOM as being restricted by its organisational size:

> Maybe the biggest difference is the fact that they have to feed 400 people, which creates a chain of events: they have to hire people who are more sales-oriented; they have a bigger insurance policy; bigger resources etc., and the personal relationships are more distant. I don't think that the big corporations will survive, since the tools of production that we have today are not the tools that produce these kinds of offices. We can easily make alliances that allow us to produce even large-scale projects, and I believe that eventually the clients will understand that when they hire a smaller firm they get a higher percentage of the creative director.
>
> (in Zucker 2006)

This focus on creativity is perhaps to overestimate the willingness of a sufficiently wide range of clients to commission 'the creative director'. Yet it does highlight the fact that SOM is on the fulcrum of functionality and design creativity, a firm that has successfully straddled architecture as business, while retaining a strong reputation for design.

## Aedas: the architectural firm as global brand

> How do 1900 creative team members in 26 offices working in 11 key sectors spread across four continents work successfully together? By sharing knowledge, expertise and cultures – and with an overwhelming desire to improve our environment – we apply our global resources through the Aedas network to deliver progressive local solutions.
>
> (Aedas 2006–7 Annual Review)

The language used in the introduction to its annual review is telling. Aedas, an amalgamation of Abbey Holford Rowe (UK) and LPT 9 (a Hong Kong based design firm, formerly part of Peddle Thorp), had over eight hundred staff in six countries in 2002, and represents the ambition of two medium-sized firms with strong presence in regional markets to operate on a larger scale (Leftly 2002). As the statement indicates, by 2007, it had grown yet further. Aedas set out with the explicit intention of creating a branded, globally operative firm which is structured to compete with major American firms (who are able to use the size and critical mass developed from their work in the major US national market to absorb foreign commissions). LPT 9 in particular had noticed the ease with which major US firms had entered the Southeast Asian market. They sought to challenge this through the application of a carefully considered business model, capable of meeting the demands of transnational corporate clients, such as Credit Suisse or JP Morgan, who look for consistent level of service and often rely on tried and trusted firms such as SOM and KPF. Through the merger, they were able to target a number of major markets, including Southeast Asia (based in Hong Kong), the UK, Western Europe, the Middle East, Russia and Eastern Europe and India. In 2006, they expanded into the US market through the integration of Davis Brody Bond, a well-regarded American firm.

The Aedas case represents the growing ability of firms to 'design at distance', as their then chairman Keith Griffiths noted in 2004:

> We thought the right way to do it would be to establish a network across the entire world. And not to have a headquarters, or a home base at all. In the electronic age you don't need to have a physical home base. You need to have a board, which is made up of different people from different cities, but you don't need a home base for it. It's a unique model. Nobody has used it before. The idea of setting up a network/necklace of offices right across the world. Nobody has used it is architectural circles. Providing a local level of service but an international level of knowledge and expertise.

So that's the model that we took to the UK, having identified a number of shortlisted people and that's the model that Abbey Holford Rowe was very interested in.

Having identified a suitable partner, the naming of the merged firm was the next key issue, given that this often revolves around the personality of the lead designers. This conscious invention of the architectural firm as global brand required that the chosen name be given the utmost consideration. Having contracted the specialist branding firm Sigelgale, the partners set out their key criteria: uniqueness, ease of pronunciation and writing in multiple languages, and maturity and status. The suggested names were reduced down to a shortlist of sixteen, which eventually settled on newly invented words. As well as fitting the criteria set out by the partners, Aedas had the advantage of being at the beginning of the alphabet, and possessing a good feng shui, important in the Southeast Asian context (Griffiths, personal interview; Sinclair 2005). The in-built resistance to renaming firms was eased by the fact that LPT had already been renamed to reflect a shift away from its derivation from the Australian firm of Peddle Thorp:[4]

> We had renamed ourselves LPT so we had no fear about renaming ourselves again. Abbey Holford Rowe were in the process of renaming themselves AHR so they had no problems in renaming themselves. So we got together and created a new name, Aedas. And the whole idea behind that was to create a name that was unique, that wasn't registered on the net, that would have some contextuality to architecture – from *aedificare*, to build, in Latin – and would be at the start of the alphabet.
>
> (Keith Griffiths, personal interview)

This search for a strong brand identity is an interesting development in architectural firm culture. In many ways, Aedas was responding to the established brand power of the 'acronymic' firms such as SOM, KPF and HOK. As Sinclair (2005) continues, as soon as the brand was chosen, it was launched at the MIPIM property fair, itself a highly significant event for commercially oriented architectural firms. I will discuss MIPIM in the following chapter.

A further striking feature of Aedas is its ability to profit from the centralisation of business services. Registered in Belgium, the firm licenses its member companies to use the Aedas name, and receives a fee of between 1 and 1.5 per cent of turnover to pay for marketing, its website, and information delivery systems. It holds quarterly board meetings, with weekly strategic meetings among the global partners. This also raises the issue of how to distribute projects, of how to link clients with particular offices. Aedas works with a referral fee of between 3 and 5 per cent of the total fee when projects are passed between offices. This is usually paid in kind, rather than through direct financial transfer. The main board of

Aedas acts in the event of dispute between the member companies. The group promotes the projects which are felt to be at the highest level of international design excellence, projects which are competing head-on with the major firms, through its Aedas Studio grouping. In addition, the firm has sectoral divisions – Aedas Education, Infrastructure, and so on – which focus on the marketing and delivery of particular sectors. As an example, Aedas Infrastructure is mostly based in Hong Kong, but bids for jobs worldwide.

Aedas is significant within the global profession as being 'instantly' global, having expanded internationally on the back of a carefully thought through business model, rather than the more sporadic approach of following clients into new markets. It provides an indication that the business of architecture – that design operates within a structured set of financial relations – is fundamental to any attempt to build on a sustained scale.

## The rise of Foster and Partners

'Design revealed for the world's first spaceport'. 'World's largest and most complete sustainable regional development announced in Libya'. 'Designs revealed for new ecological tower in Siberia'. 'Camp Nou stadium, home of FC Barcelona, to be remodelled'. 'New pen launched at paperworld'. 'New mixed use neighbourhood for Singapore'. 'New York honours for Hearst Tower'.[5] The media section of the Foster and Partners website illustrates the geographical reach of probably the most remarkable architectural firm currently operative. From the geographical spread of their projects, to the amount of fee-earning architects that they employ, Fosters (as they are generally referred to as a practice) fits neither of the two opposed categories that I have just discussed. The 'Foster model', as most architects see it, seems to do the impossible – retaining the close personal identification of a key designer, with one base design studio rather than a branch structure, together with the logistical size to undertake a vast array of projects, from pens to spaceports, simultaneously.

How has this happened? The first phase of the firm's growth came with the construction of avant-garde projects such as the Willis Faber and Dumas building in Ipswich, UK, in 1978, seen as being ahead of its time in terms of architectural properties, technical specifications and design. The second phase of growth came with the successful completion of architecturally outstanding, large-scale projects, particularly the Hong Kong and Shanghai Bank office tower in Hong Kong, Stansted airport and Barcelona telecommunications tower (one of the most striking images of the 1992 Olympics) (Abel 2000; Powell 2000). The third phase was marked by invitations to compete for sensitive redesign contracts, particularly the Berlin Reichstag, the Great Court at the British Museum in London and the Ground Zero masterplan in New York. It is also underlined by the confirmation of peer esteem, seen in Foster's receipt of the Pritzker Prize in 1999 and the

Praemium Imperiale in 2002, and in the plaudits received from architectural critics (gathered together in Jenkins 2000). The fourth phase of growth has been characterised by a shift into widely spread commercial work, a growing geographical range of commissions, and an increasing diversification in firm specialisation. It is at this stage that the firm reached a tipping point, where the close connection between Norman Foster as a figurehead and his practice's output began to dissolve.

Certainly, the firm's work is closely associated with Foster's undoubted excellence in design. In the late 1990s, when the firm was still relatively contained, one of his four partners, Spencer de Grey, outlined how the practice operated:

> Central to the organization of the practice is the strong sense of trust that exists between Norman, the partners and a number of other key members of the practice. This is crucial, especially when we have such an extraordinarily diverse range of projects, spread as they are across the world.... Thus the design in the practice is centred around Norman, Ken, David and myself. We all work here in London in a single studio so that communication is excellent throughout. Communication takes place both informally and formally. The chance discussion, the instant design comment or informal design review create a highly charged, creative atmosphere. More formally, there are regular meetings of the directors, thirteen at the moment, to review key issues, progress on projects and general financial matters. Every project is run by a job captain, who is responsible to a director – the hierarchy is therefore very broad-based with quick communications to directors, partners and Norman himself.
>
> (Spencer de Grey, partner, Foster and Partners, quoted in Quantrill 1999: 57–8)

For much of Foster and Partners' growth period of the 1990s and 2000s, the model described by Spencer de Grey would appear to have been successful. Foster had long operated with several key design partners: de Grey himself, David Nelson, Graham Phillips and Ken Shuttleworth. Each of these partners would typically oversee the day-to-day running of major project commissions – de Grey took the lead on the British Museum, for example, while Nelson led on the Reichstag, and Shuttleworth on London's City Hall and New York's Ground Zero masterplan. Phillips, along with other major project roles, had taken on the managing director's role in the company, with jobs managed as indicated by de Grey above.[6] By 2003, the practice had received commissions from eighteen countries outside the UK, including Australia, China, Poland, Saudi Arabia and the US, and was being ranked in the top ten of the world's largest architectural firms by number of fee-earning architects (over 350). It had begun to outgrow its current studio, with a fee income of US$60–9 million in 2002 (*World Architecture 300*, 2003 survey).

As a consequence of the rapid growth of commissions received, the firm announced a restructuring of its management in December 2004, dividing the practice into six teams, led by senior partners Grant Brooker, Nigel Dancey, Brandon Haw, Paul Kalkhoven, Mouzhan Majidi and Andrew Miller (*Building Design* 2004), with De Grey and Nelson becoming deputy chairmen, and Phillips the company's Chief Executive. The trade press noted that each unit would have its own accounting procedures, and had the potential to be in competition to a degree. For example, Majidi – in charge of the firm's large Beijing airport terminal project – is quoted as saying: 'I have always worked closely with Norman, and that hasn't changed ... But with the group system, it follows that you have more control over your group, which is nice' (Booth and Blackler 2004).

These organisational changes seemed to be successful in propelling the firm into new markets, with a leap in scale in the number – and type – of projects that the firm was able to undertake. With growth came a further, even more radical, restructuring in 2007. The most striking aspect of this was the involvement of 3i, a venture capital group, as a minority partner in the firm, which was valued at £350 million. As 3i's Head of UK·Growth Capital put it,

> Foster + Partners is an example of the kind of global, market leading business that 3i Growth Capital looks to work with. This is a fantastic partnership of two industry leaders with complementary global footprints and we look forward to partnering with the management team to achieve their goals of expanding and diversifying the business.
>
> (Foster and Partners 2007)

The new firm structure would have Foster as Chairman, Mouzhan Majidi as Chief Executive, de Grey and Nelson as heads of design and Graham Phillips as Chief Operating Officer. Six senior partners would also become shareholders. The restructuring also involved the closure of an employee trust scheme, which was seen to be a prerequisite of the 3i sale (Booth 2007; Pfeifer 2007).

So, Foster and Partners is an exemplary case of the tensions involved in a successful, growing practice. In the following two chapters, I will return to them to discuss the importance of the design studio in a growing firm, and the significance of Norman Foster himself as the firm seeks to balance the brand with the individuality of its design signature.

## Conclusions: the significance of the firm

### Extract from *Building*, 18 July 2033.

So, after all the speculation, the shortlist for main contractor on London One, the world's largest office complex, has been narrowed down to two candidates. It's no surprise that the global powerhouse of Bechtel Beatty made the cut for the $8bn project – it has been in pole position ever since SOM, its architectural arm, won the design contract last September. . . . The stakes are high. Stanhope BAA has a reputation as a demanding client that goes back to the 1980s. The practices they pioneered 30 years ago (project-based insurance, earned-value analysis, internet-based procurement) are now mainstream, but it remains at the cutting edge by using psychometric tests to select management teams and nanotechnology to reduce its building's whole-life costs. And whoever wins this job will be well-placed to bid for follow-up work on a string of airport and office projects that go out to tender later this year at Bucharest, Nanjing, San Jose and Bangalore.

(*Building* 2003)

This engaging piece of futurology by the UK's major construction trade magazine raises several interesting themes. It projects a landscape of full-service megafirms, encompassing the merger of two of the UK and US's leading construction, engineering and project management firms (Balfour Beatty and Bechtel, currently separate corporations), and architectural design (SOM). It highlights the scope for organisational and technological change within a traditionally conservative sector. It identifies a developer-client that has emerged from the hypothetical merger of a major UK developer (Stanhope) and a privatised major British landowner and infrastructure provider (BAA). Finally, it illuminates some likely construction hotspots in cities that are leading lights in emerging markets.

The *Building* piece was constructed as a diverting, but half-serious, scenario for the future of major architectural and development firms in a globalising economy. For architectural practice, it poses some very serious questions indeed. It highlights the significance of new sectoral markets for major design firms, in China and the US, of course, but also in India and Rumania. It raises the possible absorption of proudly independent architectural firms (SOM, in this case) into full-service corporations able to offer demanding clients seamless inter-disciplinary design and construction, probably at a guaranteed maximum price. Above all, it highlights the contrast that exists in the study of architecture between autonomous viewpoints – which dominates architecture as a profession and discipline – and a heteronomous reading (Larson 1993; Olds 2001) which sees architects as firms, operating in a market-driven environment where their designs are pulled and pushed by project managers, quantity surveyors, and property developers.

Despite this apparent trend towards mergers and amalgamations, the future of the boutique firm would seem to be assured, assuming they are able to offer something distinctive within a crowded market. Due to the cost of entering a global market (in terms of investment in technology, premises, and labour-location logistics), leading architectural CEOs such as Arthur Gensler predict a bifurcation of the market: 'The cost of entering the market is one of the reasons why the big will get bigger, and the small will stay where they are – hoovering up the boutique projects. We don't expect to see an awful lot of competitors' (in *World Architecture* 1999). However, what this *does* mean is that even small architectural firms still have a very significant role in the unfolding of these new global markets, particularly through adopting flexible organisational structures such as joint ventures.

So, we have seen that firms follow a very uneven pattern of overseas operation, with supply-side strategies and demand-side opportunities pursued and exploited in different ways. Architectural firms are well-placed to take advantage of the mobility of their product, and in the following chapter I explore how this geographical flexibility is achieved in more detail.

# 2   Designing at distance

In the study of architectural practice it is now increasingly necessary to consider the nature of design as a relational process. As with other advanced producer service firms, architects are transmitting a knowledge product, one that has specific attributes that have to travel through space from the design studio (a dense factory of embodied specialist design knowledge) to the site office, and thence to the construction site itself. How, then, are such material transfers sustained and interpreted? How are these social relations and cultural contacts – so important to client relations and repeat work – enhanced and retained? How significant is the charisma of the elite designer in all of this? How is the design studio organised and what role does it play as a node or site in a network of flows? And how are information technology and new forms of project work transforming the design process?

I propose to explore these questions in several ways. First, I examine the corporeal mobility of architects in the sense of their ability to travel, and their motivations for travel. Second, I consider the delegated nature of the design process through a case study of the design of Aurora Place, a Sydney office tower completed in 2000, with 'signature' authorship attributed to Renzo Piano. Here, I explore the nature of 'absent presence', where the drawings left by the concept designer are to be interpreted within a heteronomous design process. Third, I discuss the role of client meetings, architectural competitions and communication in terms of gaining commissions. Fourth, I explore the significance of the design studio as a 'space of practice', focusing on the studios of Norman Foster and EMTB. Fifth, I describe the importance of information technology in creating a 'seamless' design studio, describing the information strategies of Kohn Pedersen Fox, which operates a trans-Atlantic design team through two principal offices. Finally, I examine the role of temporary events in assembling some of the key players in complex construction processes in one place, at one time. In the annual MIPIM trade fair, held in Cannes, we can see the significance of face-to-face sociality for architects hoping to design at distance.

### Architects and business travel

> Do you know that in the past week I've been swimming in Lagos, in Milan, in Switzerland, in Rotterdam, in London, in L.A., and in Las Vegas?
>
> (Rem Koolhaas, in Sigler 2000)

> Although it had been arranged weeks in advance, *Building* [magazine]'s interview with Lord Foster is not carried out face to face at his riverfront office in Battersea, but by telephone to Switzerland. 'I'm at my apartment in St Moritz in between trips,' he says breezily. 'I've just come from Madrid; it will be Milan tomorrow, Beijing on Thursday and Friday and then St Petersburg. I thrive on all this travel: I love it.'
>
> (Spring 2007: 46)

Since the 1950s, jet travel has liberated major architects, allowing them to build portfolios and client bases in numerous countries in the world. Some of the key figures in modern architecture have displayed a fascination with the airplane, including Le Corbusier, who documented its form and development religiously in his writings (Pascoe 2001), and Eero Saarinen, whose terminal designs at JFK are among the most emblematic in the canon of modern architecture. More recently, Norman Foster (who pilots his own plane and once famously named the Boeing 747 as his favourite building), and Rem Koolhaas, who enthusiastically planned to relocate Schiphol airport in the North Sea, have reaffirmed the hypermobility of leading architects.

To be able to travel with frequency and reliability is an example of the changes brought about in the scope of architectural design in the last few decades. Elite architects can seemingly do so at will. As Dodge and Kitchin (2004) argue, 'Air travel provides one of the key physical supports to the global economic system by connecting together people and activities into a shared time and space, whilst simultaneously separating and bypassing other, "irrelevant", people and places' (p. 195). However, despite the apparently carefree criss-crossing of the globe enjoyed by Foster and Koolhaas, these architects cannot be everywhere at once. To think about this, I work with concepts of co-presence and event obligation, following Boden and Molotch (1994) and Urry (2002, 2003, 2004) in qualifying understandings of how often and why people move. For Urry, 'corporeal travel happens only on specific occasions, occurring intermittently, and this can be explained through a "compulsion to proximity"' (2004: 29).

Business travel is a fundamental part of the communication of knowledge within firms. As Faulconbridge (2006: 529) describes in his account of the global management strategies of advertising firms:

> The global stretching of knowledge relating to an advertising campaign is possible because of the macro-level similarities in advertising executives'

work throughout the world. This means that, although there is the need for the local tailoring of adverts, it is possible to identify globally standard approaches and elements of advertising strategy that can form the basis of the conversations involved in the social production of new knowledge.

In other words, firms will structure learning and communication around a social process which Faulconbridge calls a 'global relational space'. While colonial economies always relied upon mobile professionals, either with specialist knowledge or with a managerial role, the contemporary global economy demands a logistically more complex set of locational decisions which may see key designers moving between cities that are hubs with broader regional economies (see also Beaverstock 2002). Thus while some of the world travel being undertaken by architects involves arriving on a plane, spending a short amount of time on and around the proposed development site, and flying home to the head office, many clients demand a more permanent local presence. As noted in the last chapter, this may involve a number of strategies, from engaging trusted local representative architects, to a more permanent investment in a fully fledged design studio.

For globally operative architecture firms, the technical process of design is but the end product of a social process that involves extensive travel, a mastery of diverse business cultures, hospitality, client pitches, meetings with local contractors and representative architects and site analysis. While much of the process of designing at distance can indeed be done virtually, it is how the virtual and the material interplay that is the focus of this chapter. This issue would seem to be captured by what Urry (2002) calls 'the globalization of intermittent co-presence', where through various 'obligations', be they social (the interpersonal communication of client and contractor meetings), place-based (site visits), or object-based (working on a specific technology, such as a design computer), requires the bodily attendance of specific actors in one place at the same time. This sense of an embodiment is an important aspect of a distanciated design process. For example, Woods Bagot, which maintains offices throughout Australia, Beijing, Dubai, Abu Dhabi, Hong Kong and London, is conscious of the significance of bodily movement, particularly of highly skilled specialist staff, around their various locations:

> Our specialists tend to move to the source of the project, primarily London and Dubai, and workshop with local teams. On occasion, the work is further developed at their 'home base'. We find this works well for our clients, and is highly stimulating for our staff. From a personal perspective, I relocated from Sydney to Hong Kong and then London, and there are a couple of reasons for that. One is a market-driven decision, the other is to make a move to get our management more global, less Australian-centric, as the majority of our directors are still in Australia. But now that the large major-

ity of our revenue is generated outside of Australia, it is important for the future of the business that we get more of our leaders spread around the organization, rather than centralised in Melbourne and Sydney which is currently the situation.

(David Tregoning, Woods Bagot, personal interview)

Such executive travel is a relatively new aspect of the 'new geographies of circulation which are intended to produce situations in which creativity and innovation can, quite literally, take place' (Thrift 2005: 147). Here, however, branch office location strategies are still related to travel time:

For someone in the UK to work in the Far East, you've got to have a base office in Singapore, Hong King, or mainland China. It's just too far – to go from the UK on any kind of trip to the Far East, you wipe out a week, taking into account the travel time, the adjustment time, and doing the business over there. In the Far East, personal relationships are very important in securing the work. You can't just parachute in, throw the drawings at them, and leave. First of all, when you're securing your client you've got a lot of entertaining to do, and being with them, because they often hire you as a person, not as a firm. To try and do that from the UK, plus run the UK work, is just impossible ... Once you're there, it's bigger than Europe, so you're still into five-hour flights, you're still doing a lot of travelling, but you're not doing the fifteen to twenty-three hours. So Australian practices do well in the Far East because it's a maximum of six hours to get to most of their markets. If you're on the West coast of the US you're into a manageable time to get there – you wouldn't go from the East coast. It's too far. Because when you go on these trips, you may go for a week but only have worked for two and a half days. Then you've lost all that opportunity time.

(Nick Terry, BDP, personal interview)

The opportunity cost of travel is highly significant, as time on the road is time that cannot always be billed to clients on a specific project. And given that it takes a considerable period of time to become established in a local market, the length of time such trips take is a significantly risky investment for firms, as Bob Cioppa of KPF notes:

In terms of the global practice, if you were doing a project in, say, Indonesia, to meet with the client you do marketing calls in Indonesia. Once you've left Indonesia you might go to Singapore, do marketing with clients, stop in, go to Hong Kong, stop in, go home, so we try to piggy-back the marketing effort on top of the projects we have. At the beginning it was difficult because we didn't have that many projects, but once you're out there the hardest, most expensive part, is getting there. The visits become free after that.

(Robert Cioppa, CFO, Kohn Pedersen Fox, personal interview)

So, as practices become established in a foreign city, site and marketing visits become more time-efficient for senior partners.

As an example of the intensity of this travel, the American journal *Architectural Record* followed Brad Perkins, a partner in the New York practice Perkins Eastman (Ivy 2003). Written against the backdrop of SARS, in late March 2003, the narrator – the journal's editor Robert Ivy – describes an eight-day trip with Perkins and some of his colleagues. On day one, he flies into Shanghai, leaving by train early the next day for Nanjing, to visit the Center for Chinese and American Studies, a joint venture by Johns Hopkins and Nanjing University. On day three, they return to Shanghai, to meet the city council's vice-chairman, discussing the forthcoming 2010 Expo. After lunch, they meet a commercial client for Maxdo Plaza, a huge multi-use project in the city, a discussion that runs over two days. By day five, they have flown to Beijing to meet another client, this time for a development of 4,600 housing units. Over the following two days Perkins and his team pursue this project – Science City – in detailed negotiations. On day eight, Ivy boards a flight out from Beijing: 'Once aboard, I collapse into the seating, dumbfounded at the pace – a rotation completed monthly' (Ivy 2003: 119).

For Ivy, one of the most striking things about the trip was the importance of cross-cultural etiquette and understanding. The daily schedule is punctuated by any number of fascinating cultural tics – the serving of Szechuan food at lunch one day, sandwiches on another; the bilingual discussions in English and Mandarin; Perkins' gift of a pair of golf gloves for a client. He notes the self-assured demeanour of many of the clients, as in the case of the Shanghai City Council's vice-chairman, who 'exudes a controlled confidence, not of the bristling American boardroom type, but suggesting an inner assurance' (p. 118). Ivy also notes the means by which Perkins communicates with his clients, and the role of his senior colleagues in extending the firm's scope of operation. While Perkins travels to Jinan, Diana Sung – one of the firm's principals – remains in Beijing to accompany the Science City client to the Great Wall for a *son et lumière* and, the following day, to the city's Summer Palace. Yet direct personal friendships are also highly significant. Perkins frequently uses free moments to make mobile phone calls to other potential clients. He stresses his family's Chinese connections: his grandfather, Dwight Perkins, had designed Nanjing University; his brother is the head of Harvard's Asia Center. The Maxdo Plaza commission came from an initial meeting with the client five years previously, with Perkins working 'to gain the client's trust and friendship, returning repeatedly himself and forging strong ties with the chairman' (personal interview).

It was once assumed that improvements in information technology would decrease the need for travel. However, it seems that the opposite is true, with travel and group meetings seen as central to the construction of successful relational spaces. While firms may create spaces for formal networking and project work at such events, it is often argued that social activities enhance bonding and trust in specific cultural contexts.

## The travelling sketch: Renzo Piano and Sydney's Aurora Place

To illustrate some of the issues involved in the transmission of design ideas, this section discusses the role of Renzo Piano Building Workshop in the design of a commercial skyscraper, Aurora Place, in the central business district of Sydney. Born in Genoa in 1937, Piano's *reputation* was established in 1972 when, in partnership with Richard Rogers, he won the commission for the Pompidou Centre in Paris, which opened in 1977. In 1993 he formed Renzo Piano Building Workshop, an architectural *practice* with offices in Genoa and Paris, which in 2003 employed around 100 architects, engineers and technicians. This has been followed up by a number of highly respected projects in a range of sectors;

*Figure 2.1* Sydney skyline.

Note
'Signature' buildings are from left to right: 126 Phillip Street, by Foster and Partners; Chifley Tower, by Kohn Pedersen Fox; Aurora Place, by Renzo Piano Building Workshop; Governor Phillip Tower, by Denton Corker Marshal is second from right.

Kansai airport in Osaka, the Padre Pio pilgrimage church in Foggia, a major office building in the highly sensitive Potsdamer Platz in Berlin, and the Menil art gallery in Houston show evidence of the diversity of his work. Such diversity contributed to his winning the Pritzker Prize in 1998, garlanded in the White House before a thousand-strong throng, including most of the existing Pritzker laureates.

Piano had not yet received the Pritzker when he was approached by his clients, two representatives of Lend Lease Australia, Ross Bonthorne and Steve MacMillan, in 1996. Lend Lease had purchased a site occupied by the architecturally noted but technologically obsolete State Office Block from the New South Wales government without the possession of demolition permits. As the building, designed by Ken Woolley, was an acknowledged part of Australia's modernist heritage, it was intimated that a permit to demolish and replace it would require the construction of a superior architectural design. The appointment of a leading architectural firm was thus seen as being a way of reducing the risk. Bonthorne and MacMillan visited several leading architectural firms in the US and Europe, before finally deciding to appoint RPBW. As one local commentator suggested, and as Eugene Kohn would probably agree (see p. 20), the visit to Piano's studio on a Genoa hillside was seen as a decisive factor in his gaining the commission (Farrelly 2001).

Politicians, planning officers and the local media (architectural columnists in daily city papers, particularly) are often key stakeholders in how the design is mediated to a broader public. Then, of course, there is the client, whose ability to communicate desires ranges from individuals with a clearly articulated technical brief, to those with a vague and untutored knowledge of building process. Thus the client–architect relationship is often fragile, and will be strongly dependent on the ability of clients to gain alignment with the language of the architect. In the case of Lend Lease executives, however, the perception of Piano was that he was a contextualist, and an architect who worked well with commercial firms.

Politically, Piano's Italian ethnicity was cited as a very positive attribute, particularly given that the then Lord Mayor of Sydney, Frank Sartor, a key figure on the planning committee, was of Italian origin. In an early meeting between Sartor, Piano and Lend Lease, the Lord Mayor and architect communicated in Italian, and Piano's modus operandi clearly impressed Sartor, who commented to the press:

> He is most unassuming. He takes everything you say and analyses and argues. Or achieves what you want in a different way. 'Frank, listen to what you say. If you take that line of argument this will follow'. It is a very nice manner.
>
> (Frank Sartor, in Harley 1997)

Beyond Piano's Italian ethnicity, there was a perception that – despite the qualities of several Australian architectural firms perceived to be of 'international class' – there was a need to 'raise the bar' within Australian corporate architecture (Farrelly 2001). Furthermore, the actual cultural *reception* of the global, or international, architect was seen as being of great importance for Sydney's exterior reputation. So, the arrival of Piano was seen as being more than a clever public relations ploy to get round planning restrictions. The development application was largely successful. At the City of Sydney Council's planning committee meeting in December 1998, it was recommended that:

> 70. The proposed development is considered to be a major attribute to the City of Sydney. The proposed buildings are recognized as being innovative both in their architectural form and the proposed use of façade systems.

> 71. In recognition of the excellence in design demonstrated by the project architecture, the very significant public benefits that will arise as a result of the contributions and public works proposed by the applicant, it is considered that the request to vary the maximum floor space permitted on the site . . . is considered to be supportable.
>
> (City of Sydney Council 1998)

Thus the building was able to bypass the guidelines of the City of Sydney Local Environmental Plan which has prescribed floor-space ratios[1] and a clear statement on building to street lines, with the committee deciding that the aesthetic and public benefits given by the project outweighed the possible issues of precedent and unwanted massing. Given the primacy of the site, and the strenuous design standards pursued under the Sartor mayoralty, the design leadership shown by Piano seemed to have vindicated the decision of Lend Lease to employ him, and satisfied most of the city's media critics (Allenby 2000; Clafton 1998; Farrelly 2001). And in the project's construction phase, this would once again be an important marketing tool (McNeill 2007).

However, this is only one part of the story. As with any major project, signature architects operate within a team of construction professionals. In the case of Aurora Place, RPBW operated in conjunction with Lend Lease Design Group (LLDG), headed by Ross Bonthorne, the developer's large in-house architectural studio which had considerable experience of constructing high-rise buildings. It was agreed that RPBW would design the skins (defined as façade, wind and environmental engineering) and that LLDG would provide the core, frame and systems engineering (Metcalf and Van der Wal 2001: 34). This is a familiar arrangement in any major development involving a design-led architect, who work with production architects, engineers, and construction and project managers in the resolution of the final form.

So, central to this understanding is the idea of Piano the individual, whose time is limited, whose bodily ability to make more than occasional site visits is highly restricted by a time-distance formula, and who is reliant upon a team of similarly creative individuals to realise projects. In this sense then, Piano's initial site visit was fundamental to his ability to discuss it back in Genoa:

In September 1996, I went to visit the site with Mark Carroll and Shunji Ishida. We explored it in every possible way, flying over it in a helicopter, walking up and down Macquarie Street, sailing across Sydney Bay. We took photographs and tried to imagine the profile of our tower on the city skyline. Upon our return to the studio, at the Punta Nave, Tom Barker and the Ove Arup [engineering consultants] team arrived. They came to hear what the wind was like and how to make the best use of it. We want to capture the breezes off the sea, to improve the efficiency of the air-conditioning with a system of natural convection.

(Piano 1997: 243)

Piano was able to balance his presence in Genoa with work on the site in Sydney through a delegated design process. This involved a process of interpretation, where Piano's concept sketches are fundamental in the ultimate execution of the design. What is interesting in the context of globalisation, then, is how the sketches are passed along to his on-site representatives on the project team. In addition to the Genoa-based members of the team assigned to the project, Piano employed some former RPBW architects – Ken McBryde and Stephanie Smith (who had returned to Sydney from Europe to start their own practice, inno-varchi), and Chris Kelly, who was to play a significant role in the Sydney project team. These architects, schooled in Piano's ways of working and design language, were able to interpret and explain his sketches to other members of the design team. As McBryde explains:

The idea has got to be abundantly clear . . . and he captures that in his sketch, if you look at those sketches there's a couple of dots on them here and there, and when you've worked with him long enough you know those dots are extremely important . . . [T]hey're crucial things in the success of the project in terms of the marketing, new ways of working, all that stuff, the way the building sells.

(personal interview)

Smith concurs:

He's very skilled at reducing something complex to the essence, and that's what those sketches are about, how the concept gets used. If you can actually define your idea in 3 or 4 lines then it's going to be probably quite a success-ful project . . . you have to have a point you can always go back to through the process and say, this is the concept and this is what we're working to achieve, and if it's very complex and it's hard to defend then it's unlikely to work very well unless you've got an amazing team.

Thus Piano's rendering ability (he sketches, but doesn't work in computers, according to Metcalf and van der Wal 2001: 32) is fundamental to the detailed design and construction process. Piano works his design as a series of sketch-books:

> every aspect of the project has its given sketchbook, that's the overall concept, that's the winter garden, that's the chicken arm, the roofs, the fins, the lights, the up-lighting, the terracotta, there's a Renzo sketch for it all, because they come out in working sessions and he's clarifying in understanding the brief, understanding the budget, understanding what his team's telling him about the problems that might have been presented before, he pares it down, he understands it, he sees it, and goes OK, we'll do this, let's try this . . .
>
> (Stephanie Smith, innovarchi architects, personal interview)

Despite the significance of new technology, sketching is still a fundamental aspect of the design process (Somol 1999; Vidler 2000). Why is this? As Hill (2003: 173) suggests, 'For architects, the drawing is as real as the building. First, because the architect makes the drawing but not the building; second, because the architect has greater control over the drawing than the building; and, third, because the architect makes the drawing before the building.' Thus despite the power and apparent authorship of buildings by architects from distant shores, the realisation of the building depends on a complex process of group design. As Middleton (1967) has suggested, 'Until recent times, the artist was a workman, the commission was his starting point and excellence of craftsmanship his aim' (p. 15). With the increasing complexity of commercial buildings, however, this simple chain of command has been surpassed. In this context, how the firm's design partners apportion their scarce time is a key decision, from initial meetings with clients, through to the necessarily distanciated design process itself.

## Client meetings and performing competitions

On the 14th and 15th of November 1994, the thirteen shortlisted architects were each given twenty minutes to present themselves, followed by forty minutes of questions from the jury. There were ten assessors appointed by the Tate to choose the winner. Apart from Nick Serota [Tate's director], there were a handful of trustees and several architects . . . The architects had been asked to submit four A1-size boards responding to three issues – the setting of the building in the context of its urban location and site; planning the general layout of the building; and ideas for the display spaces. Between their visit to the building on 7 October and the date to submit their boards there was just over a month. The practices were given an honorarium of

£3,000 and expenses of £1,500 to do the work. Few of them could have worked shorter than twelve-hour days during that month. Whatever their opinion of competitions – and some were very dismissive of this method of choosing an architect – the chosen thirteen couldn't afford to miss an opportunity like this. When they turned up at Millbank, some carrying their boards under their arms after a midnight push the previous night, they were like nervous candidates for an A-level exam, rather than some of the world's leading architects.

(Sabbagh 2001: 23)

This account of the competition to design London's Tate Modern – ultimately won by the Swiss firm of Herzog and de Meuron – gives an insight into some of the challenges faced by globally operative architects. The decision to enter a competition is not taken lightly, as it involves a huge opportunity cost in terms of staff time (including those of the senior partners), not only in the studio, but also in terms of site visits and travel costs. While many firms will only enter competitions if explicitly invited to do so, and will do their own risk calculations as regards to the costs of entry and chances of success, such competitions often involve plum sites in the centre of cities, and as such provide a prime opportunity for career advancement and firm promotion (Larson 1993: 119–22; Nasar 1999).

*Figure 2.2* The Camp Nou redesign exhibition, Barcelona, 2007.

For example, as the exhibition displaying competition entries for the redesign of FC Barcelona's iconic Camp Nou stadium demonstrates (see Figure 2.2), models of important buildings will generate interest among the general public and enhance the firm's visibility.

Indeed, it is often through the design competition that an avant-garde architect makes a breakthrough. Renzo Piano and Richard Rogers are a good example of this, with their surprising victory to design a contemporary art gallery at Beaubourg in 1971. Rafael Viñoly, the New York-based architect, was similarly able to win a major convention centre job in Japan (the Tokyo International Forum, 1990–6) through competition. Zaha Hadid was less lucky, however, with her breakthrough delayed by local political opposition following her 1994 competition victory to design the Cardiff Bay Opera House (Crickhowell 1997). Similar problems have bedevilled other high profile competitions, such as the Scottish Parliament building (discussed below), and – most famously – the Sydney Opera House. While the Danish architect Jørn Utzon had been commended on his radical design, the escalating costs of the project caused local politicians to institute drastic cost-saving measures, downgrading Utzon's role in the project, preventing the holistic completion of the building as it has been envisaged, and – with blame for the continuing delays still difficult to determine – ultimately caused the architect to resign, in 1966. The building would finally be opened in 1973, completed by a new architectural team (Murray 2004).

Most of the architects involved in such high profile competitions have learned a lot about the political nature of building design. Not all of the circumstances that may hinder the realisation of successful competition entries can be predicted, including problems with contractors, physical difficulties concerning the site, and changing political and budgetary conditions. What is undeniable, however, is the need for the principal architect to *perform* in such a way as to convince sceptical clients of the merits of their proposal. For example, Norman Foster's presence was required in the public presentation of his proposed masterplan for the redesign competition for Ground Zero in 2002, held in the Winter Garden adjacent to the site. Paul Goldberger, architecture critic for the *New Yorker*, captured his delivery – and those of the other finalists including the winner Daniel Libeskind – as follows:

> He [Foster] addressed the audience with the air of a man who was accustomed to having boards of trustees, chief executives, and public officials treat him with deference, whereas Libeskind was constantly trying to please by tugging on the heartstrings. Foster was not without his own insecurities, however. One of the oddest aspects of his presentation was the frequent mention he made of specific subway lines that crisscrossed the area of Ground Zero – the 1 and 9, and the N and the R – and also the PATH trains, as if he worried that the one thing that could keep him from winning was a

perception that he was too much of an outsider, and so he had to prove that he could drop New York references like a native.

(Goldberger 2004: 10)

Along with 'local knowledge' about foreign cities, a high level and range of communicative skills are required in other contexts, as in the visit of the Reichstag's Building Committee to London to visit Foster:

> They went first to the Royal Academy to look at the Sackler Galleries [a Foster-designed building]. Mark Braun [German member of FaP] and I met them and introduced them to our former client, Sir Roger de Grey, who took them on a tour of the building. The visit over, we invited them back to the studio to get a feel for the way that we worked. It was not clear quite what the correct protocol was, but we assumed that elaborate hospitality would be inappropriate, so we had drinks, and they seemed to enjoy their visit ... I heard later that they ... had been impressed, not only by 'British understatement', but by the fact that our studio was still buzzing with activity very late into the evening.
>
> (Foster 2000: 64)

The treatment of important clients is thus given the utmost thought by Foster and the practice, even if this involves a restrained response to client hospitality, and an over-eagerness to express knowledge of local context. Ultimately, however, the choice of architect made by the client will depend on a combination of factors. As Williams (1989: 33–49) demonstrates, the commissioning process for the Hong Kong and Shanghai Bank building was undertaken by Roy Munden, assistant general manager of the Bank's management services, who drew on the recommendations of existing clients, visits to the offices of each architect, and analysis of the submitted material by each firm (which included a portfolio of written justifications for the project, models and sketches).

In their breakthrough project in the 1980s, Foster would commute every six weeks from London to Hong Kong to supervise each stage of the Hong Kong and Shanghai Bank project, meeting the Bank's managers, and visiting the on-site office staffed by trusted deputies (Williams 1989). Even given high levels of trust within the project team, the principal architect will usually wish to pay regular visits to oversee the quality of finish and to address any unforeseen construction problems that ensue.[2] Given the range of projects on his practice's books, Foster's input will – by necessities of time – be restricted. Urry (2004: 31) refers to these limitations as 'time obligations', requiring him to schedule 'quality time' with 'significant others', linked to an 'obligation to place', where a specific location – in the case of the architect, a building site, client boardroom, or design studio – must be corporeally visited.

The presentation of self in these situations is very important. For example, Chance (2001a) draws attention to the ubiquitous styling of Jacques Herzog (one half of the leading international 'star' practice, Herzog and de Meuron) as a sombre, shaven-headed aesthete, where the architect's steady gaze at the camera 'will never be altered by frivolous changes of mood and this indicates desirable qualities of both building and architect: perseverance, stamina and consistency' (Chance 2001a: 52). This is seen as important when co-present with clients, as it allows 'access to the eyes. Eye contact enables the establishment of intimacy and trust, as well as insincerity and fear, power and control' (Urry 2002: 259). Such intimacy is seen as part of a range of obligations to go 'face-to-face' in social life. In the specific case of the design process, this will vary from job to job, studio to studio. But it is undeniable that in any context where commissioning takes place through a competition, the styling of the architect and their communicative modes are very important.

## The design studio

> In order to produce a body of work with integrity, individual architects must construct avenues leading out of the disorder toward collective work and coordinated practice. The milieu of each firm is unique and in flux, but underlying their uniqueness, firms share certain structural characteristics. The first is an office's heritage, which involves the origins and founders of a firm, often recollected in legends analogous to creation myths. Other characteristics include office members' use of language, their power structure, and their prevailing practices and values.
>
> (Cuff 1992: 157)

A key aspect of architectural practice is the management and motivation of a design *studio*, that produces work of a guaranteed quality and distinction. To ensure quality control, project co-ordination, and provide design leadership, a single space is required for the success of the 'Foster model'. Contrary to other similar-sized architecture firms – such as Skidmore, Owings & Merrill or HOK, with large networks of regional offices located close to major markets – Foster and Partners is run primarily from one location, Riverside 3, designed by the firm on the banks of the Thames in Battersea, West London. The grounded physical location for the practice – the design studio – is important both for establishing a functioning space for design, and for communicating a symbolic aura to clients. As one of the firm's senior partners, David Nelson, describes, the firm's way of working changed markedly during the Hong Kong and Shanghai Bank project:

> We were spread over three floors – we couldn't expand above or below and moving is difficult when you are on the run with a major project, so the office became very dense. We took the drawing boards and positioned them

back to back and facing each other because this was the tightest possible plan and created these long tables that were independent drawing boards. Amazing things happened – people stopped writing memos, communication improved. When we came back from Hong Kong we decided to build fixed long tables, huge long desks. Our particular flexibility was that the people were going to move, not the furniture – and that has now served us well for twelve to thirteen years. Everyone was in that one space: model-makers, secretaries, me, Norman, everybody. However, as we have expanded we now occupy other buildings as well.

(Nelson in Nimmo 2004)

The significance of the space is echoed by Foster himself:

Today in our London studio you can hear perhaps 35 languages spoken. It is so cosmopolitan that I sometimes joke that it is another country . . . It is also a very young office – the average age is around 30 – and there is an extraordinary high level of motivation. The studio is open 24 hours a day, seven days a week, and you will find people working there at all hours. Two crucial characteristics of the studio and the way that we work are the democracy and freedom of communication that we enjoy. The studio has no partitions or separate rooms and meetings tend to take place informally, often around the drawing board or computer screen. And every member of the office, whatever his or her role, has an identical workplace at one of the long benches that span the width of the room.

(Foster 2000: 17)

While Foster stresses the egalitarian nature of the space, critic Kenneth Frampton likens the studio to a Panopticon, an 'unremitting panorama of order and control' (in Rose 2002). Here, logically, Foster is able to follow how his concept designs – as well as those of others – are worked on and tested. Foster's input is embodied in the concept of the 'design review', as a senior partner, Graham Phillips, testifies:

the way work is brought together for a review is crucial. When the collection of material is truly comprehensive, and it's put up on the wall, it's amazing what can be achieved in a relatively short meeting. The secret, I believe, is having Norman there, together with some other incisive people. For Norman, a design review takes priority over everything else. . . . These reviews take place at all stages of a project – not just in the initial concept phase. They continue through to Norman's regular visits to the site to see buildings under construction, and more often than not they result in detail design sessions being held on site.

(in Quantrill 1999: 59)

These may be seen as 'object obligations', which Urry (2004: 31) sees as 'the necessity to be copresent to sign contracts or to work on or to see various objects, technologies, computer screens, or written texts'. While these objects may be mobile, it is most often the design studio that is the privileged site for co-present discussions between team members involving material objects (designs pinned to walls, architectural models, the explanation of a computer visualisation on-screen). As Iain Godwin, the firm's IT director, has explained, each project has 'job captains' who work in tandem with CAD co-ordinators (whose task is to manage the huge volumes of design data on projects). As Godwin noted in 2000, however, software design technologies were still being used alongside traditional pen or pencil drawings in concept design, as well as with 3-D physical models:

> Norman has a Wacom tablet and he's still working out when it is and isn't appropriate to use. We will sketch because we don't want to be constrained by geometry in the first instance. Then the team works on how to represent the ideas in the machine in order to play with area calculations. . . . With the Swiss Re project we literally had hundreds of these 'pine cone' models in the office, as team members played with floor plates to gauge the right level of twist and work out spatial relationships. That would have been very difficult to do and get everyone's input had we done that on a machine. There was a lot of testing and area checking with the 3D modelling going on simultaneously, but the physical 'pine cone' models were essential in helping process the form.
>
> (in Day 2000)

So, as Urry (2004: 32) has emphasised, 'even electronic spaces seem to depend upon moments of face-to-face copresence for developing trustful relationships'. As a point of comparison, consider the example of the Office for Metropolitan Architecture (OMA) led by another 'star' architect, Rem Koolhaas. According to one former OMA partner, Joshua Ramus, the Koolhaas influence is felt not in creation itself, but in the management of the creative process:

> The remarkable thing of which Rem is the author, explicitly, is the office's process. . . . What the OMA process focuses on is not the creator but the critic. In our way of working, the important person is the one who is shown various options and then makes a critical decision.
>
> (in Zalewski 2005: 117)

A further example of the complexity of the design studio can be found in the following exchange involving the partner and widow of Enric Miralles, Benedetta Tagliabue, during the enquiry into the design of the Scottish Parliament. In this unfortunate case, a major public commission had soared over budget, and a legal team cross-examined the parties involved to ascertain the reasons as to why this had happened. One of the themes raised was that of the modes of co-operation between the two architectural offices engaged on the scheme, with attention focusing on the culture of each office. The transcribed dialogue is more generally revealing of how architects see their studios and work practices:

58. MR CAMPBELL QC: Can I look at paragraph 1.5 of the statement, please? You talk there about the type of studio:

59. *This architectural studio is a type of atelier, where formal experimentation was one of the main points, but always based on the most advanced technical and informatic support.*

60. Tell me what you mean by atelier; tell me about the type of the studio.

61. BENEDETTA TAGLIABUE: It is difficult to explain in words. Before, we were looking at some of the books I brought here, in which we try to explain the type of atelier. We always try not to lose the relationship with the primary creative way of doing things. We favour, for example, in the office, together with the computers in the drawing rooms; we have also the workshop where we create models. We create incredible models, which I think were very important tools for the Scottish Parliament. There are something like 15 people working there. Working together with the drawings and the models is really a very important part of how we create our architecture. It is not just that there is a sketch and this sketch is given to someone and then it is developed – it is really work in progress.

62. MR CAMPBELL QC: But making models is not unique, is it? Are you telling me that is peculiar to your studio?

63. BENEDETTA TAGLIABUE: Yes, because our models are not presentation models only; our models are really a tool to arrive at a certain shape. The shapes that we are developing, and that we were developing more and more during those years, are very unique. We were very conscious that, in the world of a certain type of architecture, we were unique. The models that we were doing were absolutely important tools to arrive at a certain kind of architecture, which was very new, very experimental and unique in the world.

64. Before we saw some photographs. Well, maybe some images of the models that we are doing are explaining that they are tools; they are not just presentation things; they are really tools in order to make the project arrive at a certain level.

65. MR CAMPBELL QC: Is it easier to evolve the project using models or using sketches and drawings – or both?

66. BENEDETTA TAGLIABUE: It is less expensive to do it using sketches, but it is really fantastic to do it using models because you can see better what you are going to do. And the people who are around you and working in your atelier also can understand better what they are doing.

67. MR CAMPBELL QC: But surely part of the training of any architect is to have a three-dimensional sense so that you can see from the plan what it will look like? Why does a model make it easier?

68. BENEDETTA TAGLIABUE: It is not so easy to give an answer to that. I think we noticed that at the beginning of the 1990s the architecture of Enric was very much a flat architecture. He produced only drawings, and then very complex buildings were coming out of those drawings. But then probably this was possible because this was in Spain and the relationship with craftsmen was very strong. The craftsmen could understand the drawings, and they could make a very complex building out of them. Then, when we became more international, the studio became bigger; we really needed tools which were more understandable to everybody, to make everybody understand where we were going. So these tools were useful inside the office and also on the outside for clients or contractors or everybody working around the project.

(Holyrood Inquiry Transcript 2004)

In the case of EMBT, the firm of Miralles and Tagliabue, a strong emphasis was placed on the office as a physical space, and as a space where design solutions are actively performed with the use of material objects. This conversation reveals a conviction that certain national construction cultures possess differing degrees of skill, or artisanal conditions. It is well established, for example, that the Japanese construction industry has a highly developed skills set in terms of how builders and architects interact in the design process, a throwback to a period prior to the establishment of the architectural profession (Buntrock 2001).

Each of the examples I have discussed here describe practices that have been dominated by single individuals: Piano, Foster, Miralles. Here, the design process and studio is central to maximising the advice and design skills of a signature architect. The arrival of 'space-shrinking technologies' has raised the bar even higher, however.

## Space-shrinking technologies

For a long time, much of the human world has been on automatic, has expanded beyond the immediate influence of bodies and has made its way into machines.

(Thrift and French 2002: 311)

The codification process alters the relationship between the *codified* and the *tacit* form of knowledge. Codified knowledge is necessarily explicit, formal, or systematic, and can be expressed in words and numbers, scientific procedures or universal principles. This codified category of knowledge is easy to transfer, store, recall and valorize. On the other hand, tacit knowledge is extremely difficult to transfer. The main forms of tacit knowledge are know-how (gathered from the accumulation of practice), mastery of a language (gathered from the accumulation of the ability to communicate), and 'representations of the world' (gathered from the accumulation of wisdom). All these forms result from complex learning processes that require considerable amounts of time to be translated from an 'emitter' to a 'receiver'.

(Amin and Cohendet 2004: 23, emphasis in original)

In Chapter 1, I described the decision by the famous US architectural firm Skidmore, Owings & Merrill (SOM) to appoint a non-architectural chief executive officer, Ken Brown, in 1999. His key objective was 'to break the link between the firm's performance and the boom-bust real estate cycle' (Fairs 2000). In particular, he sought to avoid domestic recession by having a diverse portfolio of commissions, which in turn presented logistical demands on how the company allocated its fee-earning employees. To this end, Brown launched a company intranet (SOMeThing), allowing the company's 900 staff in the US, London, Hong Kong and São Paulo to share databases and co-operate on projects. Here, the skill base of the firm is mobilised, as Brown argues: 'Our great structural engineers are in Chicago. Some of our best transportation designers are in New York. We want to access those people for the benefit of the client' (in Fairs 2000). A similar process was constructed in the Aurora Place project described above. As a complement to direct verbal communication via telephone, Lend Lease (the developers) constructed a web-based collaboration system which allowed all project participants (from designers to project managers) to access the relevant information from any point. This process had to 'address the juxtaposition between the tactile, craft-based approach of the Renzo Piano Building Workshop, the incessantly paper-based culture of most project managers and the perceived complexity of computing technology in a traditionally conservative industry' (Metcalf and Van der Wal 2001: 36).

However, while face-to-face contact is a highly significant part of the architect's job, both within design teams, with contractors, and with clients, there is no doubt that technological innovation has transformed the architectural design process in the last few years. This is a general process, of course; outsourcing has become a major feature of the new economy, fixing low-wage but skilled labour with routine parts of the production process. The willingness of major design firms to outsource is partly driven by the strength of in-house IT networks. Given the centrality of technologies for firm design, it is unsurprising that the architectural equivalent of chief information officers are now highly prized. James R. Brogan, AIA, Director, Firmwide Information Technology at Kohn Pedersen Fox Associates, outlines his personal goals as follows:

> When I began at KPF I identified a few important objectives: one was to enhance the firm's 3D modelling capabilities, second, to unify the network typology, to really bring the networks in the New York, London and subsequently Shanghai offices together, and third to create a single, unified firmwide knowledge base through our firmwide KPF intranet and unified network resources. And my ultimate goal is to create a seamless presence – we work globally, not necessarily having a single base of operations, but having the New York, London and Shanghai offices working as a seamless, single entity, with all resources and all staff being accessible globally. So wherever a KPF staff person happens to be or is working, they are able to access KPF resources through a single method of secure access.

To pursue this task requires an understanding of information technology developments outside architectural practice itself.

> All the design and documentation is done in New York, London, or Shanghai depending on the project. Then through various means of connectivity we manage the project holistically. For instance, the remote users have access, through any internet connection, to an SSL VPN [Virtual Private Network] connection enabling secure access to the KPF firmwide network, IP voice system, and the KPF intranet, our knowledge-sharing portal. We extensively use video and web conferencing, so it's how we manage projects at such a distance away. We use WebEx which is an internet-based conferencing tool, where everything seen on a person's screen in New York can be seen in one or a multiple set of offices concurrently – we'll employ these technologies in conjunction with video conferencing for multi-point conferences. We also have a document camera where one can do hand sketches, that's all transferred via the videoconferencing system. Electronic 'sketches' and ubiquitous scanning capabilities enable quick comments to be transferred in real-time. We don't necessarily use SMARTboard technology, it's not necessarily right for us at the moment. But we'll take a 3D model, use WebEx, and the client can see it as its being talked through. We are now looking at internal, individually-based video capabilities integrated with our IP-based voice system for one-on-one video/voice calls.
>
> (James Brogan, personal interview)

The ideal, therefore, is that of a virtual office, seamless and secure, that includes constant contact with designers on site visits, using handhelds (Blackberrys and

Windows-based PDAs) to allow hypermobile employees to email each other. For submission of designs, the firm uses a Linux-based File Transfer Protocol site for project file distribution and communication, for clients, consultants and contractors.

The need for a robust and reliable technology backbone for a global architecture firm thus requires a significant investment in IT staff. KPF employs ten people in New York, from Network Administrators and support staff, a Design Technology Manager responsible for modelling, rapid prototyping, fabrication tools and related tasks, a firmwide Web Technologies/Database Manager, a CAD/BIM Manager and team and a Computational Geometry Group. In London, they employ eleven people in similar roles, and also includes a Visualisation team and Director of Research and Development. The Shanghai office has a group of Visualisation specialists that work with all offices. Importantly, these specialists in each office are seen as a unified whole – as firmwide resources. These support a staff of approximately three hundred people in New York, two hundred and seventy in London and thirty in Shanghai.

Architects have thus watched the evolution of office technology closely. For John Denton, one of three partners in the Melbourne-based firm Denton Corker Marshall, while information technology has been improving rapidly, it is only from the early 2000s that full confidence can be felt in its ability to replace physical, embodied travel:

> You've been able to send emails or simple plan drawings. But the ability to send large electronic files and know they're going to get there safely and be able to be used, and have the confidence to do it, has really only come in the last few years. For us to send an 80 page full colour competition entry to London, at 5 o'clock on the day before the competition closes, and for it to get there early morning in London [to be printed], to get delivered in Manchester at 2 o'clock, you'd have to be reasonably confident about the system. You couldn't have done that a few years ago.
>
> (John Denton, partner, Denton Corker Marshall, personal interview)

Thus despite the apparent virtuality of the stretched communications system, there is a very real material process involved which is based upon calculative practices: how *confident* practitioners are in the process they have constructed. This issue of confidence in the fallibility of the design process that they are experimentally constructing applies to the growing interest in outsourcing:

> From an economic geography point of view, architectural practice has always been a local employment industry; an industry, that is, which produces its output (in this case advice and physical information) in close enough proximity to the place where such output is put to use. This is due to the socially complex and thus operatively uncertain nature of the building process.

Within it, architects are required to generate, submit, issue and transfer design information at an almost constant pace: decisions must be progressively formalised, discussed and agreed upon with a panoply of project participants coming from different directions, and eventually modified. Such a distinctive lack of operative autonomy made it traditionally difficult for architectural firms to operate beyond the territorial limits of physical transactions (essentially the space allowing drawing to be exchanged in a reasonable time) ... [...] This need for proximity generated a critical difference in the spatialisation of production in architecture ... [...] The difficulty of dividing plant (the design office), process (the drawings) and product (the building project), meant that cost minimisation strategies had to be organisational rather than geographic.

(Tombesi *et al.* 2003: 64)

The potential advantages of outsourcing are clear. It allows twenty-four-hour working, where routine design work can be carried out in a different time zone while the project team sleeps. Outsourcing has also been posited as the means by which small offices can tackle large projects, through exploiting a globally uneven division of labour: Vietnamese designers are paid £4,000 annually (Pearson 2003), allowing smaller architectural offices to avoid major staff costs during periods of downturn. As Tombesi *et al.* (2003: 85) note, web-based architectural gateways now carry adverts for dozens of Indian architectural firms, who are also directly marketing themselves to Western clients. However, this is based upon a clear-cut distinction between 'symbolic analysis' and 'routine production', between skilled and 'unskilled' architectural practice.

So, the advent of new communications technology in general, and architectural design software in particular, has revolutionised the nature of the architectural drawing and the building design process in the space of a few years. This has allowed major architectural and engineering firms to conduct complex design issues remotely. However, quality control, deliverability and cultural differences in the interpretation of designs demand careful monitoring and continuous refinement. These issues require strategic management to ensure that globally 'stretched' knowledge practices work smoothly.

## Meeting the clients: property trade fairs

As with stocks or bonds, investors are seeking to diversify their investment portfolios in both a sectoral and a geographic sense and property offers a perceived opportunity to improve risk-adjusted returns. Particular sectors of the property market that are focused on include high class ('Grade A') office space, 'trophy buildings', luxury condominium housing, hotels, vacant suburban tracts of land, rental housing, and industrial land ...

(Olds 2001: 24)

Every year, in Cannes, thousands of people descend on the brutalist concrete expanse of the Palais des Festivals, an incongruous urban monster set on the glittering shore of the Cote d'Azur. They are there to participate in MIPIM (*Le marché international des professionnels de l'immobilier*), a trade fair for property professionals, regeneration officials, mayors, and those who seek them out, the much-prized investor. Among the year-round procession of trade fairs that come to Cannes, it lies second in size to the film festival, but consumes – so it is claimed – the most champagne by far. By the early 2000s, MIPIM was attracting anything in the region of 15,000 to 17,000 delegates, and while its profile is primarily European, there are delegations from North America, China and Southeast Asia, and the Middle East. It is also, gradually, becoming seen as an essential destination for architectural practices, certainly those operating in Europe. Along with other trade fairs such as Cityscape, MAPIC, or Exporeal, MIPIM offers architects specialising in commercial design access to a targeted group of developers, politicians, and property professionals.

In this context, MIPIM is important to architectural firms for a number of reasons. For large firms, there is the need to be seen to be *there*, as expressed by Nick Terry of BDP:

> It's like a chicken and egg situation with MIPIM. You go there and you already know loads of people who are there. It's like if you're not there, where are you? It's a great opportunity when you go to meet all the people that would normally take months to get hold of, if you're in London to get meetings, suddenly you've got all the key decision-makers in one place all at the same time, you can actually make contacts, have meetings, make decisions on projects you're doing or hoping to do all over this 4 or 5 day period. So it's a great use of time. If you're going for the first time, you're not necessarily going to get any work out of it, because in a way you've got to be in the club before you start, but it's a great forum. It's like a huge market, effectively, but you have to go with a real focus.
>
> (personal interview)

So, at moments when there is a large amount of surplus investment capital, architectural firms can pick up significant commissions, particularly in major master-planned projects with multiple actors. Furthermore, the presence of major politicians with significant influence over the winning composition of competitive bidding teams provides architects with an efficient networking platform to showcase their existing work, and to talk to partners in complicated development proposals.

For the architect accustomed to fairly small commissions, trade fairs such as MIPIM can be a confronting experience, providing direct exposure to the atmosphere of commercial development. As one 'boutique' architect, Kathryn Finlay, describes in her diary in *Building Design*:

Tuesday and Wednesday saw us deluged with queries on the stand. We had conversation after conversation with Chinese, Russians and Germans. Some clients were interested in our highly crafted design approach, others, with eyes set only on profit, were unconvinced. There were some time wasters and a few competitors wanting to smell us out. There were also plenty of people selling to us – engineers and landscape architects, in particular. But we felt positive about being part of this kind of market. I like to know every-thing to do with the process: why people build and how the profit motive works. You get that in spades at MIPIM with all the accountants, lawyers and developers around.

So, we can see MIPIM as being an arena where a particular branch of capitalism, namely the property development industry, helps to reduce the complexity and precariousness of its operating environments. As Thrift (2005; 3) has argued, 'The whole point of capitalism … is precisely its ability to change its practices constantly, and those who run corporations must be able to surf the right side of the constant change that results'. To this end, capitalism must be 'known', and as a result is 'performative: it is always engaged in experiment'. Economic geo-graphers have referred to this kind of interaction as 'buzz': 'the information and communication ecology created by face-to-face contacts, co-presence and co-location of people and firms within the same industry and place or region' (Bathelt *et al.* 2004: 38).

MIPIM provides the 'buzz', the 'untraded dependencies' that allow the gradual, time-consuming development of trust-based 'global pipelines' of associ-ation. Despite the rhetoric surrounding the hypermobile signature architect, the fact remains that for all firms, global reach in building design requires a multi-sectoral logistical coalition which will include engineers and interior designers as well as architects.

## Conclusions

How do we make sense of the impact of such extended knowledge networks? How important is distance as an impediment – or advantage – to architectural practice? How significant for the practice of a globalising architecture profession is the interweaving of corporeal travel, virtual co-presence, technological enabling, and tacit knowledge? One solution might be to use the language of 'cyborg urbanism', to consider the office and the Blackberry as being an exten-sion of the architect's human faculties. As William Mitchell (2003: 19) puts it in his book *Me++*: 'Embedded within a vast structure of nested boundaries and ramifying networks, my muscular and skeletal, physiological, and nervous systems have been artificially augmented and expanded'. The individual architect is thus involved in a network of relations facilitated by a mix of face-to-face meetings and socialising, telephone conversations, video and web conferencing, emails, and project intranets. The design process requires the co-presence – real or virtual – of many bodies, from concept design, through to the labour intensity of the construction process. Large architectural firms are thus faced with a challenge common to all professional services firms, which is to ensure that the knowledge required to produce their services exist (in the form of skilled employees), is retained (by stopping employees leaving work for rivals) and is leveraged (through knowledge management) (Lowendahl 2000, in Faulconbridge 2006: 523).

With this in mind, it may be prudent to consider how – particularly in large firms – senior architects are required to be authors of a design *process* rather than as authors of designs per se. In other words, how the senior partners, job captains, and CAD managers work to realise concept designs, and how well this is communicated to team members, contractors and clients, defines the output of the practice. 'Corporate organization, with all its devices, is the banal means by which knowledge spaces made up of bits and pieces from all over are mobilized' (Amin and Cohendet 2004: 99), and architectural firms – of whatever size – must work out how best to put them together to achieve and fulfil the practice's standards, design concepts, and ethos.

# 3 Architectural celebrity and the cult of the individual

## Daniel Libeskind as 'starchitect'

EVENTS

**Daniel Libeskind lecture.** Barbican Theatre £9/£7. Joint ticket with exhibition £15/£11. Daniel Libeskind discusses his architectural vision. This will be the only opportunity to hear this influential and thought provoking architect speak in London this year. Early booking highly recommended 0845 121 6826.

(from Barbican Art Gallery promotional leaflet to 'Space of Encounter: The Architecture of Daniel Libeskind, 16 Sept./04–23 Jan./05')

In 2004, Daniel Libeskind released an autobiography entitled *Breaking Ground: Adventures in Life and Architecture*. The style is light, often jocular, and fairly emotive. It describes Libeskind's childhood, his years as a student and his major professional challenges. It has few drawings, but does have a collection of photos, of buildings, models and of family life. He describes the creative process like this: 'Sometimes, I can be working on a drawing for weeks, making hundreds of sketches, when, with no warning at all, it happens: A perfect form emerges' (Libeskind 2004: 7). The personality that emerges from the book is one that has been carefully crafted and tuned. The book also carries a credit to Sarah Crichton, presumably a ghost writer. *Breaking Ground* is in stark contrast to his earlier manifesto, *Daniel Libeskind: The Space of Encounter* (2001), which articulated his design philosophy in a highly stylised, even obscurantist, mode of writing. In the latter book, there are pages and pages of complex diagrams, models, sketches and plans, explaining his design philosophy in a very different way.

Lecture tours, exhibitions and books are all important contributions to the construction of an architect's public image. And the rush of publications in the early 2000s reflected Libeskind's sudden emergence on the 'A' list of world architecture. He has had an interesting life story. Arriving in New York in 1959 from Poland as a thirteen year old, Libeskind would – after studying in the city –

return to spend much of his time in mainland Europe, 'winning dozen of awards and showing his work – ruptured, counterintuitive spaces in complex geometries, all of it on paper – at more than sixty exhibitions in the following years' (Nobel 2005: 136). As a predominately theoretical architect, his only significant built work took years to complete, but was of great importance: the Jewish Museum in Berlin, which he and his wife Nina patiently pushed through to completion in the midst of heated and tortuous debate over how Germany may most appropriately commemorate the Holocaust.

His autobiography tells this story with wit and passion. But its publication came at a very significant moment in Libeskind's professional career. In 2002, the Lower Manhattan Development Corporation (LMDC), responsible for co-ordinating the rebuilding of Ground Zero, announced that it would be holding a competition for the masterplanning of the highly sensitive site (Filler 2005; Goldberger 2004; Nobel 2005). The brief was complex: it had to satisfy both the requirements for a memorial to those that perished in the terrorist attack, as well as restoring the huge quantity of commercial space that had been present on the site in both the World Trade Center towers and in surrounding buildings that had to be demolished subsequent to the attack. Unsurprisingly, the competition attracted many of the major names in world architecture. In December 2002, the architects presented their schemes in the World Financial Center's Winter Gardens adjacent to the Ground Zero site. As Paul Goldberger describes, Libeskind made a distinctive contribution:

> Libeskind went up to the lectern. His first words were not about architecture at all. 'I believe this is about a day that altered all of our lives', he said. And then he went on to describe his own arrival in the United States forty-three years earlier. 'I arrived by ship to New York as a teenager, an immigrant, and like millions of others before me, my first sight was the Statue of Liberty and the amazing skyline of Manhattan,' Libeskind said. 'I have never forgotten that sight or what it stands for'.
>
> (2004: 8)

Libeskind's masterplan – which he dubbed 'Memory Foundations' – contained other highly emotive spatial interventions. He would introduce a 'Wedge of Light' in one of his proposed plazas, which would be designed to funnel sunlight through the skyscrapers in such a way that the site would always be in sunlight on 11 September, between the times of the first plane attack and the collapse of the second tower. He proposed a Park of Heroes to commemorate those lost. His central skyscraper – the Freedom Tower – provided a strong visual connection with the Statue of Liberty, an asymmetrical antenna mirroring that of Liberty's flame. And the tower itself was projected to stand 1,776 feet in height, a commemoration of the founding year of America (Nobel 2005: 137–9).

The Ground Zero design competition was one of the few occasions where architecture became a matter of general public debate. The architects and their designs were the focus of considerable media attention. Libeskind's design was particularly approachable for a broader public. For some, his evocation of an American spirit was rousing; for others, he was wrapping himself in the American flag in a fairly cynical attempt to win the competition. They began to see Libeskind as having created a 'niche' in suffering, a competitive position, as it were. As Deyan Sudjic notes, 'For the cynics . . . he was becoming a therapist as much as an architect' (2005b: 314). Although his Jewish Museum in Berlin was seen to be a sensitive, thoughtful attempt to materialise memory and recover suffering, there was a contrary argument to this. As Karen Till has described in her book about Berlin's memory politics:

> Günter Morsch, director of Sachsenhausen Memorial Museum and Brandenburg Concentration Camp Memorial Museums Foundation, argued that 'the discussions about the Jewish Museum, the Topography of Terror, and the Holocaust Memorial result[ed] in a turning away from the authentic sites of terror and destruction. . . . The spectacular architecture [of these three places] finds more attention among feuilletonists [art and cultural critics in the media] that we could ever have won for our [memorial museum] projects' (interview, 2000). Morsch, like other memorial museum experts, is concerned about the public attention these places receive for their world-famous architect-stars rather than their social functions of critically coming to terms with the past. He fears that the 'spectacular' memory district signifies a troubling direction in German public commemoration, a centralization of memory that may undermine the existing national, decentralized network of memorial museums.
>
> (Till 2005: 196)

This is a deep, nuanced debate that I cannot fully explore here. Yet it makes an important point in its implicit critique of iconic building solutions that attempt to resolve major traumas. And it highlights the complaint that architectural celebrity can interfere with the reception of the building itself, particularly important when it is designed as a mode of commemoration. Sudjic (2005b: 314) makes an interesting observation about this in respect to the Ground Zero competition:

> Of all the architects taking part, Libeskind was the only one not to be afraid of using the 'I' word. Strangely enough for a profession that cannot be anything but egotistical, the first person singular personal pronoun is almost always finessed away. It's always 'we' did this, when an architect means 'I'. But not Libeskind. 'I went to look at the site', he said, 'to see and feel what it is like to be standing in it, to see people, to feel its power, and to listen to its voices, and this is what I heard, felt and saw'.

Libeskind would thus use his life story as a central aspect in the performance of his competition entry, and in subsequent media pronouncements. As it happened, he would be sucked into a high profile media debate over the subsequent design control of the building with David Childs from Skidmore, Owings & Merrill, so the retention of public sympathy became as important a part of his repertoire as his design skills.

This brief profile of Libeskind gives a hint of the importance of differing types of social recognition to the success of architects, 'Starchitects' – as they are increasingly known – share a number of characteristics. First, they are identifiable individuals, with a name, a face and perhaps some kind of authored book. As with the advert that started the chapter, they have a particular charisma that will draw a paying audience to a high profile cultural institution to hear them explain their designs. As Philip Nobel has pointed out, Libeskind 'looked the part. . . . Topping out in a gray brush cut at not over five feet, invariably [dressed] in black from his cowboy boots to his thick, shieldlike designer frames' (2005: 135). Second, they are often associated with striking shapes, surfaces, or concepts. In other words, their buildings become famous, more so than the individual, at least to the broader public. Interestingly, critical evaluation of their contribution to the discipline can only be made after many years in which the longevity of both their aesthetics and their structural design can be assessed. So the term 'starchitect' often carries a negative connotation, implying an attempt to make an immediate, populist impact. Third, many of these individuals have a strong capacity for self-promotion. This is not necessarily a pejorative term, but simply a reflection of entrepreneurial zeal, communicative skills, innovative design partners, favourable economic cycles, or strong institutional embeddedness. They are, effectively, embodiments of the adage that celebrities are made not born, that they are social products of history rather than geniuses whose intrinsic skills have surfaced through an evolutionary impulse.

The relationship between fame and architecture practice is a fundamental aspect of the contemporary building process, particularly in the context of high profile civic commissions (Chance and Schmeideknecht 2001). This fame can be demanding. As Charles Jencks has noted, 'if you disappear from the scene for six months people think that you are dead, so you have to keep your name in front of the public in some way' (2001: 17). This fame can be posthumous. The likes of Frank Lloyd Wright, Charles Rennie Mackintosh and Antoni Gaudí have all been promoted mercilessly by their supporters and local marketing departments, their designs appearing on everything from mugs to ashtrays to towels. And this fame can be modish. For Jencks, 'architects have to reinvent themselves every ten years . . . this transformation is necessary because technology, society and fashion change' (p. 16).

# The cult of the individual architect

> Star power is frequently cited as the defining feature of transnational action films; a cohort of action stars includes Jean-Claude Van Damme, Arnold Schwarzenegger, Sylvester Stallone, Mel Gibson, Jackie Chan, Bruce Willis, Chow Yun Fat, Nicholas Cage, and Wesley Snipes. These figures help to 'pre-sell' a film.
>
> (Acland 2003: 35)

The star system has been a major part of the film industry for much of the twentieth century, and the use of star actors has long served to reduce the investment risk of film productions, underpinning the rise of film genres (Dyer 1998; McDonald 2005). In Hollywood, it is easy to track the waxing and waning of 'stars', by virtue of their box office takings. And certainly, just as star power pre-sells films, so developers are very conscious of the importance of world-renowned architects to pre-sell buildings to a sometimes sceptical public or market.

Yet carrying over the notion of a star system from Hollywood to architecture can be problematic. As Jeffrey Williams has argued with reference to 'star' academics, the Hollywood model is often 'framed as a homology, the academic following its template' (2006: 373). This creates a misleading binary, where the notion of celebrity is either dismissed out of hand (how can Jacques Herzog be compared with Robert de Niro?) or else overplayed (does public fame dictate esteem and power within architecture?). Despite the significance of name recognition, architects – unlike major sports, film, or music stars – can rarely be considered 'household names'. For one thing, it is often buildings that become famous, rather than their designers. With the possible exception of Frank Gehry (who, as we shall see in chapter four, played himself on an episode of *The Simpsons*), while the image of famous buildings will usually prompt recognition by the general public, the face of the architect would likely pass unnoticed in a crowd. Such is the problem of engaging with the notion of architectural celebrity or reputation.

Yet, this does not mean that the idea of an architectural star system should be dismissed. There are parallels with what has become known as the 'celebrity industry' (Gamson 1994; Rein *et al.* 1997). Film stars with breakthrough roles become stereotyped, condemned to replicate their first roles to satisfy risk-averse producers. Similarly, architects are often expected to reproduce a similar style or outcome for risk-averse clients. A producer or director will know the individual foibles, work ethic, temperament and modus operandi of the movie star, and know the broader celebrity apparatus – the hair stylists, agents, publicists, and supporting, secondary cast members – that will ensure the success of the final product, the movie. In a similar way, clients will be drawn to the doors of particular architects partly by their reputation for flexibility and teamwork with particular engineers and project teams, and will be less well-disposed to firms whose work modes do not suit them.

However, we can agree that the Hollywood star system is the result of a systematic, industrialised process of promoting individuals with a particular uniqueness or distinctiveness, requiring audiences to differentiate one star from another. And in this sense, the production of architectural celebrity is no different. As Andrew Saint (1983) has argued, the image of the architect has shifted little from the 'hero and genius' label attached to Frank Lloyd Wright and mythologised in Ayn Rand's novel *The Fountainhead* (with Gary Cooper taking the Howard Roark part in a subsequent film). In an amusing satirical article, Mornement's (2000) identifies four 'breeds' of global architect: the thirty to forty-five-year-old 'visionary', a manifesto-writing, loft-dwelling centre-leftie wearing miniature glasses and 'anything tight-fitting and black'; the 'businessman', a sixty-plus-year-old with a permanent tan and tailored suit, typically designing retail malls and airports; the 'contender', with a practice name of 'Me and Partners', 'a pragmatic balance between promoting the name of the dominant design partner, and acknowledging the contribution/presence of colleagues', who appears '50% academic/50% business guru – black linen suit (no tie), gracefully greying hair and a subscription to Fortune', and finally the 'untouchable', with a practice name of 'Me, Me and Me': 'An exclusively male bastion, the Untouchable is a wise and wealthy man. He will confirm his status as a driven genius by developing eccentric habits in his later years – distinctive hat, flying a helicopter...'. His typical projects include 'The world's largest airport, the world's tallest building, the world's most sculptural museum, or a foundation for the world's wealthiest man'.

This portfolio – written to entertain the 99.99 per cent of qualified architects who fail to fit these stereotypes – is nonetheless telling, as it does build upon a composite of psychological traits, bodily appearance, and charismatic performance that many in the broader world of property and construction will quickly recognise. From the visionary to the pragmatist, the subjectivity of the architect is important in the professional's public image. The conditions for the emergence of a star architect have long been in place, but the nature of architectural 'stardom' is a complex issue.

Here, the tension between architectural design as a team process clashes with the desire to attribute artistic autonomy to a single individual. The architect Denise Scott Brown, business partner *and* wife of Robert Venturi, documents how the critical response to the practice's output (which included the renowned *Learning from Las Vegas*) is usually solely attributed to Venturi, despite proactive attempts by the practice to spell out the nature of each individual's contributions to projects and writing. She reflects that 'A body of theory and design in architecture apparently must be associated by architecture critics with an individual; the more emotional their criticism, the stronger is its focus on one person'

(1989: 238). For Scott Brown, the gendered nature of these representations is fundamental. There remains only one female architect – Zaha Hadid – on an international 'A' list of name brand architects. Hadid, herself a female role model in magazines such as *Vogue*, explains the relative lack of leading female architects as follows: 'Really you have to go at it full-time, not dip in and out. When women break off to have babies, it is hard for them to reconnect on the big scale' (in Niesewand 2008: 145)

Yet this problem is not confined to the smaller firms. For Nat Owings, one of the founding partners of Skidmore, Owings & Merrill, the secret of SOM's success would be in the cultivation of a culture of anonymity, a 'modern "Gothic Builders Guild"' as he put it (Owings 1973: 66). Nonetheless, alongside the founding triumvirate of Nathaniel Owings, Lewis Skidmore and John Merrill, successive generations of high-profile design leaders have emerged in the three main offices of New York, Chicago and San Francisco. In New York, it was first Gordon Bunshaft, then David Childs; in Chicago, it would be Bruce Graham, and the structural engineer Fazlur Khan, and latterly Adrian Smith; in San Francisco, it was Charles Bassett. The firm has had to fight the perception that craft, individuality, signature and innovation are subordinate to their reputation for efficiency and ability to harness industrialised building methods. Gordon Bunshaft recalls one such incident, arguing that the press would simply not be interested in a depersonalised architectural product:

> Take Lever House. Bill Brown played a great, important part of it. But they would not mention him. They only wanted what I used to call 'the decorator', the designer. They wouldn't accept anything else. It was a difficult battle. In my case, it was these three other partners. I didn't want to hurt their feelings, and I couldn't avoid what was going on.... There was a big article in Newsweek, I think, about the firm. They came to see me, and I said some things, and right after that I went to Europe. I didn't see the article. I got a telegram from Walt Severinghaus saying that the firm's partners were terribly upset ... I don't know whether I'd seen the article or whether they sent me a copy, but the essence of it was I sort of casually said, 'Well, I do the design and the rest of them do all the work, all the other partners carry it out.' You know, like I'm the prima donna and they're slaves. Not quite like that, but it was bad. Owings earlier had once seriously tried to fire me, and Skid wouldn't let him. But this time, the partners of my own group – we were closely knit – asked me to leave when I got home over this remark.
>
> (Art Institute of Chicago 1989b: 184–5)

Bunshaft recalls the incident as being a learning experience, that this 'was the final blow of this publicity business with the partners'. He then pushed on to address the issue of architectural creativity.

*Figure 3.1* Lever House, New York, by SOM: sole authorship is often attributed to Gordon Bunshaft.

BLUM: But I think everyone, historians included, understands that a building doesn't get built by one man.

BUNSHAFT: I know, but they only want to talk about one man.

BLUM: Well supposedly that's the man with the creative idea.

BUNSHAFT: Oh creative nothing. They have the idea that I tried to explain to you that a creative idea comes out of some brilliant, imaginary mind. It doesn't. It comes out of [...] sweat [...] ... That's how it comes out. You add something to it, which is your architectural training and a certain amount of imagination or a concept.

(Art Institute of Chicago 1989b: 186)

The issue of anonymity as opposed to individual credit has been one of the major challenges facing SOM from its earliest days through to the present. The head of its San Francisco studio for many years, Chuck Bassett, had a clear understanding of authorship:

I didn't think of it as anonymity. I thought of it as appropriate recognition. One would have to go to great pains to be unaware of how many talents and energies share in the creation of a fine building, or of the discrepancy between that truth and the myth kept alive by an obvious cynicism that a building is born full-blown out of a single person's head. To perpetuate that myth, when it takes so many people, so much talent, so much technical expertise, so much dedication and commitment to a professional work ethic of a profession they love, it has always bothered me.

(Art Institute of Chicago 1989a: 130)

Nonetheless, it remains the case that partners within SOM and similar firms do not have the same recognition as celebrated designers within their own boutique firms.

## The signature architect

Both the aesthetics of the signature and the aesthetics of the brand are ideologies: they are regimes of marketing and authorization which draw in rather similar ways on an imaginary of the unique person or of personality; brands have a 'personality' because they make use of strategies of personalization (the use of characters, celebrities, direct address) to create something like a signature-effect; signatures stand as metonyms of an originating author or artist, even though the making of any work of art involves an extended number of participants (editors, publishers, proofreaders, printers, paint-makers, curators...) and a complex commercial apparatus.

(Frow 2002: 70–1)

It is increasingly common to hear mention of the 'signature' architect. However, the meaning of this term is not always clear. The signature as a statement of value has emerged from the norms of fine art and painting, where 'the signature is a guarantee of originality and its converse, the repudiation of forgery' (Frow 2002: 58; Lury 2005). By contrast, the emergence of the brand in forms of cultural production has a different meaning: 'the brand is a corporate rather than a personal signature: it is a *quasi-signature* ... Brands are typically *managed* to ensure that products are consistent with brand image and that competitors do not encroach on it' (p. 63). This imposes a tension between meeting market expectations ('the aesthetics of the brand'), and the need to produce original, or inventive, work ('the aesthetics of the signature').

It might be useful to compare the signature architect with two other professions that have had to reconcile market expectations with innovation: the couturier, and the celebrity chef. As Guillaume Erner (2005) has argued, female high fashion has increasingly become subordinate to brands, as evidenced in the trend for most major couturiers – Dior, Givenchy, Chanel – to respond to the branding opportunities associated with the lucrative perfume sector, associating their name with an industrial product markedly different from their core business of high quality tailoring and dressmaking. In this case, brand association is developed through the creation of standardised, mass marketed products that need no further monitoring for quality beyond regular industrial quality control methods.

We can also consider the small number of chefs who are rapidly expanding their worldwide presence in top-end dining: Gordon Ramsay, Alain Ducasse, Joel Robuchon, Nobu Matsuhisa, Alan Yau and Jean-Georges Vongerichten. Each has rolled out a restaurant chain on the presumption that diners will know that they are eating the auteur's concept, and that it will be of an assured quality. Yet the problem remains of *how* to assure this, of how to avoid simply being the 'name above the door'. A continuous process of monitoring may be one solution. Rayner (2006) quotes the irascible Ramsay, who has opened restaurants in London, New York, Tokyo and Dubai: 'I'm putting an £80,000 webcam in my kitchen. I'll be able to see what's going on in all my restaurants around the world. It will look like a f***ing investment bank in there' (p. 42). Effectively, Ramsay has attempted to solve the problem facing all elite designers – whether of food, clothes, or perfumes – which is the challenge of brand management, of quality control, while rapidly expanding output in destinations that are physically remote to the (food) designer. This places a premium on the training of trusted deputies. Ramsay regularly pushes forward 'his' staff to oversee the new satellite restaurants, allowing them a degree of individual style and autonomy.

There is an interesting parallel here with architecture, in that this version of brand expansion is based upon a successful apprenticeship or mentoring system. Ensuring a successful 'passing of the torch' will both relieve partners of any indefinite personal liability for lawsuits brought against their buildings, and should also enhance the value of their own shares in the firm. For the younger partners, the advantages of maintaining a firm's name recognition, reputation, and an established client base (given the significance of personal recommendations and repeat business for many clients) are strong (Dunlap 1999; Knutt 2001; Hay 2004). There are some interesting examples of this, such as the legacy of I.M. Pei. His sons, C.C. and L.C. Pei, left their father's practice to set up Pei Partnership, which would design the prestigious Bank of China headquarters in Beijing. The name is retained for purposes of recognition, yet altered slightly, but significantly. Richard Rogers Partnership changed its name in 2007 to Rogers Stirk Harbour + Partners. And the de facto use of 'acronymic' firm titles such as SOM, KPF and HOK reflect a subtle move away from the names of the original founders, as the firms expand to include multiple partners.

I want to consider this further by returning to the discussion of Foster and Partners. Foster's firm has achieved recognition through a series of visually striking buildings in some of the world's most mediated cities, including Berlin (Reichstag), New York (Hearst Tower) and London (City Hall, Wembley Stadium and the Swiss Re 'erotic gherkin' office building, among others), and infrastructural projects, as in the Millau viaduct in the South of France, or the Torre de Collserola in Barcelona.

*Figure 3.2* Swiss Re building, London, by Foster and Partners, seen from the Tower of London.

However, being identified as a signature architect requires confirmation of authorship. There are two interesting issues here. First, as we have seen, the relationship between the individual designer and the firm will gradually evolve to a point where sustained growth can only be achieved by the appointment and/or promotion of other elite designers, who may be frustrated at a lack of name recognition (as in the 'Me and Partners' model). Foster had long relied on a small number of key design partners, such as David Nelson and Ken Shuttleworth, in overseeing major projects. In January 2003, in an interview with Marcus Fairs that would appear in both the trade magazine *Building*, as well as the *Guardian* newspaper (Fairs 2003a, 2003b), Shuttleworth made a striking claim. Asked about his role in the firm, he responded that his major projects had been London's City Hall, Wembley Stadium and the Swiss Re building. These three projects were notable for their exuberant, strongly expressed design, and critics had suggested that a hand other than Foster's was responsible. Asked outright if he was the designer, Shuttleworth responded:

> Everything comes from the office. We work together, we'll all be toying with ideas with Norman and the others. You won't get what you get at some office – mentioning no names – where each partner produces a completely different type of architecture. We want to make sure there's consistency across the board. *Having said that, a lot of the sketches and the initial ideas have come from me. Swiss Re, for example. I don't know where they come from really; I sketch them out and they get worked up.*

He was then asked if he was concerned that his role was rarely credited:

> No, not at all. I've never sought publicity. I'm happy when Norman takes the credit. That's fine. He owns the company. He's the chairman. He had the guts to set the company up in the first place; he put his reputation on the line. *Architects are trained to be individuals, with a one-man-and-a-dog practice; they're trained to be artists. But in reality you can't do it on your own. It has to be as part of a team.*
>
> (in Fairs 2003a, emphasis added)

In the week following this article, Shuttleworth e-mailed a response to the magazine stating that he was embarrassed at the emphasis given on his design leadership in the article, and asked that the team-working aspect of the Foster studio be re-emphasised (Shuttleworth 2003). In November of that year, however, Shuttleworth resigned from the practice to set up a new firm – Make – with several other Foster and Partners architects. While the circumstances of his departure were publicly presented as being amicable, several commentators argued that the issue of credit for the Swiss Re building was a key reason for the split (Kirwan-Taylor 2004; Sudjic 2004).

A further point of relevance here is the role of structural engineers in the realisation of built form, a role that has assumed particular importance with the recent trend for stylistic expressiveness. The input of engineers is rarely acknowledged publicly, however. As Glancey (2006b) notes, the spectacular Millau Viaduct in the South of France is often attributed to Norman Foster, yet the engineer of the bridge – Michel Virlogeux – is nearly anonymous outside construction and design circles. A similar identity issue arises in the work of Cecil Balmond and Terry Hill, the chiefs of Arup's building and infrastructure divisions respectively. Balmond has worked closely with both Libeskind and Koolhaas, and is credited with the structural calculations behind some of their most noted projects, namely the Freedom Tower and CCTV project respectively (Arnold 2004).

The second interesting issue in terms of signature arises when the lead individual's name may eventually become redundant, or merges into a corporate, depersonalised product. While the popular press may continue to individualise the design process and refer to 'Norman Foster's design for Beijing airport' or suchlike as a possessive adjective, the specialist architectural and trade press will increasingly refer to 'Fosters' as a *noun*, a subtle, but hugely significant shift in meaning that signifies the *firm* – a shorthand, in other words, for Foster and Partners. Evidence of the power of the signature came as a footnote to the sale of a minority shareholding in the firm to venture capitalists 3i. As the official press release noted,

> The value of the company is directly linked to Lord Foster, the use of his name and his ongoing presence. As part of this transaction he has therefore agreed to assign his personal 'Foster' trademark to Foster + Partners. This provides significant present and future value as well as long-term stability to the business. It also guarantees that all projects will continue to be inextricably linked to the Foster brand with its tradition of design excellence, innovation and client service.
>
> (Foster and Partners 2007)

Such a distinction has been made in many other firms, such as Arup, and is perhaps an inevitable result of growth and/or the retirement of the lead designers. Once Foster retires, the transition of 'Fosters' to a brand will be complete. The next question will then be over his legacy, and whether he will achieve the posthumous fame that some architects retain.

Here, the 'brand' suppresses the 'signature', to continue Frow's (2002) analysis. A key feature of the firm's growth has thus been its ability to move into a number of commercial sectors, yet while maintaining a reputation for civic commissions. Some have noted the firm's remarkably deft grasp of business practice, publicity and strategy. As Martin Filler (2007: 229) argues:

even when his job list passed the one thousand mark, he was still careful to maintain the illusion that his was a design boutique with an artistic soul, not some impersonal corporate operation. Foster's publicists further cultivated that impression as they promoted not the firm's commercial work but its far smaller number of cultural commissions.

His reputation has been furthered through successive honours bestowed by the British state (a knighthood in 1990, the Order of Merit in 1997, a Life Peerage in 1999, when he became Lord Foster of Thames Bank) (Melvin 2001). And as Rowan Moore argues: 'Foster is popular because he supplies the look of innovation without the pain of actually changing anything; the establishment likes him because he lets it feel daring at minimal emotional expense; he is the purveyor of radical architecture for people who want no such thing' (Moore 2002: 52).

These issues are central to the production of the ultimate design product, the 'Foster building'. Here the building means more than a homogenised house style, but also the cost and creative regime used in the design and construction *process*. On the one hand, some clients are buying a 'look' and may be disappointed if they are not presented with what they expect. Other clients may be buying into a cost-benefit formula, which takes into account a complex matrix of building performance, process, site analysis, sectoral expertise and aesthetics calculated against fees. In this sense, pressure is put on the firm to supply a cost-efficient and unified brand, an identifiable style, whether in use of materials, organisation of space, or expressive features.

## Critical representations

Visual images often travel before or with the architect's name or personality. Kazuo Akao of Japan's Obunsha Group, client for the Foster-designed Century Tower in Tokyo, provides the following testimony:

> I first came across Foster's work in the spring of 1982. The Japanese news-paper *Nikkei News* issued a special edition about Hong Kong which included a full-page advertisement for the Hongkong and Shanghai Banking Corporation showing a photograph of its proposed new headquarters building. The image was very powerful and, for some time afterwards, I found myself thinking about the building. The name of the architect was not mentioned, but I was able to find that out for myself.
>
> (Akao: 2000: 285)

As Akao continues, he then made a 'pilgrimage' to the completed building to see it for himself, which led to Obunsha commissioning the office tower from Foster.

This vignette is revealing of the visuality of architectural recognition, and explains the significance of the firm's strong publication output (seen in artefacts such as *Foster Catalogue 2001* (Foster and Partners 2001), *On Foster ... Foster On ...* (Jenkins 2000), and the ongoing set of volumes that lavishly document the practice's output, *Norman Foster: Works* (Jenkins 2004), and the presence of the firm's PR chief on the board of directors (Illoniemi 2004).

Travel – both of images and of bodies – is thus a central part in the diffusion of architectural knowledge. Travelogues form a part of many architectural autobiographies or biographies, from *Le Corbusier in America* (Bacon 2001) to Harry Seidler, the late Australian modernist, whose *A Grand Tour: Travelling the World with an Architect's Eye*, collates decades of photographs of buildings both famous and remote (Seidler 2003). In a similar vein, *On Tour with Renzo Piano* is a fairly blatant attempt to turn the publicity-conscious architectural monograph into a consumable travelogue (Piano 2004). Both illustrate the importance of visualisation and travel in the appreciation of an architect's output.

Architectural 'gazing' is also a central feature of peer recognition, in terms of the role of the critic. Visiting buildings is thus central to the process of evaluation. Bill Lacy of the Pritzker Prize jury records his experience on the 'grand tour' of some of the buildings of the short-listed applicants:

> As compelling and seductive as photographs are, the buildings themselves in their context and spatial reality are the primary basis on which the prize is awarded each year. Photographic representations of architecture are always misleading, since they represent only two dimensions of a three-dimensional art form. . . .
>
> (1999: 24)

There is thus a political economy of criticism and publicity that critics may find difficult to escape from, particularly given that in assessing the output of a global architect, one must travel widely. Deyan Sudjic, architectural critic of *The Observer* notes the power this endows:

> I would . . . rather not accept financial support from owners or architects to travel to see projects, but in the current climate of reduced budgets at newspapers and ever-more far-flung projects it's hard to avoid it if you are going to keep up with the key buildings. Of course seeing them gives you a strange world view: Nobody else, not even the architects themselves, see Herzog and de Meuron in California one week, Daniel Libeskind in Tel Aviv the next, Norman Foster in Beijing the month after, followed by Rem Koolhaas in Porto.
>
> (Sudjic 2005b: 20)

The Pritzker Prize is one of the most important forms of professional recognition. Established in 1979 by the Pritzker family of Hyatt hotel fame, the prize was seen as a means of raising the visibility of architecture as 'a strategy for honoring a profession whose members were often overlooked, even at dedication ceremonies of buildings they had designed' (Lacy 1999: 21). The prize – which can only be won once by a single architect – has emerged as a key indicator of professional recognition, and is recognised far beyond the profession itself. While dominated by American-based modernist architects for its first decade (four of the first six awards went to American architects), the Prize has increasingly been expanded to include figures from nations such as Japan, Spain, Brazil and Australia. Thus we can surmise that Pritzker Prize winners are usually, though not exclusively, practising on a worldwide scale. Certainly, after several years of awarding prominent American modernist architects, prizes were given to a geographically diverse, but at times puzzling, set of architects. Filler (1999) singles out the cases of Sverre Fehn and Christian de Portzamparc, as exemplars of 'wild cards [that] seem aimed at demonstrating that the Pritzker is not the handmaiden of the international star system' (p. 92).

The awards ceremony is often held in a forum of cultural esteem or even political power. For example, in 1998, the twentieth award (given to Renzo Piano) was made at the White House, the world's architectural elite gathered in audience with Bill and Hillary Clinton. As such, the Pritzker is something of a hybrid, between professional acclamation and media projection. This is, as James English (2005) argues, part of an increasingly intense awards industry which feeds a growing 'global economy of cultural prestige': 'it is the prize, above all else, that defines the artist: it was an "Academy Award-Winning Actress" who died last night at age eighty-six, or a "Pulitzer Prize-Winning Author"' (English 2005: 21). So, the Pritzker reflects the growing economic significance and marketability of cultural products. For English (2005: 260): 'We can readily observe ... how the most ambitious prizes are more and more obliged to reach beyond national boundaries both for objects of esteem and for (other) sources of legitimacy.' Such is the case with the Praemium Imperiale prizes of Japan, which seek to attain the same level of global standard as the Nobel Prizes.

Such awards highlight the importance of a second major factor in recognition systems, the power of architectural critics. There exists an infrastructure of critics who are able – at the top end of the market – to travel frequently and pronounce judgement on buildings, either as jury members on design competitions or as newspaper or magazine critics. As Bill Lacy describes, the awards are based on a fairly intense period of site visits:

> We were travelling to Venice to meet and select the twenty-first Pritzker Architecture Prize winner. The sleek white private Canadair jet with 'N831CJ' neatly lettered on the tail ('CJ' for Cindy and Jay Pritzker) was

parked in its place at the Marine Air Terminal at LaGuardia at 7.00am as scheduled. Members of the jury were assembled in the small waiting room ... J. Carter Brown, the longtime chairman and director emeritus of the National Gallery of Art; Jorge Silvetti, head of Harvard's architecture program and partner in the Boston firm of Machado and Silvetti; Toshio Nakamura, former editor of the Japanese magazine *A+U*, now with the Japanese Institute of Architects; and Ada Louise Huxtable, author and noted doyenne of architectural criticism, critic at the *New York Times* for many years and most recently at the *Wall Street Journal*; and myself.... We would be joined at our destination in Venice later that evening by Charles Correa, a much-honored architect from Bombay, and on the following day by Giovanni Agnelli, the senior corporate leader of Italy's Fiat empire and a member of the jury. Lord Jacob Rothschild had been excused due to pressing Heritage Fund business in London.... On this particular trip we would cover eleven countries and seven cities in nine days. We would ride in numerous vehicles to see two dozen buildings by architects from Italy, Switzerland, the U.S.A., Finland, Spain and the Netherlands.

(Lacy 1999: 23–4)

As can be seen, the jury for the award is the key to delivering the prestige, requiring an international composition. Similarly, the fields of recognition for architects are now far wider than ever before, reflected in the focus of the profession's major publications:

Once upon a time, most trade and professional journals confined their reportage to local and perhaps national issues. Now, a quick preview of magazines such as *Architectural Review* in England, *Architectural Record* in America, *A+U* in Japan, or even *World Architecture* in China shows greatly expanded reporting.... The number of magazines that deal exclusively on an international scale has also risen, and, when combined with images from nonprint media, the upshot is a rather constant and, at times, unfortunately narrow presentation of design practice as being only international.

(Rowe 1996: 221)

However, while critics and magazines are important shapers of architectural reputation, there is a strong grassroots community that architects have to address: that of the architectural student. The importance of travel to examine built exemplars has been enshrined in architectural programmes through travelling scholarships, field visits and so on (Jones 2001). Joan Ockman (2005: 160) calls this 'the architect's gaze': 'architects by training and trade look with attention and knowledge, even on vacation'. This is important, because they 'differ from their fellow travellers by being active rather than passive spectators, observers for whom the consumption of places has a direct or indirect link to future production' (p. 161). The cultivation of reputation and fame can be as significant within the world's schools as anywhere else:

> Schools ... are central institutions for all fields that claim to produce and transmit specialized theoretical and applied knowledge. Besides teaching standard technical competence, architecture schools teach conceptions of design, relying less on abstract theory than on the analysis of great exemplars, on the studio, and on the critical evaluation of students' work.... Schools, then, are both an audience of choice and a recruiting pool, especially for practitioners with design reputations.
>
> (Larson 1993: 10)

In this sense, institutions such as the major American design schools of Harvard or Yale, or London's Architectural Association (established to encourage the development of avant-gardism in British design), have proved to be breeding grounds for the ideas and practitioners that gradually percolate into mainstream commercial design. Such institutions form what Larson (1993: 8) terms the 'discursive centre' of any profession, powerful, yet possibly very distanced from the mass of practitioners in the base of the profession. In a very material way, the links that architects have with architectural schools is an important channel for the recruitment of new talent, and the propagation of particular design styles and ideologies.

## Signature architects and value added

The purest expression of using renowned architects in the design of corporate office towers once came in the owner-occupied building popularised in the post-war period, from foundational examples such as Frank Lloyd Wright's Johnson Wax Building or SOM's Sears Tower to more recent cases such as Foster and Partners' Hong Kong and Shanghai Bank or Commerzbank towers in Hong Kong and Frankfurt respectively, I.M. Pei's Bank of China in Hong Kong, Phillip Johnson's AT & T building in Manhattan and Kenzo Tange's Fuji Television building in Tokyo (Pearman 2002: 258). However, the commercial logic of commissioning owner-occupied buildings is being rethought. Many developers – especially property trusts – will try to reduce risk by negotiating a pre-let, where a substantial portion of the building's space is anchored by a renowned, established corporation. To gain such a commitment, the building will have to possess some aspect that clearly differentiates it from competitor buildings, which will act to lure key tenants from their existing premises. By contrast, major corporations – which once saw bespoke buildings as central to their company ethos – are increasingly valuing capital liquidity to maximise returns, rather than tying up capital in property (O'Neill and McGuirk 2003). As Larry Malcic, a director of HOK puts it (in Young 2003):

> Now developers want to build something special for clients; they recognize that architecture matters, not just space. They want something iconic to set their development apart. Conversely, corporate clients are looking for flexibility and adaptability, which are traditionally developers' priorities.

In some office markets, the 'branded', landmark, or iconic building can make a significant impact on the commercial success of the building. Of New York, for example, Ada Louise Huxtable has written that 'rental response relates directly to a building's recognition factor on the skyline. Identity and novelty give a builder a different product and a competitive edge' (Huxtable 1984: 68–9, in Dovey 1992: 173). At the time in which Huxtable was writing, when owner-occupied buildings were still in fashion, this may have been the case. And it is certainly relevant to the current boom in high end residential condominium developments in Manhattan, designed by architects such as Richard Meier and Santiago Calatrava. Fein (2007: 2) captures this moment as follows:

> To lure prospective buyers into ownership of one of the myriad condominiums available to them, marketing teams have set up elaborate sales centers replete with full-scale mockups of the dwelling units, videos meant to educate the laity about the significance of the starchitect whose brand they are about to support, and freebees contributing to the cult of personality surrounding the marketing of these luxury commodities. Marketing teams comprised of model look-alikes dressed in chic attire tour visitors around their potential purchases while handing out things like tote bags emblazoned with images of the architect's face. These goodie bags often contain hard-bound portfolios of the designer's previous projects, carefully folded copies of presentation-size drawings of each unit type, and select caches of articles about the respective starchitects to further illuminate the masses. Some marketers even go so far as to bring prospective clients out on yachts to better see a project from a waterside vantage. These starchitect-branded condos exude more than good design; they become signifiers of an entire lifestyle.

In less prominent global cities, though, the market for signature architecture is seen as being very different, particularly when applied to commercial buildings. For example, the Foster and Partners office tower at 126 Phillip Street in Sydney is a striking feature of the city's famed skyline (see Figure 2.1). It features a large public atrium of 15 metres in height, and an unusual 'remote core' design (where lifts, toilets, etc. are placed at the corner of the building, thus allowing an open-plan space) (Nimmo 2004). However, the fact that the project was financed as an investment vehicle meant that the commercial office sector – unlike educational or cultural institutions, for example – is driven by strict profit calculations, and any interest in 'premium', 'signature' or branded office developments have to be clearly reflected in yield differentials. It is argued that design can give added value to developers, reflected in the higher rents paid by tenants who in turn have value added to their operations. This can be measured in a number of ways, but may include brand enhancement, or retention of skilled employees through the communication of the firm's status and prestige. As office markets are counter-cyclical, developers often respond to supply and demand in leased space, but as construction and planning permission takes time, buildings may be ready just when demand is falling. They need to decide whether investing money in a premium design product is worth the risk: it may provide a critical edge in a saturated market, but rents may fall to such levels as to threaten yield when set against costs (including design and materials costs). Nonetheless, it is clear that clients perceive long-term benefits from the larger fee income justified by international class architects, which comes in their superior technical ability and project experience when calculating the best technical solution to, say, a commercial building in a historic downtown. More than this: many city councils incentivise strong architectural design through bonuses in floor-space ratio allowances, thus giving developers the potential for sustained extra rental income in return for the initial investment in a prestige design.

Thus in seeking anchor tenants for pre-lets (where leases are signed by tenants before the building's construction is completed), or for relocations, the 'blue chip' or prestige building is likely to carry significant marketing weight. The symbolism and centrality of certain locations adds both gravitas and agglomeration advantages to the tenant. However, 126 Phillip Street was marketed without 'headline' reference to the role of Norman Foster, being distinguished instead by its remote core floorplate, which allowed uninterrupted views of Sydney Harbour. The marketing for 126 Phillip Street included a quarterly newsletter, a webcam following on-site construction, a website and, at street level, eye-catching billboards featuring thought-provoking quotations. More targeted approaches to tenants included a CD-ROM explaining the building with video clips of Norman Foster, shown sketching the floorplate, Ken Maher, partner of the well-known Sydney practice Hassell (acting as representative architect), and Frank Duffy from DEGW talking about how the new building was at the forefront of new office design. Significantly, the communication with clients focused on the floorplates of the buildings, the flexible spaces for occupiers, and the amenity that would help drive workplace productivity. While Norman Foster as a visiting figurehead was an important element in the public legitimisation of the building, for the developer and prospective tenants this would be a secondary consideration to the product they offered, namely a column-free floorspace and outstanding views. I discuss the examples of Aurora Place and 126 Phillip Street at greater length elsewhere (McNeill 2007).[1]

Thus developers remain sceptical of the role of architects in the design process, unless they are prepared to meet fundamental cost constraints and economic rationalities. To be sure, most architectural firms are very conscious of these constraints, and many developers – often working on the recommendation of consultants – are also highly aware of the reputations and cost efficiency of particular design firms. Recognition is of a different form to that of their peers or the public.

## Conclusions

This chapter began with a discussion of the emergence of 'star power' in the architectural profession, and hinted that while famed individuals have long been part of the production of the built environment, there is an intensity in the current system of globalised circuits of knowledge, investment and design styles that has helped to systematise the likelihood of particular firms gaining major prizes and commissions.

Given the august history of architecture, and its association with the apparently timeless values of beauty and art, or else with scientific and technological rationalism, there is a feeling that calling architects 'celebrities' is *a priori* problematic. There is a parallel with the case of celebrity academics:

> at the milder end of the spectrum, it is taken as a version of gossip and thus dismissed, sometimes with amusement and sometimes with irritation, as superficial. Under more serious consideration, it is seen as a popular cultural phenomenon imported to the academic sphere, and then criticized as a foreign or specious measure imposed on scholarly work.
>
> (Williams 2006: 371–2)

The implication is that by endowing architects with celebrity status, it follows that their design must be flippant, corny, gestural. This is difficult to sustain. In architecture, design fashion does not

> depend as much on the general media as on the organized profession, the specialist press, and especially the system of training institutions. The design process is still too complex and too highly professionalized, and, above all, building is still too expensive for clients and banks to permit momentary fads.
>
> (Larson 1993: 249)

Architecture as art is not like painting or sculpture or even film-making, given the incredible complexity of the design process (from the need to engage with construction professionals and quantity surveyors, to satisfy client taste, to meet planning regulations and site conditions). Thus the public narrative developed by architects, be it their comportment or dress sense, or their position within a publicity regime, is a fundamental aspect of their professional life, and one that cannot be avoided. For Gutman (1988: 70–7), competition between architects has been an increasingly noticeable phenomenon, reflected in the attention to business practice, an intensified participation in competitions, a growing awareness of niche and expertise, and an understanding of how to manipulate or use media sources to position their firm or project. As Gutman acknowledges, this is not confined to the architectural profession: medical and scientific research institutes attached to hospitals and universities have each developed public relations machines to better position themselves in a race for endowments.

This chapter has suggested that architects face the problem of operating in an artistic field where self-publicity is not an accepted aspect of the social rules: 'There is a desire to be acknowledged without being seen to desire acknowledgement' (Chance and Schmiedeknecht 2001: 5). Yet architects are now increasingly implicated – however unwillingly – in the production of branding strategies for clients. The most noted recent example of this was Frank Gehry's design for the Bilbao Guggenheim, as the following chapter explores.

# 4    The 'Bilbao effect'

A spectre is haunting the global village – the spectre of the iconic building.

(Jencks 2005: 7)

*The Simpsons* is well-known for its use of celebrities. Kelsey Grammer, Larry King, Danny deVito, Dustin Hoffman, Britney Spears, Ringo Starr, Aerosmith, Tito Puente and Rupert Murdoch are only some of the famous personalities to have featured in the cartoon series since its inception.[1] The appearance of Frank Gehry on season 16, episode 4, however, was a noteworthy moment for architects, rarely acclaimed as popular icons. Gehry provided a voice-over for his character. The episode – entitled 'The seven-beer snitch' – begins with Marge and family visiting neighbouring Shelbyville. They are ridiculed as hick residents of Springfield (a town notable only as a site of a nuclear power plant), lacking in culture. An infuriated Marge responds by sending an invitation to Gehry, who accepts a $30 million commission to design a concert hall. Gehry provides sketches and models of an unorthodox and complex design of jagged, interlocking walls. When the town leader calls the vote: 'All in favour of a $30 million "screw you" to Shelbyville?' the response is unanimously in favour.[2]

In 1997, the opening of the visually striking Bilbao Guggenheim art gallery made the front pages of the world's news media, a rare event for a new building. With its sharply interacting planes, curved galleries and fragmented glass panelled walls, the gallery was immediately striking. Covered by titanium panels, which create a stunning effect when placed against the backdrop of central Bilbao's lush river valley, the museum – sited on an ex-steelworks – was like very little that had gone before. The impact on the three key actors involved – the Basque regional government, the Guggenheim Foundation and Frank Gehry's design firm – was remarkable, not least for the de-industrialised Basque city which saw a sudden rise in tourist numbers, as well as shining a spotlight on its broader urban regeneration initiatives. The building itself has created a 'Bilbao effect', which has brought together deeply politicised place marketing, the architectural branding of an aspirational art institution, and the worldwide projection of Frank Gehry as a celebrity architect. In this chapter, I suggest that the power of the icon as architectural discourse is reliant on the intensified circulation of visual images, combined with an embodied, performed set of tourist practices on the part of architects and their professional critics and journalists.

I begin by considering the specific reception of the building in the Basque country, and note its initial contextualisation as being an agent of American cultural imperialism. Second, however, I argue that a strong argument can be made to see the Bilbao Guggenheim as an indigenised global cultural artefact. To illustrate this, I sketch the geopolitical debates which framed the decision to commission the gallery. Then, briefly introducing 'the Bilbao effect' itself, tracing out its immediate impact in both architectural and political circles. I conclude by suggesting that these agents coalesce and mutually benefit from a branding exercise, drawing critical disdain in the process.

## Cultural imperialism?

I begin by exploring the charge – made frequently by some Basque critics after the negotiation process became public – that the Guggenheim's arrival in Bilbao was an example of the latest stage of American cultural imperialism, a corollary of inward investment by American multinationals, the dominance of Hollywood in televisual and film production, the increasing hegemony of English as a global language and the long-term military interests of NATO and the US in the Iberian peninsula. Critics such as Mattelart (1979) and Schiller (1976) have documented the impact of various forms of American cultural product which, by virtue of the strength of American economic and diplomatic muscle, introduces commodities which usurp or replace existing, indigenous products. And as Tellitu et al. (1997: chapter 3) describe, many in the Basque artistic community explicitly identified this threat.

The Guggenheim Foundation had, since the early 1990s, undertaken a forcefully proactive policy of global geographical expansion. With some parallels to Ritzer's (1996) McDonaldisation thesis, the Guggenheim director, Thomas Krens, set out his intention to establish a chain of museums throughout the world operating on a franchise basis. This involved the Guggenheim selling itself as a brand, allowing local operators to pay for new premises in their locality, to pay for the curatorial skills offered, and to benefit from a continuous circulation of the museum's stock (the central branch can display less than 5 per cent of its total holdings at a time) (Thorncroft 1998). The 'Guggenheim' name would benefit the franchisees as a tourist magnet, bestowing instant cultural kudos in the global culture circuit.

Appointed in 1988, Krens came to the Guggenheim facing a difficult financial situation, with its famed Frank Lloyd Wright headquarters in Manhattan requiring repairs, a shortage of storage space for its art holdings, and with limited funds for expansion. His response was controversial, particularly his decision to sell three key works – by Modigliani, Kandinsky and Chagall – for $47 million. A further, equally controversial, fundraising measure involved the issue of $54 million in public bonds. These revenues were used to drive a strategy of opening satellite museums, away from Fifth Avenue, beginning with MassMOCA in Massachusetts and a new gallery in SoHo in downtown Manhattan (Kimmelman 1998). However, Krens made it clear that his aim was to search for partners in cities across the world. In 1991, Robyn Cembalest was noting in *ARTnews* the 'surge of rumors that have Guggenheims popping up like McDonald's all over the globe'. Venice – which already held a Guggenheim collection, but was earmarked for a possible new museum – Osaka, Salzburg, Graz, Vienna and Seville were all linked to the Guggenheim with varying degrees of veracity (Cembalest 1992; Thorncroft 1998). But towards the end of 1991 came the news that the Basque regional government, the Comunidad Autónoma Vasco (CAV), had signed a preagreement with the Guggenheim to establish a franchised museum in Bilbao.

The Basque interest had emerged from the leadership of the dominant Basque nationalist party, the Partido Nacional Vasco (PNV), which was exploring ways in which it could move Euzkadi (el País Vasco in Castilian) out from the dual bind of de-industrialisation and crippling terrorism which had effectively devastated its local economy. The PNV bear many similarities to what Harvie (1994) refers to as 'bourgeois regionalist' parties, centre right in stance with a strong degree of indigenous business participation, along with a fierce defence of cultural particularism and demands for far-reaching political and economic autonomy. Unlike many other such parties in Europe, however, they had considerable executive power to negotiate directly with the Guggenheim. Electorally, they had dominated the key institutions in the Basque country such as the regional government since its establishment in 1980. In addition, they possessed a remarkable degree of financial autonomy. Historically, Navarre and the three provinces that constituted the CAV had – until 1876 – collected their own taxes. The post-Francoist constitutional settlement allowed provincial assemblies (Diputaciones) to retain and administer taxation within the Basque country, paying a reverse block grant to the central government for services provided. As Ross (1997: 81) describes, this means that negotiations over funding are conducted directly with central government and are independent of the broader regional financial regime in Spain, and means that any delays in the negotiation process are harmful to central government, giving the CAV and Navarre an upper hand in the negotiations. The PNV elite thus had considerable scope to finance a cultural policy distinctive within Spain, and linked this to their attempts to regenerate the ex-industrial areas of its territory, particularly the province of Bizkaia which contains the Bilbao metropolitan area. As such, once Krens was informed of the seriousness of the PNV's interest, he was able to convince them to pay $100 million for a landmark building in Bilbao, but also to pay a fee of $20 million for the services rendered – the franchise. In addition, the Basques would create a fund of $50m to build up the museum's own collection.

The negotiation process began with the intercession of Spanish ex-minister of culture, Carmen Giménez, who was by 1991 employed as a curator by the Guggenheim in New York, and which by May of that year had led to the signing of a 'memorandum of understanding' between the two sides. As well as the fee demanded by the Guggenheim, they also put pressure on the Basque institutions to fund a flagship building through an architectural competition. Gehry, strongly favoured by Krens, was successful. The contract was finally signed in December 1994, after a considerable amount of amendments on the Basque side (provoked by criticisms from the PNV's socialist coalition partners in the CAV and an unfavourable response in the press). These conditions included a restriction on Guggenheim expansion in Europe without the prior consent of the Basques, and the requirement that the Foundation provide at least three exhibitions per year of equal merit to those being staged in New York (Bradley 1997). Despite these concessions, critics such as Zulaika (1997) and a couple of notable interventions in the press by Basque academics suggested that the deal was not in the best interests of the Basque country; the local PNV grassroots and the CAV president, Ardanza, all initially needed to be convinced of its viability and suitability (Tellitu et al. 1997: 86–9); and all the opposition parties in the CAV were at some point opposed to the project.

The overriding concern was that the Basque institutions were the weaker partners in the negotiating process, on the wrong end of an aggressive cultural imperialism. There were, I suggest, four reasons for this perception. First, the Guggenheim Foundation was able to play upon the structural weakness of the Basque economy in a way similar to the strategy of any transnational corporation that demands favourable conditions in return for their investment. Krens was already negotiating for new branches in Venice and Salzburg and had attempted to use the rivalry between European cities to force an early signing of the contract in terms favourable to the Guggenheim. This strategy would, it appears, have been successful had it not been for the political opposition of the socialists and sections of civil society. Second, fears raised about the impact of the flagship museum on indigenous cultural production had echoes of the opening of Euro Disney outside Paris in 1992. The dilemmas were similarly clear: in the latter case too there was a contradiction between cultural policy and economic policy; fears of a dilution of French culture by an Americanised homogeneity; the repackaging of 'European' tales such as Pinocchio and Cinderella, just as the Guggenheim was commodifying European artworks; the French government had similarly fought off strong competition from Spain to be chosen as the site of the theme park (Pells 1997: 306–13). Third, there was a difference in cultural capital between the two negotiating teams. Zulaika (1997) argues that the individuals participating in the Basque negotiating team drawn from the PNV were naïve with respect to Krens' self-stylisation as a 'professional seducer'. They had a poorly developed knowledge of art markets, all but one had weak English, and lacked negotiating ability, doing little more than meekly accept the terms of the contract initially offered by the Guggenheim (which was vague in a number of key aspects, and would subsequently be modified following local pressure). Fourth, the accord signed between the Guggenheim and the regional government was also vague in specifying which artworks would be coming to Bilbao: there were fears that the work of 1960s and 1970s conceptual artists such as Donald Judd and Joseph Beuys would be more likely to appear than the blue chip Modiglianis or Picassos of Manhattan. Indeed, some local critics argued that had the Basques gone it alone they could have afforded a modern art collection that outshone what the Guggenheim was able to offer. Furthermore, it became clear that the Guggenheim would absorb all the resources that had been dedicated to a coherent plan for museum funding throughout the Basque region (Tellitu *et al.* 1997: 126–7).

Can we accept the process of the Guggenheim's establishment as being an example of how an institution from the core of the global cultural economy is able to dictate terms to an actor in the periphery? A clue to the veracity of this is given by the (PNV) director of the Bilbao Guggenheim, Juan Vidarte, speaking shortly after the museum's opening:

> With this unique space and this important collection, we can be playing a role in the periphery that we could not do otherwise. . . . To play in this league, you have to be associated with someone in it. Otherwise, it's hard to get there.
>
> (cited in Cembalest 1997: 64)

The obvious allusion is that of the strategic corporate alliance, a realisation that for a political elite to compete in a globalising world requires a critical awareness of one's competitive weaknesses, and a strategic alliance – widespread in the airline industry, for example – may be the most profitable way forward. It is important, therefore, to consider the establishment of the Bilbao Guggenheim not as a simple power-play between core and periphery, uneven though the bargaining process was, but also as part of a manoeuvre by the ruling party in the Basque regional institutions to enhance its relative strength within its immediate political space – Spain.

## Indigenisation and 'bourgeois regionalism': the Basque state as client

As Appadurai (1990) has noted, the thesis which sees globalisation as being synonymous with a commodity-led Americanisation, as a one-way flow of cultural and financial influence and power is misleading:

What these arguments fail to consider is that at least as rapidly as forces from various metropolises are brought into new societies they tend to become indigenized in one or other way: this is true of music and housing styles as much as it is true of science and terrorism, spectacles and institutions. . . . But it is worth noticing that for the people of Irian Jaya, Indonesianization may be more worrisome than Americanization, as Japanization may be for Koreans, Indianization for Sri Lankans, Vietnamization for the Cambodians, Russianization for the people of Soviet Armenia and the Baltic Republics.

(Appadurai 1990: 295)

Notwithstanding the explicit critique of American imperialism which has influenced many Basque groups such as Herri Batasuna (reflected in, for example, opposition to Spanish membership of NATO), it is clear that the 'historic nationalities' of Spain – Basques, Galicians and Catalans – have faced a more pressing threat to their culture – Hispanicisation. The negotiation of the post-Francoist constitution in Spain thus reflected political demands to restore a strong degree of autonomy, with the CAV, Navarre and, to a lesser extent, Catalonia and Galicia being given differing levels of autonomy from the rest of Spain's 'autonomous communities', which has included provisions for interventionist linguistic policies in the fields of education and media.

Aside from language as a source of identity, however, certain aspects of territory take on symbolic value for regionalising or nationalising elites, a continuation of long-established processes of nation formation. Yet as the above examples suggest, in contemporary Europe, symbolic value can be found not just in romanticist landscape ideology, battlefields, statuary or castles. They may instead be found in all-seated football stadia, reinvented cuisine, science parks, new art galleries, many of them symbols of a rejuvenated post-industrialism. In this vein, the PNV's decision to bid for the Guggenheim gave the party a powerful totem, a statement the Basque identity was at home in the contemporary world, rather than being mired in pre-modern ethnic bloodshed. To understand why this was so important to the party, however, requires a brief survey of recent Basque political history.

In many ways, Basque identity was reinforced by the industrialisation of the country in the late nineteenth century. The founder of modern Basque nationalism, Sabino Arana, constructed a racial theory of the Basques which held them to be superior to the rest of Spain, mobilising language as a the essence of Basque 'purity'. While Arana's racialist theories were abandoned for a number of reasons by all the Basque nationalist parties, the Basque language – Euskera – has remained the defining point of identity. Under the fiercely (Castilian) centralist Francoist dictatorship (1939–75) which emerged from the bloody Spanish civil war, it was not only Basque political autonomy which was proscribed, but elimination of the use of Basque in all public spheres – at church, in school, in print, and even on tombstones

(Conversi 1997: 81). This paralleled the repression of Catalan culture being carried out at the same time. As much of the West recognised this dictatorship in the post-war years, the PNV-dominated Basque government in exile was left isolated, and lost legitimacy within the Basque country itself, especially among radical youth (Conversi 1997: 80–90). The attempt to build a more effective resistance movement to this Hispanicisation culminated in the formation of ETA (Euzkadi 'ta Azkatasuna, Basque Land and Freedom) in 1959. Without wishing to document the complexity of Basque politics following this period, it is important to note two things: first, the role of ETA in developing an armed opposition to the Spanish state, most notably with the 1973 assassination of Carrero Blanco, Franco's anointed successor, which ultimately proved very influential in ensuring that the dictatorship crumbled after Franco's death in 1975; second, the ideological split that opened up between the centre-right, 'bourgeois' PNV, and the often Marxist-inspired groupings on the Basque nationalist left such as ETA and its political wing, Herri Batasuna (HB) (Conversi 1997).

Upon the restoration of an autonomous regional government from 1980, the PNV won a succession of majorities in the regional elections, and throughout the 1980s and 1990s has pursued an ambivalent strategy of hostility to the Spanish state's legitimacy, while distancing itself – precariously – from extremist terrorism. It remains far more committed to independence than many other nationalist groupings in Europe, and its calls to strengthen institutions of economic autonomy, such as proposals for a Basque Central Bank, have been at the forefront of its policy programmes (and reflect its 'bourgeois' profile). For a number of reasons the party split in 1986, and as a result almost lost its status as leading party in the regional government. By the mid-1990s, it had recovered and continued as the dominant Basque party, though having to work in coalition in most regional institutions (Ross 1996, 1997).

Simultaneously, the Spanish nation state had been dramatically reinvented, a succession of social democrat (PSOE) governments between 1982 and 1995 professionalising the army, joining NATO and the European Community, and dismantling the corporatist state machinery through privatisation (Holman 1996). After the cultural archaism of Francoism, there was also an attempt to internationalise Spanish culture, central to which was the *annus mirabilis* of 1992, when Barcelona held the Olympics, Seville a World Expo and Madrid the European City of Culture title. The events of 1992

> were explicitly intended to celebrate Spain's coming of age as a modern, democratic European nation-state, marking the end of a period of political transition (and uncertainty).... But these popular celebrations of Spain's new status tended to neglect the past and glorify the present. Indeed this seemed to be part of an official attempt to represent Spain's new, 'modern', democratic national identity as if it were built on a *tabula rasa*, thus avoiding

confrontation with the cultural, social, regional and political tensions that have plagued Spain since its emergence as a nation-state.

(Graham and Sánchez 1995: 406)

The Basques were noticeably absent from these events. Xabier Arzalluz, the PNV leader, made reference to the 'pomp' of 1992 (Zulaika 1997: 27), and it was clear that the Basque elite was both desirous to be excluded from any association with a 'New Spain', but was equally keen to retain its political strength relative to the other Spanish regions. In this context the Guggenheim acts as the PNV's own 1992, but with negotiation conducted independently of the central government. As noted above, the relative financial autonomy of the Basques – similar to that of a small nation-state – was something which convinced Krens of the seriousness of the Basque application (Zulaika 1997: 163).

Aside from the sensation of being left out of Spain's renaissance, the PNV had to address the de-industrialisation of the local economy which had proceeded apace during the 1980s. Bilbao and its hinterland in the province of Bizkaia had seen 94,766 jobs lost in manufacturing between 1979 and 1985, particularly in shipbuilding, heavy engineering and iron and steel production (Gómez 1998: 109). By 1993, unemployment in the city had reached 25 per cent, far worse than at any time in the 1980s. Furthermore, the rate of joblessness in the municipalities on the left bank of the river Nervión, the traditional working class districts of Bilbao, was three to four points higher than the average for the metropolitan area as a whole (Gómez 1998: 116–17).

In seeking solutions to these problems, the Basque government had identified the need to pursue a strategy aimed at turning Bilbao into a post-industrial centre for services, finance and tourism. They used a number of planning strategies, pushed primarily by Bilbao Metrópoli 30, a public–private partnership aimed at implementing a metropolitan plan. This was augmented by the creation of Bilbao Ría-2000, an urban development corporation dedicated to clearing old industrial land for new property investment. These strategies identified the need for a transformation both of Bilbao's image and its physical environment, centred around the removal of its port functions from the heart of the city to new facilities at the mouth of the Nervión river estuary. A riverfront area at the heart of the central city was zoned to site various new leisure, shopping and office developments, and it would be here that the museum was located, on the site of a former steelworks at El Campo de los Ingleses, at the Abandoibarra section of the river.

The Guggenheim had stipulated that the new museum building be a high-calibre architectural project. As such, Gehry's competition victory over Arata Isozaki and Coop Himmelblau would soon allow Bilbao Metrópoli 30 to put the museum at the centre of its place-marketing strategy. The Basque country had an image problem with parallels in Western Europe only in Northern Ireland, de-industrialisation and economic weakness combined with a reputation for violent civic strife. Along with strategies to stimulate new economic functions and improve infrastructure, the metropolitan agencies had already sought leading architects to design their major projects – a new metro system designed by Foster and Partners; a footbridge over the Nervión by Santiago Calatrava; a transport interchange by James Stirling and Michael Wilford. The Guggenheim would form the centrepiece, the magnet of regeneration, a choice vindicated by its astonishing promotional and pulling power.

The reimaging strategy drew strongly on European experience (Gómez 1998: 113). As such, the refurbishment of the central city and an aggressive place-marketing strategy was seen as being the key to attracting service industries and tourist expenditure. The development of a European economic space which transcends national boundaries allowed Bilbao to be modelled as 'capital of the Atlantic axis'. Furthermore, Zulaika (1997: 123–9) notes that the PNV leadership had watched jealously as Pasqual Maragall in Barcelona slotted himself and his city into international political and diplomatic circles during the 1992 Olympics. They had also seen how Frankfurt had used a combination of new museums and a strong financial sector to become one of the leading cities in Europe in terms of economic muscle.

Their desire for change was motivated by a need to escape from the problems of separatist isolation implied by Basque identity. The PNV had already split in the mid-1980s over its ambivalence towards terrorism, and its newly-formed 'sister' (Eusko Alkartasuna) remained an important electoral consideration. Pushed on one side by Herri Batasuna, which represented a radical, pro-ETA popular nationalism, on another by the social democracy of the Partido Socialista de Euskadi (PSE) and on a third by the steadily more popular pro-business, Spanish nationalist Partido Popular, the PNV had to find a spatial fix which retained its (conservative, christian democratic) hegemony over Basque identity yet which avoided it being trapped within a separatist isolation from both the Spanish and global economies. In the late 1980s it was explicitly invoking the Europe of the Regions as a potential model, but with the anti-Maastricht climate of the 1990s it began once again to flirt with HB and a ceasefire (Ross 1996: 106). The Guggenheim offered a Basque-controlled flagship which advertised Basque difference (and financial autonomy) to the world, yet which represented Euzkadi not as a primordial backwater but as a society at ease with global modernity.

## Mapping the 'Bilbao effect'

If you want to look into the heart of American art today, you are going to need a passport. You will have to pack your bags, leave the U.S.A. and find your way to Bilbao, a small, rusty city in the northeast corner of Spain. The trip is not convenient, and you should not expect to have much fun while you're there. This is Basque country. A region proudly, if not officially, independent from the rest of Spain, it is also bleakly free from Spanish sophistication. Oh, and by the way, you might get blown up. Basque country is not Bosnia. But it's not Disney World, either.

(Muschamp 1997)

The idea that Bilbao was placed 'on the map' recurs in discussions about the Bilbao Effect. What might this mean beyond mere metaphor? First, the building generated a significant amount of tourism. Although there are debates about the opportunity costs of the public investment in the gallery, the number of visitors entering Bilbao soared to record levels after the Guggenheim's opening, particularly among foreign visitors (Plaza 1999, 2006). Measuring success is not a straightforward process. The museum had more than 600,000 visitors in its first six months, and had its millionth guest well before its first anniversary, far exceeding the half-million projected for the first year, with the tourist board registering a 28 per cent rise in tourists in the first quarter of 1997 (Burns 1998; Webster 1998). By the end of the first year, a Peat Marwick survey suggested the following, glowing, figures: 1.4 million visitors, three times the original projected first year figure; 85 per cent of visitors who had travelled to the city to visit the museum had prolonged their stay; which all contributed to 0.47 per cent of the annual GNP of the Basque country (*Cashing in . . .* 1999).[1] By the mid-2000s, even cautious observers were accepting that the museum had certainly come close to providing a positive return on investment, and with a contribution to local employment in associated tourist sectors, such as restaurants and tour guide services.

Second, there is the sense of being placed on the map in discursive or cognitive terms. For example, Herbert Muschamp's rather patronising essay in the *New York Times Magazine* – 'The Miracle in Bilbao' – has been seen to have an influential role in the positioning of the building in the minds of international cultural elites (Ockman 2004):

Bilbao has lately become a pilgrimage town . . . people have been flocking to Bilbao for nearly two years, just to watch the building's skeleton take shape. 'Have you been to Bilbao?'. In architectural circles, that question has acquired the status of a shibboleth. Have you seen the light? Have you seen the future?

(Muschamp 1997)

The blanket coverage of the building's opening in general news magazines was enough to kick-start its reputation. Its subsequent appearance in a James Bond film and as a backdrop to car adverts and Spanish tourist board promotions helped to sustain its impact.

Third, the 'Bilbao Effect' is a phrase which itself has entered popular usage among policy-makers. Type it into Google and up comes currently, in order, a CNN article entitled 'The Milwaukee Effect' (about a Santiago Calatrava art gallery for the city), followed by pieces in *Forbes*, *The Atlantic Monthly*, *Village Voice*, and the *New York Times* each debating the pros and cons of such buildings, along with articles on Montreal, Baton Rouge ('"We'll be better than Bilbao," predicts a half-serious André Mika, executive director of the Shaw Center for the Arts, Baton Rouge's $55 million entry in the high-design arts-center derby', in Cohen 2004), and, inevitably, of a Gehry building itself, Bard College in up-state New York ('Goodbye Collegiate Gothic and vintage campus Brutalism: Bilbao has hit the quad.') (Byles 2000). This type of copying has been a central part of the toolkit of urban policy-makers for a number of years, despite the fact that such 'fast policy' (Peck 2005) is not always as carefully considered as it might be.

Fourth, the building had a huge impact on the Guggenheim Foundation itself. By 2005, Krens was boasting that he was regularly contacted by city councils and governments seeking to 'share in the so-called Bilbao Effect' (Vogel 2005). Potential suitors were ranged around the world: Guadalajara, Las Vegas, Rio de Janeiro, the Hermitage in St Petersburg, Singapore, Hong Kong, Geelong, Taiwan, Abu Dhabi, adding to the small Berlin museum sponsored by Deutsche Bank, and the long-established Peggy Guggenheim gallery in Venice. The expansionist strategy

*Figure 4.1* Santiago Calatrava's extension to the Milwaukee Art Gallery is a good example of the use of a signature architect to make an eye-catching museum project.

of Krens has always been controversial within the art world, and within the Guggenheim's own board of trustees. In the aftermath of the attack on the World Trade Center and the drastic downturn in tourism that accompanied it, the Krens strategy was suddenly exposed to a harsher climate. In November 2001 the Foundation's budget was slashed, leading to staff cuts from 339 to 181 full-time posts,

*Figure 4.2* Frank Gehry's 'Fish' sculpture, Barcelona. SOM's Hotel Arts is behind it to the left.

and with a cut in operating hours. The Guggenheim SoHo, one of the first outposts in a shift away from Fifth Avenue, closed its doors in late 2001. The strongly touted Gehry design for a huge downtown Manhattan branch on the banks of the East River, was shelved. In January 2003, the Guggenheim Las Vegas closed its doors for an indefinite period until further corporate sponsorship could be found. These setbacks occurred against a backdrop of growing discontentment within the Guggenheim's trustees. As Peter Lewis, the Foundation's principal benefactor, insisted, Krens would have to balance the budget before further expansion took place (Bohlen 2002). Ultimately, Lewis would lose the stand-off with Krens, and would tender his resignation.

Fifth, the key decision that underpinned the museum's success was the engagement of Frank Gehry. Adding to the Loyola Law School, the Dancing House in Prague, the American Center in Paris, and a prominent Fish sculpture next to SOM's Hotel Arts in Barcelona, the Bilbao Guggenheim both projected Gehry into the big-time, and would gather reflected credit from Gehry's subsequent worldwide commissions. With the Walt Disney Concert Hall in Los Angeles, and flagship projects such as the Art Gallery of Ontario in Toronto, the Museum of Tolerance in Jerusalem and the controversial Atlantic Yards redevelopment in Brooklyn (which I discuss in Chapter 7), Gehry has emerged as one of the key 'celebrity' architects of global renown.

However, along with the celebrity recognition came a sense that the success of the Guggenheim (and the Los Angeles Concert Hall) would effectively stereotype Gehry. Leon Botstein, president of Bard College, who commissioned the architect to design a new performing arts centre, recalls that 'People would say to us in New York society, "Don't you know that Frank Gehry is passé?"' (in Nobel 2003). Gehry is now working within a framework of expectations, as he himself recognises:

> since Bilbao, I get called to do 'Frank Gehry buildings'. They actually say that to me. We want a 'Frank Gehry'. I run into trouble when I put a design on the table and they say, 'Well, that isn't a Gehry building.' It doesn't have enough of whatever these buildings are supposed to have – yet.
>
> (in Jencks 2005: 9)

There exists, then, a paradox – that the more celebrated a building, and by extension, its architect, becomes, the more beholden that architect is to produce a design that strongly resembles, or achieves the same effect as, the celebrated structure. This is particularly problematic when one considers the diversity of Gehry's output. As Ada Louise Huxtable argued in 1989, long before his Bilbao success:

> If there are many facets to Gehry's work, there are also several Gehrys. There is the media Gehry as defined and promoted by the press: the casual,

laid-back Californian whose work is touted as fashionably 'pop' or 'punk,' who uses funny materials – chain link, exposed pipe, corrugated aluminum, utility-grade construction board – in a funky, easy, West Coast way. The image is part of the media-chic of Venice and the seductive charms of Santa Monica, the places he has made his habitat; this is nouveau California at the cutting-edge of style. It is the fashion to admire his offbeat spirit but to wonder how well the work will travel. And then there is the real Frank Gehry, who is all and none of this: an admirer of the quirky, the accidental and the absurd, tuned in to the transient nature of much contemporary culture, while he is deeply involved, personally and professionally, with the world of serious art and artists.

(Huxtable 1989)

The danger identified by critics is that in the architect's desire to capture an increasingly fickle public and rapid cycles of architectural fashion, she or he seeks the most obvious, first order metaphorical statement that s/he can muster.

One architect who has aroused a lot of critical ire in this regard is Santiago Calatrava. I have already mentioned how his extension to the Milwaukee Art Museum (the Quadracci Pavilion) has been seen as an attempt to achieve some of the same success as Bilbao. This was part of a general demand for his services, partly as a reaction to 'the stultifying rigidity of the late International Style' (Filler 2007: 294). His designs for the City of Arts and Sciences in his home city

*Figure 4.3* Santiago Calatrava's City of Arts and Sciences, Valencia.

of Valencia, the Tenerife Concert Hall, the Ground Zero transportation interchange, a telecommunications tower in Barcelona, a Bilbao airport terminal and the Athens Olympic Stadium provided an immediate recognition factor for these localities, particularly important for public works.

For Filler (2007: 296), Calatrava's 'flashy contours, flamboyant engineering effects, and mechanical flummery' border on kitsch. Charles Jencks, while sympathetic in his search for a 'structural expressionism', suggests that 'something in him always pushes beyond this basic poetry, exaggerating a cantilever a bit too far, tapering a concrete section just a little too elegantly, repeating a structural unit once too often'. That something may well be the client, eager for a self-consciously iconic design. But for many critics, iconic buildings are unhealthy, not least because they attempt to upstage each other, are often disrespectful to urban context, can be excessively expensive, and – the greatest crime of all? – can reduce architecture to mere surface decoration, and the architect to confectioner.

## Conclusions

The opening of the Bilbao Guggenheim has achieved something of a paradigmatic status in the minds of both public and commercial clients. Yet I have hoped to show in this chapter that this was a highly contingent process. We might profitably conceive of the Bilbao gallery as a site, located in a number of cross-cutting spatial arrangements, as a consumption space, as networked temporally and transculturally, but as much dependent on local political will as on global circuits of recognition. This is particularly important when one considers the 'Bilbao Effect' as something materially different from the building itself. There are three aspects to this.

First, there is a growing interest in seeing place as something that acquires value over distance. This literature on the 'traffic in things', which derives from theorisations of commodity culture, expands the concern with traditional commodities – sugar, say – into the increasingly diverse set of artefacts that are being sourced, packaged, and marketed. From this perspective, 'the value of commodities cannot be reduced to an intrinsic property of objects, but exists in the space or distance between our desires and our enjoyment of these objects' (Jackson 1999: 98). Here, the Guggenheim *brand*, firmly associated with the Fifth Avenue location, its Frank Lloyd Wright icon, and its exemplary art collection, was heavy in the minds of the Basques as they parted with their hard-earned tax revenues. It was precisely the distance – cultural as much as physical – between the two institutions which actively mediated the commodity exchange in the purchase of the Guggenheim as brand, collection, and curatorial knowledge. It is interesting to reflect upon what this means for the future of the art museum, which itself has always acted to house and fix and display a market for art, that indeed moves periodically. New York's centrality in contemporary art, one which it inherited from Paris, may indeed shift to a city in Asia, such as Hong Kong.

Second, and relatedly, this distance also involves a metaphorical or mental mapping of the Basque state. As Harvie (1994: 2) argues, by the late 1980s 'certain regions . . . now seemed at the sharp-point of European consciousness: areas of sophisticated technology, environmental awareness, local democracy, and a culture and civil society *which integrated the intimate and the cosmopolitan*' (my emphasis). As well as drawing on the symbols and scripts of ethnic particularism – history, cuisine, language – such movements embraced many of the most intensively 'global' sectors of the economy such as high technology and the media. While this has made such regions economically dynamic, it has far-reaching consequences for their cultural identity. And it is also crucial to note that globalisation as a process of capitalist development has advanced quickest in the domain of symbols. As such, it has been the major producers of symbols – film and television corporations, advertisers, satellite news agencies, software and games companies – that have had the greatest intensity of global penetration. It is clear that those corporations carry a particular symbolic message from a producing to a receiving culture, and that some degree of alteration of the receiving culture will occur. As a consequence, such developments in globally influenced cultural production have had an unsettling impact on the geographical imagining of territories. As Edensor (1997: 191) has noted, with reference to Scottish nationalism,

> disembedding processes [the heritage industry] . . . place-marketing, and mediatisation [think of Braveheart] have a profound effect on national and local identities. On the one hand, they remove aspects of the production of identity from the local stage and transform situated characters and events in transmitting them to a local audience. On the other hand, they provide reworked narratives and images *which can reignite debates over identity and be repatriated.*
>
> [my emphasis]

I hope to have shown that the debate over the Guggenheim encapsulated this paradox. The museum clearly absorbed resources which would otherwise have been allocated to locally based cultural producers. Simultaneously, however, the process of obtaining the museum is a profound message from one section of the Basque nationalist family as to their preferred vision of Basque cultural identity.

Third, the Bilbao Effect has impacted not just on the site. It has also worked within the intensely visual fields of contemporary culture, and here we see the significance of the Bilbao 'effect' in terms of its locus as an icon. However, the icon works not just to mark out the Bilbao site, but also of its protagonists. As one of the key aspects of the event was the intention to establish the Guggenheim as a global art brand, setting it in competition with other players such as the Metropolitan or MOMA, this also included cross-branding, the New York gallery selling 320,000 tickets – a record – for an exhibition about Gehry himself:

> It called it a retrospective but the reality, stretching all the way up the sea-sickness-inducing spiral at the heart of the museum, was nothing less than Gehry's coronation by Thomas Krens ... as 'the most important architect of our time'.... If Gehry really was the most important architect in the world, then that would clearly make Krens its most important architectural patron.
>
> (Sudjic 2005b: 274)

This cross-branding is revealing of how architectural fame and reputation is increasingly associated with corporate self-promotion. It is interesting to consider Thomas Frank's assessment of the popularity of Gehry in the context of the 'New Economy' moment:

> his trademark computer-assisted curves representing the giddy religion of entrepreneurial 'creativity' in the same way that the Beaux Arts works of McKim, Mead & White radiated imperial grandeur, in the same way that the office blocks of Skidmore, Owings & Merrill symbolised efficiency.
>
> (Frank 2005: 64)

It did not escape Frank's notice that the New York Guggenheim's celebration of Gehry was sponsored by Enron: an unfortunate association, but one that seemed to encapsulate the popularity of Gehry in the hot years of the dot.com boom.

Gehry's appearance on *The Simpsons* ends with a salutary commentary – the concert hall project is a failure, as no one in Springfield actually likes classical music. After sitting derelict, the building is sold to Mr Burns for use as a prison. This is the hidden side of the Bilbao Effect – the instant appeal of the Basque case perhaps overlooked some of the factors aiding the Bilbao's popularity: its location in the temperate North of Spain attractive to tourists seeking to escape the heat of the rest of the peninsula; the arrival of budget airlines at just the moment when the museum was seeking visitors; the burgeoning reputation for Basque cuisine as among the best in Europe. Thus the three actors have each been altered profoundly by the unlikely, even serendipitous, coming together of a fiercely financially autonomous region, one of the few in Spain not to have benefited from a major event in the 1990s, a 'globetrotting' museum director determined to break moulds but masking a less-than-cosy domestic financial situation, and an architect who had spent most of his career in the avant-garde. This historical conjuncture may be difficult to replicate.

# 5   Rem Koolhaas and global capitalism

## Koolhaas and the Office for Metropolitan Architecture

> There are moments, for instance, when the decline of the yen has a direct impact on my professional and personal situation. The outcome of the French elections might dictate where I live and work.... The most crucial project I ever worked on fell through because a politician had accepted an illegal trip to Thailand as a bribe. Some days Cable News Network seems like an oracle, a kind of private bulletin board, as each story hits nerve endings directly related to my work and my private life. For the modern architect, this condition is a twenty-four hour source of anxiety.
>
> (Rem Koolhaas 1996: 238)

Rem Koolhaas expresses what every internationally operative architect knows: that the 'autonomous' design of architecture on paper or in the studio, a process which can take countless hours of team-working and experimentation, can be swept away by any number of unpredictable political and economic events. His anxiety reflects the fact that his firm had struggled to get established for a long period. In the mid-1990s Koolhaas was more famous for his publications – *Delirious New York* and *S, M, L, XL* – than for his built projects. OMA's early output was characterised by a handful of small commissions, such as the National Dance Theatre in The Hague (1987) and Rotterdam's art gallery (1992). The firm's breakthrough in terms of scale came as masterplanners for EuraLille (1994), a bold attempt to reposition the Northern French city within an emerging European high-speed rail network.

By the mid-2000s, Koolhaas and OMA had achieved worldwide success. The firm received a major commission to redesign the headquarters of Chinese State Television in Beijing, was involved in large masterplanning projects in the Gulf, and had completed a select number of high profile commissions in the US and Europe. These included a Campus Center at the famed Mies-designed Illinois Institute of Technology in Chicago, a branch of the Guggenheim in Las Vegas,

Prada stores in New York and Los Angeles and a new library for Seattle. Their European work expanded too, with projects such as the Dutch Embassy in Berlin, and a Concert Hall in Porto. The radical, distinctive designs achieved were sufficient to place OMA and Koolhaas at the forefront of the architectural star system.

My interest in this chapter is in how Koolhaas revels in redefining the role of the architect in all the social and technological messiness of the contemporary world economy. In what follows, I describe how OMA's fluctuating fortunes in getting their commissions built has inspired an acute self-examination over the ability of the architect to operate in conditions of 'fast production'. His challenging narrative style in expressing his work, the embrace of branding – facilitated through the creation of sister company AMO – and his geographical adventurism in China and Nigeria provide a fascinating set of insights into the search for architectural autonomy.

## *Content* and the architect's book

Born in Rotterdam in 1944, Koolhaas had an early career as journalist and screen-writer, but soon moved to architecture. Educated at the Architectural Association, he became exposed to the work of Archigram, the iconoclastic futurists that would influence many of his ideas. This was followed by a move to the US, another foundational influence. There, he began work at Cornell University, where he was exposed to the city-scale architectural vision of Oswald Ungers. He then moved to New York, settling in Peter Eisenman's Institute for Architecture and Urban Studies, where he developed and subsequently published *Delirious New York* (1978), hailed by his peers as one of the most influential architectural books of recent times (see, for example, Moneo 2004: 308–9).

In many ways, this helped project him to prominence within a modernist architectural world seeking to move beyond the impasse of corporate building and post-oil crisis dystopianism. In *S, M, L, XL* – dubbed in *Time* as 'the ultimate coffee table book for a generation raised on MTV and Derrida' (Luscombe 1996) – he worked with the graphic designer Bruce Mau to mash together a series of parallel stories, manifestos and theories around each of the firm's projects. The book endeared Koolhaas to new generations of architectural students worldwide that gagged on the solemn manifestos of the modernist movement, or the tedium of official corporate monographs. Its silver cover and splashy graphics woo the reader into a series of OMA design projects, organised around the four scales indicated by the title, from Small (for houses, etc.) through to Extra Large (the Lille masterplan, primarily). Koolhaas showed the influence of the Architectural Association and Archigram in this. Yet as Martin Filler has acidly observed, while Archigram's attempt to 'to convey a breakaway energy conspicuously lacking in corporate modernism' was expressed through cheap, cheerful and ephemeral pamphlets, *S, M, L, XL* 'is closer in spirit to the deluxe boxed CD sets of aging

60's rock stars' (Filler 2006). The book was influential, yet expensive and heavy. While it sought to reinvent the architectural monograph, it still retained an aura of grandiosity and permanence.

In 1999, Koolhaas formed AMO as a twin studio to OMA, one which represented 'the liberation of architecture from practice'. For Koolhaas:

> AMO doesn't stand for anything specific, but it could be Architecture Media Organization. OMA and AMO are like Siamese twins that were recently separated. We divide the entire field of architecture into two parts: one is actual building, mud, the huge effort of realizing a project; the other is virtual – everything related to concepts and 'pure' architectural thinking. The separation enables us to liberate architectural thinking from architectural practice. That inevitably leads to a further questioning of the need for architecture, but now our manner of questioning has changed: first we did it through buildings; now we can do it through intellectual activities parallel to building.
>
> (in Sigler 2000)

The idea of AMO as a thinktank, where design solutions emerge from a period of brainstorming of the urban, social and economic context of the project, fits with Koolhaas' rejection of the idea of architect as auteur: 'It is an insult to me, as well as to the others, to make it all seem like just my work. . . . If I pride myself on one thing, it is a talent to collaborate' (in Lubow 2000).

In 2004, OMA and AMO published *Content*, a chunky, glossy bricklet of a magazine. *Content* is cheap, subsidised by colour adverts for Prada, Gucci and Volkswagen, among others. It would, in itself, be of little lasting significance were it not for its muscular exertion of the latest stage of Koolhaas' thought and action. Indeed, its editor is quick to note its ephemerality, its air of being something cheap enough to be thrown away in the recycling.

> *Content* is a product of the moment. Inspired by the ceaseless fluctuation of the early 21st century, it, inevitably, bears the marks of globalism and the market, ideological siblings that, over the past twenty years, undercut the stability of every facet of contemporary life. This book is born of that instability. It is not timeless, it's almost out of date already. It uses volatility as a license to be immediate, informal, blunt; it embraces instability as a new source of freedom . . . *It is an attempt to illustrate the architect's ambiguous relations with the forces of globalization*, an account of seven years spent scouring the earth – not as business traveller or backpacker, but as a *vagabond* – roving, searching for an opportunity to realize the visions that make remaining at home torturous. *Content* is, beyond all, a tribute to what are perhaps OMA-AMO's greatest virtues – its courage, its dogged, almost existential

pursuit of discomfort, its commitment to engaging the world by inviting itself to places where it has not authority, places where it doesn't 'belong'.

(McGetrick 2004: 16, emphasis added)

*Content* is a hybrid of book and magazine. Its cover is garish, plastered with sensational slogans ('Perverted Architecture, Homicidal Engineering, Sweat shop demographics, Big Brother skyscrapers, Paranoid Technology, Al Qaeda fetish, Martha Stewart urbanism, Slum Sociology'), and with a montage of grotesque figures (George Bush with a McDonalds fries-hat, next to Saddam Hussein disguised as Rambo, and so on). The only clue that this is an architectural output is the backdrop: the distinctive ziggurat of OMA's Chinese State Television building. Inside, among the adverts, are a series of interviews, opinion pieces and feature articles, many of which contain Koolhaas polemics.

Throughout *Content*, Koolhaas disappears and reappears, though his presence is felt everywhere. He interviews Martha Stewart, Venturi and Scott Brown and the editor of *Der Spiegel* (de Graaf and Koolhaas 2004b). His peculiar and pithy essays pop up in between adverts. There is even a swipe at the Pritzker Prize, which Koolhaas received in 2000 in Jerusalem, and which is illustrated not with the grateful acceptance of the garland, but with a blurred photo of a pair of Israeli army officers, looking down on a target below. As the caption reads: 'the architect regretted "that political obliviousness is now assumed to be part of the architect's equipment," and was subsequently declared the most ungrateful winner in the history of the prize by its PR person' (p. 418).

Interspersed among the Koolhaas jeremiads are presentations of the OMA projects, both built and unbuilt. Indeed, they are – as often as not – about projects that worked on paper, but failed to be realised. *Content* is a counterpoint to the well-established format of the architectural monograph, with completed work precisely photographed under azure skies, and accompanied by minimal textual clutter. Its ironic tone contrasts with the post-rationalised summaries of favourite buildings found in the output of most practices. For example, OMA's design for the headquarters of Universal was cancelled as a result of the corporate merger of a competitor, America Online-Time Warner. Universal pulled out of the deal when its market positioning suddenly changed. It had originally engaged OMA to provide a rebranded HQ in order to overcome its own perceived brand dissonance, after conglomerating Seagram (a drinks company), with MCA, the entertainment corporation that included Universal Studios and MCA Music. However, rather than consigning the unfortunate project to the company's archive, *Content* revels in telling the story of its demise with some wicked humour. Photos of the model are arranged alongside four of the company's brand-name bottles, which replace the four pillars of the projected structure (AMO/OMA 2004: 121, photo). *Content*'s presentation of OMA's Dutch Embassy in Berlin uses a montage of grainy, poorly lit interior shots. One shot has the building creepily framed through a telescopic lens, ringed in red as if in a sniper's sights. Even OMA's output is listed in the manner of property small ads at the end of the publication.

*Content* had been prefigured by AMO and Koolhaas's guest stint as editors of the June 2003 edition of *Wired* magazine. The cover portrays an austere, black-clad Koolhaas, gazing off-camera into the distance. The main headline is 'Koolworld', the strapline 'Guest Editor Rem Koolhaas presents the ultimate atlas for the 21st Century' is emblazoned across his body. The magazine's inside pages document the preoccupations of this age: the editor's invited contributors cover twenty 'space' related capsule essays including 'nano space', 'golf space', 'DNA space', 'Atlas space' and, inevitably, 'Space space' (www.wired.com/ wired/archive/11.06/). In his editorial, Koolhaas sets out the context for this spatial turn:

> Our old ideas about space have exploded. The past three decades have pro-
> duced more change in more cultures than any other time in history. Radic-
> ally accelerated growth, deregulation, and globalization have redrawn our
> familiar maps and reset the parameters: Borders are inscribed and perme-
> ated, control zones imposed and violated, jurisdictions declared and ignored,
> markets pumped up and punctured. And at the same time, entirely new
> spatial conditions, demanding new definitions, have emerged.
>
> (Koolhaas 2003)

Koolhaas's presence in *Wired* was evidence of his growing recognition within 'new economy' industries, from entertainment (as commissioned architect for the new Universal headquarters), to fashion (Prada) and culture (the Guggenheim Las Vegas). Yet it also showed his willingness to move beyond the traditional pre-occupations of architects to engage with new forms of urban spatiality, cyber-space not least. *Wired* magazine has, for many, embodied the story of the recent cyberculture. From its origins in 1993, its techno-utopianism and libertarian outlook made it a bible for young dot.commers. Its own corporatisation – from 1998 firmly embedded within the Advanced Publications/Condé Nast publishing fortress – mirrors that of the sector as a whole, as the idealism of the Web 2.0 pioneers is gobbled up by giant media conglomerates. As Thomas Frank captures so well in his account of the dot.com collapse, *One Market Under God*, the boom period of new economy companies between 1996 and 2001 was played out in such magazines:

> In *Wired* itself hipness, and the free-market politics to which the Web was
> wedding it, came together in a mixture of boastful 'radicalism' and an almost
> deranged optimism. The magazine's fifth anniversary issue showed this
> stealth-reactionary style at its most blaring: someone from the libertarian
> Cato Institute declaring the lifespan of *Wired* to be the 'five greatest years for

humanity' ever; software designer Jaron Lanier announcing that 'we are witnessing the most productive, intelligent, and optimistic example of youthful rebellion in the history of the world'; ... and an editorial broadside booming, 'In this economy, our ability to create wealth is not bound by physical limits, but by our ability to come up with new ideas – in other words, it's unlimited'.

(Frank 2000: 85)

This would presumably be the intended audience for *Content* – a technoliterate, vaguely counter-cultural youth. Critics were generally kind. A reviewer in *Spike* magazine placed it in the same league as Le Corbusier's *Towards a New Architecture*, and Robert Venturi's *Complexity and Contradiction in Architecture* (Hardy 2004). The editor of *Icon* magazine proclaimed that: 'The visuals might consist of clip-art graphics, grainy photography and rough collages but the articles see Koolhaas at his incisive best. The range of subject material is awesome' (Fairs 2004).

So, Koolhaas uses the book as a provocation not just about architecture, but about the whole nature of visual, as much as textual and verbal, communication in the contemporary world. While *Content* is designed as a disposable novelty, an OMA fanzine, it is also a bold statement on the messiness of architectural production. The publication of the book by the German-owned Taschen is, in this context, entirely apt, given the publisher's reputation for the mass reproduction of art books (Berens 2001). For some critics, Taschen's impact on art and design publishing has been negative, undercutting the 'serious' architectural monograph, 'leaving an uncritical consumer demanding little more of its heavily illustrated books than that they respond to the lowest possible price-to-colour-plate ratio' (Eerme and Kinross 2002). Yet for OMA/AMO, enamoured of pop culture and aesthetics, Taschen's populism sits well. This book-in-performance (after Barnes 2002) in many ways 'surfs' (to use a favourite Koolhaas verb) the capitalist mode of Anglophone publishing. These 'immutable mobiles' help spread the Koolhaas message, filtered through numerous magazine or newspaper interviews and features, university lectures, and student gossip (Barnes 2002; Latour 1987). The ultimate expression of this? The decision to accept advertising in *Content* as a means of selling the book for £6.99, and to capitalise on Taschen's global distribution network.

## Rebranding architecture

JS: Where does your practice begin and end? With AMO, you can also be an architect of concepts, right?

RK: I'd say that my profession ends where architectural thinking ends – architectural thinking in terms of thinking about programs and organizational structure. These abstractions play a role in many other disciplines, and those disciplines are now defining their 'architectures' as well. There's a kind of multiplication of architectural activities. I don't feel that I'm becoming less of an architect, but more.

(Rem Koolhaas, interviewed by Jennifer Sigler 2000)

Miuccia Prada's decision to commission Koolhaas for stores in Los Angeles, New York and San Francisco (along with Herzog and de Meuron for a Tokyo shop) was part of a broader strategy of avant-garde artistic patronage. Prada engaged artists Elmgreen and Dragset to design a faux Prada boutique at the side of a desert highway, I-90, close to the environmental art mecca of Marfa, Texas. They invited photographer Andreas Gursky to provide a major work to adorn its New York epicentre. They commissioned controversial sculptor Tom Sachs (who had earlier designed a Prada hatbox in the form of a concentration camp) for a single show at Fondazione Prada in 2006. This canny strategy feeds the cultural premium of the Prada brand: just as the epicentre stores acted as loss-leaders for the brand (a form of 'experiential retailing'), so the association with avant-garde artists and architects allows the firm to enhance the mysterious form of commodity fetishism that luxury consumption items possess. As Nicky Ryan has argued, 'By aligning themselves with the values of artists positioned in opposition to established middle- and upper-class canons is to make visible their membership of a particular cultural elite' (Ryan 2007: 21).

The opening of the New York Prada store coincided with the publication of the *Harvard Guide to Shopping* in which Koolhaas had embraced the science of shopping with an enthusiasm matched by few other architects except, perhaps, Robert Venturi and Denise Scott Brown, and sector leaders such as Jon Jerde. For Anna Klingmann, such an approach involves 'brandscaping', which redefined accepted ideas of the role of architecture in relation to commerce:

> OMA's projects, each in their own way, express the narrowing gap between commercial culture and cultural production accelerated by the experience economy of late capitalism. More implicitly, they seem to challenge the notion of architecture as a self-fulfilled cultural object, now eroded by commodification.

(Klingmann 2007: 122–4)

As Ole Scheeren, an OMA partner, described, 'for the first time there was an articulated commission by a client not only to produce architecture but also to simultaneously produce a body of research; to investigate broader conditions, in this case of shopping and of Prada as a brand in itself.' Thus while OMA worked on the design and spatial programme of the retail space, AMO were able to work in tandem on Prada's brand, making 'a series of very precise or intertwined links between these domains' (Scheeren 2003). In many ways, OMA-AMO is following the kind of work done by the strong service firms, who increasingly offer consulting services to clients – should they renovate, lease, move, rebuild? – based on their knowledge of the development and design industry.

The Prada commission would be quickly followed by another big breakthrough. In 2001, Romano Prodi (then President of the European Commission), and Guy Verhofstadt (Belgian prime minister, and then President of the EU) invited a group of public intellectuals to brainstorm two issues: the need, or otherwise, for the EU to have a capital city; and the suitability, or otherwise, of Brussels for that role (European Commission 2001: 8). Among the intellectuals called upon to expound were Umberto Eco and Koolhaas. Eco outlined his vision of a 'soft' capital:

> Brussels should become a capital of European culture.... The organisation of a European book-fair (not on the model of the Frankfurt one, which works very well as far as commercial issues, exchange of rights and translations are concerned), as a playground where European publishers and readers would meet to discuss the European state of the art. The same should be done for films and television. Thus, the capital of the European Union should become a 'foyer culturel', a centre for the confrontation of diversities.
>
> (European Commission 2001: 11–12)

Koolhaas countered with a focus on a 'hard' capital, advocating the redesign of the infamous EU District, conventional terrain for an invited architect. Yet he quickly extended his analysis into the representational field occupied by the European Union's typical historiography and publishing norms (Shore 2000, ch. 1). In contrast to Eco's interest in the cultural output of the EU, Koolhaas was interested in how it could be branded. As he put it: 'The representation of the European Union as one entity is often flat and without eloquence. It is possible to represent both the diversity and unity of Europe in a more attractive way' (European Commission 2001: 13).

In his slideshow presentation, Koolhaas then revealed a whole range of playful visual reworkings of European territory. Conventional 'flat' maps of the European territory are enlivened by overlays: flat, uninterrupted official blue for 'Blueurope'; the 'mosaic' (which appears to conform to a European of the Regions); €urope (a pastiche of brand-names joined to country of origin – from Absolut, Ikea, Volvo and Ericsson in the North down through KLM, Chanel, Prada and Camper); a whimsical 'cool Europe' of cultural celebrities (Abba to Saramago and Victoria Abril); and a further – fascinating – iconography of religious diversity (European Commission 2001: Part III).

However, it was the tongue-in-cheek proposal for a new European flag – where each of the national flags of the member states are condensed into a single 'barcode' design – that gained most attention. In an aggressive riposte to 'blueurope', the barcode is advertised as 'new symbolism for a new coalition: Europe shown as a sum of the cultural identities of its current and future members. Whereas the number of stars in the current EU flag is fixed, the barcode can accommodate newcomers and gain impact' (AMO/OMA 2004: 384). Of course, there is a subtext: the barcode can be seen as an allusion to a European integration project based upon economic rationality and the neo-liberalised movement of goods and people (as enshrined in the Single European Market ideal). As Jameson (2003: 71) notes, the barcode or Universal Product Code is powerful as both signifier and actor: 'Analyse its functions and see how the statistics it immediately provides the retailer transform the whole structure of inventory, resupplying, marketing and the like'.

The media backlash – in the UK at least – was swift. 'Call that a flag? It's just like a deckchair!' screamed Britain's *Sun* tabloid. The pro-European *Independent* ran the barcode in full colour on its front page, proclaiming 'The new symbol of the EU'. As AMO and Koolhaas respond in *Content:*

> No work of AMO-OMA ever came close to receiving so much attention. The hype that ensued testified to the urgency of the issue of Europe and its representation. Apparently the 'flag' had hit a nerve of pent-up Euro-sentiment throughout Europe. In a reaction to the barcode, Britain ... emphatically professed its loyalty to the old European flag, symbol of every-thing it had loved to hate.
>
> (de Graaf and Koolhaas 2004a: 385)

The barcode served to destabilise a debate on European identity that is often con-ducted in the realm of idealism, rather than materiality. Koolhaas does much to *visualise* the economic-material processes that are reshaping Europe, and in particular the nature of its changing territory. This entry into the realm of Euro-pean iconography has been underpinned by irony, by provocation, in the finest surrealist traditions.

## Architect as anthropologist

The Project on the City began in 1996 as an endeavour to decipher virulent and escalating changes to the contemporary city. The intention is to examine ways that what was previously defined as the city has undergone wholesale change. At the start, two factors made the need for such a study critical. First was the realization that there was a renewed interest in the city coming from outside the profession: the city as an idea had been resuscitated not by architects, but by market-driven investment. Second, through the influence of the market, urban conditions around the world were mutating at unprece-dented rates; new urban conditions were emerging that the vocabulary of architecture was simply unable to capture. We, inside the profession, were forced to clumsily grope for concepts, constrained by the outdated, cultur-ally specific tools of architectural language.

(Inaba 2004: 256)

In 1995, Koolhaas was appointed as a professor to the Harvard Graduate School of Design. Instead of lecturing, he established a series of research projects addressing areas where the market dictated architectural output in a way that existing theory failed to consider, as the project co-ordinator, Jeffery Inaba, describes above. Koolhaas had already developed an aesthetics of 'dirty realism', or, as Charles Jencks has put it, the 'poetry of the botch' (Jencks 2002: 183). In his first large built project, Congrexpo Grand Palais convention centre in Lille, he pursued the low budget commission with characteristic enthusiasm. 'God is not in these details, but rather in the zeitgeist of late Capitalism and bricolage' says Jencks (2002: 188). This reflected a growing interest among a whole gener-ation of Dutch architects – such as MVRDV, for example – in seeing archi-tecture and its products as being, effectively, *structured* by a commercial rationale based on demographic analysis, market research and geographic information systems. This perspective requires an understanding of building at a metropolitan scale, rather than being limited to the immediate context of the site. This is in part developed from a statistical methodology, the datascape, deriving the specific form of a building from its wider territorial context (Jencks 2002).

The 'Project on the City' book series, published by Taschen, initially con-sisted of two volumes: *Great Leap Forward* (Chung et al. 2001) and *The Harvard Guide to Shopping* (Chung 2002). Both books are edited collections of high quality essays and photoreportage developed by individuals from within the Harvard group. The latter is concerned with artificiality, homogenisation, the Generic City and (over)consumption, leading to a foray into the netherworld of the architecture and practice of shopping, something of a taboo for 'serious' architects. The former addresses the Pearl River Delta, where the astonishing pace of rural to urban migration, combined with double digit economic growth, has dramatically reshaped the conditions for architectural production: Shenzhen with its overnight skyscrapers, Qingdao with its golf courses, Guangzhou with its old core and its new space juxtaposed, Dongguan, the industrial hinterland of Hong Kong and so on. The astonishing rates of urban building in Shenzhen, for example, reputedly see a masterplan for 300 houses completed in just one night by a team of five architects. As a professional figure, the Chinese architect 'designs the largest volume, in the shortest time, for the lowest fee. There is one tenth the number of architects in China than in the United States, designing five times the project volume in one-fifth the time, earning one-tenth the design fee' (Lin 2001: 161). Such 'fast production' became a growing fascination for Koolhaas, seemingly negating the role of architects in shaping these cityscapes.

Koolhaas fused these approaches – that of fast production and dirty realism – in his ethereal essay 'Junkspace', versions of which have appeared in a number of publications, including the *Harvard Guide to Shopping*, the cultural theory magazine *October* and *Content* (Koolhaas 2002a, 2002b, 2004, respectively). With the barest of punctuation, and written in a breathless, aphoristic monologue, it is a list of gripes, jokes and wordplays that wheelies around the central concept. Frederic Jameson, the esteemed pioneer of Marxist-infused postmodern literary criticism, was moved to hail 'Junkspace' – 'this sustained and non-stop "performance" of built space' – as 'an extraordinary piece of writing ... the point of the exercise is ... to find synonyms, hundreds upon hundreds of theoretical synonyms, hammered one upon the other and fused together into a massive and terrifying vision' (Jameson 2003: 73). 'Junkspace is ...', sentences often begin. It starts with the airport and ends with vague references to the cyborg: 'Will Junkspace invade the body? ... Is each of us a mini-construction site?' (Koolhaas 2004: 171). It rattles through many of the favourite Koolhaas motifs – air-conditioning, interior design, neon, lunch-boxes, escalators, stretched things ('limousines, body parts, planes', p. 167), building finance, brands, work-life balance, globalisation, Las Vegas, golf courses, East Germany, art gallery design, television screens – without stopping for pause. It is an encyclopaedia of the heteronomy of architecture, a celebration of the visual, the structural and the hidden systems of building technology.

It also reflects Koolhaas' restlessness, and his envisioning of the world through his travels. As was discussed in Chapter 3, travel and the architect's 'gaze' has always been an important part of architectural practice, whether an examination of the best of the best, or an understanding of the origins of form (Ockman and Frausto 2005). Yet what is as interesting is, as Joan Ockman has suggested, the emergence of a 'paradigm shift' in how architects understand the 'other' in an anthropological sense. This has more to do with mass tourism, which in turn has always been complicit in trailing and plundering the sites of the world, bringing them home on photographs and on t-shirts. Koolhaas is not innocent in this process:

> If we may characterise the objective that underlay the journeys of the most emblematic architect-tourists of the twentieth century as *cognitive mapping*, that of the globe-trotting Koolhaas (300 hotel nights a year) might be described as *global positioning* ... it is clear that as the global horizons of difference have receded in the onslaught of advanced capitalism, requiring ever more exotic 'trips' to satisfy the tourist's appetite for new stimuli, the architect's gaze too has become more refractory to experiential mediations. Thus Koolhaas coolly surveys the contemporary global condition from a totalizing

vantage point that confirms and celebrates it in advance as junkspace. In contrast, the modernist gaze was frequently naïve and misguided, but there was no doubt where its heart was.

(Ockman 2005: 183–4)

Koolhaas is not alone in his endeavour, for in urban theory, more broadly, there has been a tendency to impose a Western-centric viewpoint on 'other' less industrialised societies. As Jenny Robinson has argued, such a colonisation has been part and parcel of Western urban theory for decades. Interestingly, she suggests that the global cities discourse which has become dominant in urban studies of globalisation has tended to pathologise African cities, demapping them as irrelevant to a global economy. Here, she argues for a cosmopolitan urban theory, where 'scholars in privileged western environments will need to find responsible and ethical ways to engage with, learn from and promote the ideas of intellectuals in less privileged places' (Robinson 2002: 550).

For the Harvard team, the exciting thing about Lagos is that it 'represents a developed, extreme, paradigmatic case-study of a city at the forefront of globalizing modernity' (Koolhaas and Harvard Project on the City 2001: 653).[1] It stands in for a possible future of cities: 'the fact that many of the trends of modern, Western cities can be seen in hyperbolic guises in Lagos suggests that to write about the African city is to write about the terminal condition of Chicago, London or Los Angeles' (p. 653). In an interview with *Index* magazine in 2000, Koolhaas describes how he and Edgar Cleijne

> borrowed the helicopter of President Obasanjo and flew over the city for two days. . . . We made an unbelievable video about a traffic jam in Lagos, which is really scary because the sheer pressure makes everything liquefy. There are these jams that are mostly buses – rivers of yellow trying to go through arteries that are too narrow. Huge trucks – almost everything is public transport and trucks – really colliding and squeezing. And in between them, there are these people – almost like cement. . . . So it's not just a traffic jam. It's actually a traffic jam turning into a car market, turning into spare parts turning into a smoldering ruin. All in consecutive phases. It's really about metabolism and flows and scale. And unbelievable organization.
>
> (in Sigler 2000)

With this focus on the latent energy of the city's poor, who recycle almost everything and utilise the nooks and crannies of the metropolitan transport network as a site for trade and barter, Koolhaas and the Harvard team seize upon Lagos as the epitome of urban efficiency, a perverse urban model of success. Here, a schematic outline of their argument must suffice: Lagos is understood as 'both paradigm and pathological extreme of the West African city'. Its fascination lies in what the Harvard team call its 'conundrum ... its continued existence and productivity in spite of a near-complete absence of those infrastructures, systems, organizations, and amenities that define the word "city" in terms of Western planning methodology' (Koolhaas and Harvard Project on the City 2001: 652). The sweeping aerial photographs which accompany the narrative trace out the team's interest in Lagos as a laboratory of unplanned, informal transactions. After a brief introduction to the material topology of the city's form – its property and plot norms, and its taxation structure, seen as determinants of the city's land use – there follows a discussion of traffic networks, and of its market places, primarily Oshodi, a largely chaotic site of exchange that sprawls across a junction between a major motorway off-ramp and a railway line. For the Harvard team, the striking finding is that 'Oshodi somehow works' (p. 693), despite the fact that it breaches most of the regulatory prescriptions for the city's governance.

Bregtje van der Haak's fifty-five minute documentary Lagos/Koolhaas (2002) contributes to this myth. The opening frames split the screen in half, splicing a close-up of Koolhaas' *eyes*, holding a studied gaze over the Lagos cityscape, which in the lower segment of the screen is depicted in a long, slow pan. The screen changes quickly to footage of 'The New Dawn at 10', a popular Nigerian breakfast television show, where Koolhaas and his Harvard accomplice Edgar Cleijne are interviewed about the Lagos project. As the Koolhaas exposition unfolds, we hear his favourite mantras – the 'self-sustaining organism' of the city, an ordered efficiency – played over the city's street life. Traffic cops battle with sweat to keep the traffic moving, as bright yellow minibus-taxis clog the streets. A rough and ready social geography of the city emerges, from the comfortable, if mildly annoying, drag of life on Victoria Island, to the daily fears of the child water and newspaper vendors, vulnerable to kidnap or arrest. The crude commerce of Alaba electronics market – lauded by Koolhaas for its almost total self-sufficiency (it even has its own jail, he comments approvingly) – makes good camera copy, unboxed VCRs and television sets stacked high, Herculean porters moving towering stock on their shoulders.

Of course, what makes this poignant is the state of economic governance in Nigeria. Asked by the television host if he would return to Lagos to help solve some of its urban problems in practical terms, Koolhaas is evasive: 'he answers that that would entail a different kind of project' (Ockman 2005: 183). The desperate lack of foreign investment and development in the area is mirrored in the absence of opportunities for indigenous architects and any conception of aesthetic beauty is replaced by an aesthetic of noir. The ruthless pan of the camera over sweeping vistas of oil drum repair yards, sofa markets, choked expressways and potted roads evokes an otherness rich in texture for those used to the ordered life of contemporary urbanism. Street photography has its own contested history, and it is difficult to find a balance between prurient exploitation and empathy with

the subject. This is a balance that Koolhaas seems unaware of. It is evident, says
Joan Ockman, that

> what has led him to its wild urbanism – armed with digital camera, film
> crew, Ivy League entourage, and the Nigerian president's helicopter – just as
> to China's construction boom and Prada's high fashion runways, is an aes-
> thetic and intellectual fascination with contemporary spectacles of global
> culture, whether of under- or overdevelopment.
>
> (2005: 160)

This is an interesting intellectual agenda, but it is pursued in a rather offensively
dilettante manner. As Matthew Gandy has pointed out, the enthusiasm with which
Koolhaas greets the ingenious use of space in Lagos street markets ignores the structural forces that continue to keep so many in the city mired in poverty:

> If Koolhaas and his colleagues, soaring over the city, can claim that the sight
> of the traders crammed beneath the Oshodi flyover is 'proof and evidence'
> that Lagos urbanism is 'one that works', the conclusion is inescapable: in
> their perspective, it is the city's ability to sustain a market that is the sole sig-
> nifier of its health.
>
> (2005, 52)

For Gandy, this reflects an ignorance of recent Nigerian history:

> The informal economy of poverty celebrated by the Harvard team is the
> result of a specific set of policies pursued by Nigeria's military dictatorships
> over the last two decades under IMF and World Bank guidance, which deci-
> mated the metropolitan economy.
>
> (p. 42)

The Koolhaas team is seemingly unaware of, or else chillingly conscious of, the
political instability which has brought that city to 'the brink of a cataclysm
brought about by ethnic strife and infrastructural collapse' (Gandy 2005: 38).

The documentary will be an intriguing artefact for future generations. We do
see Koolhaas in the streets of Lagos, not always in situations of great personal
relaxation as the young street vendors that so fascinate him from afar push in on
him and the camera. There are vague references to the oil-rich background of the
city, with footage of the Shell Cup football tournament and car radios reporting
business news involving the World Bank. Yet the overall impression is that Lagos
is being aestheticised in all of its dysfunctional grandeur in a way that rather over-
looks the geopolitical structures that have consciously underdeveloped a once
booming city.

## Conclusions

AMO, the Harvard Projects and *Content* thus reflect what Koolhaas has cheekily described as his 'exit strategy' from architecture, a means by which he escapes the self-referential field of architecture and steps out into the wilder world of economics, culture and politics (Dyckhoff 2004). Thus he can perhaps be seen to be pushing the boundaries of architectural professionalism in an age of increasing globalisation. I will discuss his controversial design of the CCTV building in Beijing in Chapter 7. What is clear, however, is that Koolhaas has simultaneously subverted (even undermined) the status of the architect as an autonomous professional, and has embraced the power of the client in determining the process (Jencks 2000).

Accepting that the client's goals and budget define the architectural response is not new. However, what Koolhaas does is work *through* the architect's lack of autonomy. The irony employed as a central part of the Koolhaas performance is a feature common to contemporary celebrity with popular culture, particularly in the entertainment industries. As Joshua Gamson argues, irony has 'become a common piece of celebrity public personas' (1994: 52). It is common for film stars, actors and even politicians to engage in controlled self-deprecation, particularly of the supposed glamour of their jobs as constructed by the celebrity industry. Here, 'the ridiculing of glamour by celebrities is another star turn ... updated to accommodate the visibility of glamour production ... The reader, armed with a cynical knowledge about image-manipulation strategies, is being told how to read the pose as a pose' (Gamson 1994: 52). Koolhaas is aware of the force of his own personality and celebrity. *Content* was accompanied by an exhibition, or retrospective, held in the Mies van der Rohe-designed National Gallery in Berlin. As Deyan Sudjic describes:

> If you ventured inside, you found an effigy of Koolhaas himself. It was a doll, made by the artist Tony Oursler, impaled on a steel rod emerging from the middle of a pile of discarded and broken models. Its miniature black shirt and its grey striped trousers, just like Koolhaas's, were clearly meant to suggest that they came from Prada. A digital projection of the architect's face played over the doll's blank white head. If you listened carefully you could catch snatches of him reading from one of his essays about Junk Space.
>
> (Sudjic 2005b: 111)

This is an important redefinition of the role of the architect in an intensely mediated age. For Aaron Betsky (2004: 27), 'Though he plays the role of the dashing half-businessman, half-artist jetting around the globe, he has turned that image into a self-conscious construct'. As Arthur Lubow, who profiled Koolhaas for the *New York Times Magazine* (itself an indication of a degree of celebrity status) suggests: 'if his denunciation of the cult of personality has only enhanced his own mystique, that is the sort of contradiction that he relishes' (Lubow 2000). As a result, Koolhaas argues that the architect 'must not become the hermeneutic savant of space, but operate in it like a virus, between forms, social conditions, economic structures, political ideologies' (Enwezor 2004: 111). In a similar way, the artificiality of the autonomous approach to architectural production is stripped away in Koolhaas's tales of commissions won and lost.

# 6 The geography of the skyscraper

## Relational geographies of the skyscraper

> For the skyscraper is not only the building of the century, it is also the single work of architecture that can be studied as the embodiment and expression of much that makes the century what it is.... For better or for worse, it is measure, parameter, or apotheosis of our consumer and corporate culture. No other building type incorporates so many forces of the modern world, or has been so expressive of changing belief systems and so responsive to changing tastes and practices. It romanticizes power and the urban condition.... The tall building probes our collective psyche as it probes the sky.
>
> (Huxtable 1984: 11)

As Ada Louise Huxtable captures so precisely, skyscrapers have a fundamentally expressive function. They act as icons of modernity, collectively form a scenographic backdrop that defines a city's identity, and usually involve the clearance of older, less profitable, land uses. The tall building is often dismissed as the ultimate product of faceless, rationalised capitalist modernity. In this scenario, global architectural firms are seen as agents of cultural imperialism, and in particular as conduits of American business culture.

In contrast to the idea that skyscrapers are *only* functional outcrops of globalising capitalism, the 'faceless' corporation, or the abstract flows of capital that undermine place, there is an argument that tall buildings give cities identity through 'skyline', an identifiable array of icons that provide orientation for walkers and drivers, and narrative markers for urban historians (both professional and casual). They have played an important role in the visual history of the twentieth and twenty-first centuries, witnessed in countless films, postcards and adverts. And they provide a poignant reminder of social visibility, both of the powerful, who buy, sell, design or promote the buildings, and of the hidden labourers who construct and maintain them.

Skyscrapers are important to debates about globalisation because they can act as switches for globalised flows, whether metaphorical or material. The most expressive of these buildings, those that stand out in the financial districts of some of the world's most affluent cities, may seem to be designed for highly skilled, highly paid knowledge specialists, with their associated consumption choices in hotels, apartments, restaurants, shops and gyms. Yet these workers require support, and the complex ecology of the skyscraper will also include bicycle couriers, photocopier maintenance specialists, cleaners, lift engineers, receptionists, security guards, software and systems specialists; those who deliver sandwiches, wash the windows, drive taxis and so on. The social impact of this should be obvious: as Graham and Marvin (2001) explore in *Splintering Urbanism*, contemporary skyscrapers are often designed as nodes in 'premium' infrastructure networks – 'high speed communications, "smart" highways, global airline networks [that] selectively connect together the most favoured users and places, both within and between cities' (p. 15). From this perspective, these buildings have tiny foot-plates but huge aggregate impacts on urban form.

The chapter has three sections. First, it traces the development of the 'tall building race', following the intense competition that has seen height records shift from the US, to Malaysia, to Taiwan and now to Dubai over a period of a few years. Second, the chapter sketches a rough outline of some of the links between architects and oil, between architectural form and colonial production sites, suggesting that the representational form of architecture can only be understood through a holistic vision of the supply chain. It draws a tentative link between the kinds of architectural production that characterised colonial economies, and the current beanfeast being enjoyed by architects in the Gulf, particularly in Dubai. Third, it considers debates surrounding contextualism in skyscraper design, and explores how architects articulate the relationship between the form and structure of their buildings with vernacular forms.

## The world's tallest building

[T]he economic success of nation-states such as Malaysia emboldened political elites and cultural authorities to articulate their own visions of modernity. The location of the world's tallest building in Kuala Lumpur added credence to such imaginings. Not only had Malaysia and other economies in a rising East achieved a Rostovian 'take off', but the evolutionary charts of socio-economic 'progress' which had staged the West as the end-point of being modern now continued their ascent to a new apex of A(/Malay)sian development. Thus the building height charts so popular in Malaysia and the international media in the 1990s appeared to corroborate the civilisational arguments of Mahathir and other proponents of 'Asian values'.

(Bunnell 2004a: 74)

The striking impact of skyscrapers on urban landscapes around the world has often been associated with discourses of progress. As David Nye suggests, skyscrapers were part of an 'American technological sublime', generating the same popular excitement as such events as bridge dedications and World's Fairs. These events are, he argues, a mirror of classical antiquity's celebration of sublime nature. This captures that 'essentially religious feeling, aroused by the confrontation with impressive objects, such as Niagara Falls, the Grand Canyon, the New York skyline, the Golden Gate Bridge, or the earth-shaking launch of a space shuttle' (Nye 1996: xiii). And so: 'Those operating within this logic embrace the reconstruction of the lifeworld by machinery, experience the dislocations and perceptual disorientations caused by this reconstruction in terms of awe and wonder, and, in their excitement, feel insulated from immediate danger' (Nye 1996: 282). Skyscrapers were central to this process through the twentieth century, yet even then, their continual technological progress, invention, and advance coincided with a growing public disinterest: 'The once dizzying and disorienting view from atop the Flatiron Building became familiar, and higher towers were needed to upset the sense of "normal" spatial relations' (Nye 1996: 284).

Such buildings are both sites and sights, therefore, an amalgamation of financial power with symbolic presence, popular with the new commercial elites of modern America. By the 1920s, 'the olympian perspective from their offices was immediately recognized as a visualization of their power' (Nye 1996: 97). The race to construct the world's tallest building was a manifestation of this, one which seeped into the popular consciousness with the often secretive battle over the final height of the Empire State Building and the Chrysler Building. For Nye, this 'geometrical sublime and its fantasies of domain thus altered the phenomenology of the city' (1996: 108). For New Yorkers, such buildings – and their successors, particularly the World Trade Center – allowed the boastful claims of world centrality.

Unsurprisingly, these monuments to national state prestige have proliferated in the post-colonial world. As Tim Bunnell has shown, Malaysian Prime Minister Mohammed Mahathir prioritised the Petronas Towers, in Kuala Lumpur, as a means of advertising Malaysian modernity, a material demonstration of the government's determination to 'leave a mark in global urban imaginaries' (Bunnell 2004a: 68). The Petronas Towers represented a material intervention in both the urban landscape and economy, forming part of a more widespread project of redeveloping and cleansing the city's old racetrack and squatter settlements. They acted as a symbolic gateway of a corridor, the Multimedia Super Corridor (MSC) to be more precise, which ran from Malaysia's colonial capital, Kuala Lumpur, along a newly constructed motorway spine to Kuala Lumpur International Airport, a mammoth construction designed to reach full capacity in 2020. In between was a new administrative capital, Putrajaya, which would neighbour a technopole called Cyberjaya, itself planned as an attractive site for high technology firms.

The towers were designed by an international architect (Cesar Pelli) with Islamic motifs incorporated into the façade and floor-plans, an attempt to fuse standardised western production methods with a locally sensitive design vocabulary, sending 'intentionally mixed ethnic messages ... while obfuscating the metaphors so that a single one does not dominate' (Steele 1997: 381). While some critics have seen these motifs as simplistic, Bunnell (1999, 2004a, 2004b) argues that this was the actual intention, that the towers were explicitly designed to be easily quotable iconic architecture that would feature in adverts, in-flight magazines, postcards and even Hollywood feature films.

Höweler (2003) sees such buildings as 'mediatic' skyscrapers, which are 'choreographed, not designed' and involve 'a shift from the purely quantitative (i.e. how tall) to the design of urban effect (i.e. how spectacular)' (pp. 160–1). The façade of buildings such as the KPN Telecom tower in Rotterdam, The Centre in Hong Kong or 5 Times Square in New York are designed to allow light shows and high-resolution animation, in effect becoming projection screens for a new form of urban sensation, that 'manifest a presence in excess of their physical dimensions – a kind of hyper-presence' (p. 160). The impact of these designs can be dramatic, but can also be seen as a simple extension of the ways in which major buildings have always dominated their surroundings through projection, traced back to the bell-ringing of medieval cathedrals (Höweler 2003: 160). So, the claiming of the height record by the Petronas Towers was enough to ensure worldwide media coverage with a bold narrative theme – that the quintessential icon of American modernity, the skyscraper, was now most prevalent in Asia, not in the US. This was but one aspect of a wider strategy:

> The reorientation of Kuala Lumpur in the 1990s was not reducible to attempts to connect up to a global modernity centred elsewhere. . . . Proponents of the KLCC project clearly saw their developmental contributions in terms of regional- (Asian, Southeast Asian, East Asian, Asia-Pacific etc.) as well as national-scale modern transformation. [. . .] the site/sight itself was actively bound up in the (re)formation of geographical subjectivities in 1990s Malaysia – new ways of seeing, and being in, the world.
>
> (Bunnell 2004a: 74)

Thus the site – the redevelopment of 'marginal' urban uses – was combined with the sight (the visual expression of Malaysian transformation for the benefit of the world's media and the citizenry alike). However, this carefully crafted plan was to be undermined in an unpredictable fashion. In Fox's film *Entrapment* (starring Sean Connery and Catherine Zeta-Jones), Mahathir's ambition for the towers to 'project' a new image of Malaysia to a world audience seemed to have been quickly fulfilled. However, as Tim Bunnell argues, the film had the opposite effect, effectively 'orientalising' Kuala Lumpur by cutting in scenes and frames of underdevelopment filmed 150 kilometres away in Malacca, splicing them with the hypermodern backdrop of the Petronas Towers:

> Kuala Lumpur here remained imaginatively entrapped within a 'third world' that had motivated Mahathirist postcolonial redevelopment. 'Slums', 'pollu- tion', 'poverty' – all those signs of underdevelopment that a decade of urban investment had sought to erase or, at least, render out of sight, had been col- lapsed into a single cinematic frame alongside Kuala Lumpur's world class architectural centrepiece.
>
> (Bunnell 2004b: 300)

Such cinematic license provoked a diverse range of responses among the Malaysian public and political class. Yet more broadly, too, the film was merely replicating a 'slums and citadels' trope that has prevailed in urban discourse for centuries. The Petronas Towers had only a brief period as the world's tallest buildings, before being overtaken by an emblem of another strongly emerging economy, Taipei 101, in Taiwan. It did not reside for long in Taipei, as by 2008 Dubai had taken the title.

## Dubai and global imagineering

In 2008, Emaar Properties were on the brink of launching the Burj Dubai tower, the centrepiece of their Downtown Burj Dubai development. At over 600 metres, the tower – looking a little like the Empire State Building fused with Sears Tower – smashed height records, easily surpassing its nearest contenders: Taipei 101 (509 metres), Shanghai's World Financial Center (492 metres) and the Petronas Towers (452 metres).

As architects, SOM had the distinction of designing two of the early twenty- first century's most iconic towers – Burj Dubai, the crowning glory of Gulf eco- nomic strength, and Freedom Tower in Manhattan, on the site of the World Trade Center towers. It did not escape the attention of some critics that Dubai's building boom was based upon the millennial fears of 'peak oil', the same combi- nation that had swirled around successive US presidential entanglements in the Middle East, and that ultimately implicated downtown Manhattan with global terrorism. Dubai, a mere 100 miles from Iran, has considerable geopolitical significance within the Middle East as a bolthole for dissident Iranians. This was underpinned by the Bush administration's establishment of an 'Iran desk' at the US Consulate in Dubai, set up to encourage regime change in Iran and intelli- gence gathering, playing a similar function to the Riga station in Latvia set up to act as a 'window' on the Soviet Union during the Cold War (*New York Times* 2006c).

There has always been a close relationship between US foreign policy and commercial export goals, especially in the immediate aftermath of the Second World War. A triumvirate of major policy initiatives – Bretton Woods (1944), the Marshall Plan (1947) and Truman's Point Four Program (1949) – set out an interventionist role for American governments in post-war reconstruction and economic development programmes. The export of the skyscraper is thus tightly linked to the post-war capitalist economies, their early dominance by American interests, and subsequent post-colonial expressions of sovereignty (initially in the Middle East of Nasser and OPEC) and more recently in Southeast Asia. For SOM, and other major architecture and engineering firms, the growing reliance of the US economy on Middle Eastern oil supplies brought considerable commercial benefit. Between 1945 and 1975, from the end of the Second World War to the emergence of a newly powerful Middle East, war and peace brought significant demand for architectural, engineering, and construction expertise. As Cody (2003: 124–5, 136–9) has noted, the reach of American firms extended to port-building, US army and naval base construction, and dam and road-building. In his study of the 'export of American architecture' between 1870 and 2000, Cody argues that

> one of the distinguishing features of post-World War II architectural exporting was how U.S. government institutions began to play more significant roles, becoming what one might term 'public gloves' in bolstering the transfer of American architectural skills – and its tools for war and peace – to countries where those institutions exerted increasing influence. In so doing, the protective 'glove' of the U.S. government facilitated American architectural exporting by a proliferating number of 'private hands'.
>
> (Cody 2003: 123)

By 1975, SOM had begun a programme of masterplanning oil towns in Iran, in Khuzestan, at Bandar-Shapour, and in Saudi Arabia, at Yanbu on the Red Sea. This could often entangle the firms in geopolitical conflicts. William Hartmann, a leading partner in SOM's Chicago office between 1945 and 1981, gives one such example:

> We undertook probably the biggest project in the world. It was a new town. The Japanese and the Iranians were building a petrochemical complex at Bandar-Shahpur, and they had to build a town to provide places for workers to live. . . . We established an office in Teheran. I used to go over quite frequently to establish that office. Finally Jim de Stefano was there with twenty or thirty people. And then, of course, the Shah was kicked out, and that was

the melodrama of all melodramas. We were very, very fortunate. It was nip-and-tuck, cloak-and-dagger when our fellows escaped out of Iran. Escaped! It was touch and go. Didn't sleep those nights waiting to hear.

(Art Institute of Chicago 1989c: 170)

However, while Iranian political change had become a national preoccupation, friendlier relations with Saudi Arabia brought the firm one of its most famous overseas commissions: the Haj Terminal at Jeddah. And the firm continued to develop strong links into the Middle East, as well as landing some major US embassy commissions (in Ottawa and Moscow). In an essay reviewing SOM's output in the 1980s and 1990s, Joan Ockman points out the irony that

> the modernist aspiration to a world architecture is being realized within a 'postmodernist' cultural climate. It is also remarkable that precisely the areas that have witnessed America's greatest conflicts – Germany, Japan, Russia, China, Korea, Vietnam – are now offering SOM some of its major opportunities.
>
> (Ockman 1995: 9)

The Middle East has certainly been a defining feature of US foreign policy for several decades. But under the leadership of Sheikh Mohammed bin Rashid-al-Maktoum, the Emirate of Dubai has become a 'new global icon of imagineered urbanism' (Davis 2006: 50). As Mike Davis continues: 'Although compared variously to Las Vegas, Manhattan, Orlando, Monaco and Singapore, the sheikhdom is more like their collective summation and mythologisation: a hallucinatory pastiche of the big, the bad, and the ugly' (p. 51). It is, he says, 'not a hybrid but an eerie chimera: a promiscuous coupling of all the cyclopean fantasies of Barnum, Eiffel, Disney, Spielberg, Jon Jerde, Steve Wynn, and Skidmore, Owings & Merrill' (p. 51). Dubai is the latest manifestation of a technological sublime, its complacent mastery over nature reflected in a culture of great luxury. The clients for many of these towers, major developers such as Nakheel, Sama Dubai and Emaar, have had their coffers swollen by a curious historical moment of financial liquidity. Given the Emirate's relative lack of oil, much of Dubai's investment is heavily leveraged, and much of it is provided by Arab investors relocating capital due to the post 9/11 instability in the US, and over-accumulation brought about by rising oil prices. Key individual clients such as Sultan Ahmed bin Sulayem, of Dubai Ports and Executive chairman of Nakheel; Mohammad al-Abar, chairman of Emaar and head of Dubai's economic development department; and Moham-mad al-Gergawi, Chief Executive of Dubai Holding (the government's key investment arm) form a major part of the estimated $100 billion that have been invested in new projects (Sherwood 2005; Timmons 2006).

The links between the oil economy of the early twenty-first century and the

*Figure 6.1* A development site of Emaar Properties, in Dubai.

steady globalisation of architectural practice has a precedent. In *Modern Architecture and the End of Empire*, Mark Crinson describes the role of the Anglo-Persian Oil Company (APOC, subsequently the Anglo-Iranian Oil Company [AIOC], British Petroleum, and BP) in the construction of a colonial settlement in Abadan, in the southwest of what was then Persia. The emergence of APOC from a relatively humble beginning was a good example of colonial economics: 'From the Persian point of view they had given a mining commission to a private individual in 1901 only to discover that within fifteen years they had virtually a colonial mini-state on their doorstep' (Crinson 2003: 53). By the 1920s, this small company town served as a microcosm of the inequalities of the colonial system – the neatly planned villas of Abadan contrasting with the oil-drum shacks of its associated shanty, Kaghazabad.

If the discovery of oil in Abadan underpinned the rapid corporate expansion of BP, so its architecture was expressive of the hidden nature of oil within a globalising economy: 'Abadan's refinery was the end of a pipeline,' writes Crinson,

> collecting the liquid and passing it through plants for all stages of refining before pumping it onto tankers to be sent around the world ... By the late 1940s it had become the largest refinery in the world, with the AIOC's assets in Abadan representing Britain's single most significant overseas investment.
>
> (p. 53)

With its growth came a huge increase in the town's population to around 200,000, requiring housing and a range of services. However,

> while the works dominated the site, as with most definable company towns, they were given no symbolic dimension; beyond a functional office building the company felt no necessity to establish architectural representations of the unity of its enterprise centred on the place of industry.
>
> (p. 56)

The company town that grew up around the refinery was a reflection of the spatial division of labour under colonialism, large plots of land with high quality housing for European workers contrasting with the shanty towns and cheap housing of the refinery's workers.

At the other end of the pipeline, metaphorically speaking, lay APOC's head-quarters in London, the Lutyens-designed Britannic House. Drawing on a review of the building from APOC's company journal (1925), Crinson summarises how the firm saw its headquarters 'as a metaphor for the company':

> Britannic House is a combination of beauty, exemplary business practice and utility, but above all it is a manifestation of high intelligence organizing the building and its technologies ... and of concentrated manual skill carrying out specialized tasks and ornamenting the product. The building is a highly efficient machine but one that is also finely tuned to its occupants' needs: twenty-eight telephone exchange lines serve communication, 250 clocks are

synchronized by a master clock, a thousand radiators heat the building and a thousand cups of tea slake the employees' thirst. This intelligence, prudence and skill is in the very nature of the company, the article intimates, and the building is the exemplification of its larger purpose.

(2003: 61–2)

Crinson's account underlines the fact that the colonial system is constructed around an international division of labour, with a strong symbolic dimension often expressed in architectural form (Jacobs 1994). His co-location of the refinery town with the architectural beauties of the London headquarters, at two ends of a production process, is an important imaginative construct. It implicates the symbolic power of the head office within a deeper system of exchange relations that underpin the management of different parts of a commodity chain. These oil-related design and construction opportunities emerged at a turning point in world politics – the decline of European colonialism, and its replacement by an American hegemony in world politics and culture. As Crinson continues, architectural modernism

arose at the peak of European colonial empires, even if its own histories barely acknowledge this and even if empire seems like one of those things it consigns to history. . . . Did modernism mark the end of empire or its continuation by other means?

(Crinson 2003: 1)

Certainly, there are some strong continuities between the conditions underpinning SOM's current work in Dubai, and the earlier work of architects such as Lutyens in the colonial economy. For Mike Davis, Dubai is where 'the super-profits of the international oil trade are intercepted and then reinvested in Arabia's one truly inexhaustible natural resource: sand' (2006: 53). Enjoying only a fraction of the oil reserves enjoyed by its large neighbour Abu Dhabi, Dubai's government has instead focused on diversifying its economy across a number of sectors, from real estate to tourism, financial and media industries and logistics. This has triggered a further trend in upmarket residential construction, usually in high-rise developments. As with APOC's headquarters in London, visually unconnected with the raw image of the desert oil-well, so Dubai uses its architectural emblems – such as the sail-like Burj al-Arab hotel – as a means of advertising its corporate success. And just as Abadan had its Kaghazabad, so too does Dubai rely upon an exploitative international division of labour. The Dubai construction boom is underpinned by low wages and limited worker rights, including non-unionisation. Of the 1.5 million residents of Dubai, two thirds are immigrants, with the largest group being construction workers. In March 2006, workers in a central construction site rioted, reportedly smashing cars, upturning offices and damaging equipment. Housed in

*Figure 6.2* Burj al-Arab hotel: an icon of Dubai.

peripheral work camps, labourers – primarily from India, Pakistan and Bangladesh – are paid 150 dollars a month, many feeling that they are poorer than if they had stayed at home (Davis 2006; *New York Times* 2006a, 2006b).

   Nonetheless, relaxed architectural design guidelines, a lack of historic urban context, ambitious clients and seemingly limitless amounts of building sites mean that architects have a rare freedom to push concept designs into built form. A range of new skyscrapers, from – among many others – SOM, Zaha Hadid and

Make are currently providing a palette of shapes and textures unseen in any other city in the world. While most architects would argue that they relish being in the historical centres of major cities, jousting with the existing fabric, context and scale of long-established landscapes, few enjoy the planning battles that go with such projects. As much of the territory of Dubai is desert, and with a long straight coast-line giving onto the Arabian Sea, the opportunities for unencumbered construction are plentiful. Indeed, architects in Dubai face the opposite problem – lack of context.

## Essentialism, and the International Style

It is rather ironic that SOM have been involved in the design of two major towers in Dubai's architectural phantasmagoria (Adrian Smith's Burj Dubai and Ross Wimer's Infinity Tower), given the firm's prominence in the evolution of the International Style, a movement associated with an aesthetic minimalism that stripped away ornamentation. By the late 1990s, the firm's various partners had shifted away from this style towards a more commercially popular aesthetic, with a strong interest in contextualism, combined with technological advance (Filler 1990; Ockman 1995). Many of SOM's designers had tried hard to reorient the firm's approach to skyscraper design and large-scale commercial projects. Larry Oltmanns, the design director of the London office, sets out his personal interests as being the:

> development of new architectural prototypes, definition of an urban mission, and recognition of cultural identities. I am intrigued with the invention of new prototypes that re-define how building types should work functionally. I continue to believe that the design success of a built project should be judged more by its contribution in improving the quality of urban life than in its qualities as an object. *And I am adamant that as international architects we should bear the responsibility for helping to preserve cultural identities.*
>
> (Oltmanns 2002: 32, emphasis added)

It is worthwhile tracing back how SOM got to this point. One of the firm's first major overseas commissions was as architects for the huge building programme undertaken in West Germany after the war. Leland King, of the Office of Foreign Buildings Operations (FBO), saw in SOM a firm with the necessary size, experience and style to represent the US in reconstruction efforts in war-torn Germany. According to Jane Loeffler, King 'saw the use of the Bauhaus idiom, transformed into an American icon, as a fitting goodwill gesture towards Germany' (Loeffler 1998: 88). Led by Gordon Bunshaft, SOM rolled out several consulate buildings in a style similar to Lever House, their Mies-inspired masterpiece in mid-town Manhattan. However, their designs for the Munich consulate seemed to exemplify the negative attributes of the International Style. On a site adjacent to an early nineteenth-century palace and the city's cherished Englischer Garten, Bunshaft famously stated that his building would work as well in Alaska as in Munich, a claim too bold even for this moment in post-war optimism (Loeffler 1998: 94). And the predominance of glass in many of these buildings was unsuitable for a situation of political tension: many panes were smashed during incidents of unrest. By the time official liking for their designs had waned, they had nonetheless succeeded in transforming the original, socialistic message of the Bauhaus that had been imported to the US by figures such as Gropius, and had re-exported it with a profound, if subtle, change in substance:

> A specific commitment to an egalitarian society was replaced by a more general commitment to democracy, and the political agenda was replaced by one that was almost exclusively artistic. Outwardly, the architecture looked the same, but to those who claimed to understand it, its meaning had changed. Modernism now represented capitalism – corporate capitalism – not socialism.
>
> (Loeffler 1998: 101)

So, the export of so-called 'International Style' modernism was in many ways a watered down version of the socialist ideals of its European pioneers. As Filler (2007: xv) puts it: 'the International Style – the cartoonishly simplified version of Modernist architecture most familiar to the American public – was as American as apple pie'.

Yet what has replaced the deracinated style has also been controversial. The move towards contextualism has arguably become a new International Style. As we saw in the case of museum architecture, the search for an identifiable style which allows the building to speak, or to brand its occupants, is an important prerequisite for many clients. The skyscraper is no different. For example, Jean Nouvel's Torre Agbar in Barcelona makes a clear break with the modernist skyscraper. Standing 144 metres high, with thirty-three floors, the façade of the building is coated with bris soleil, using forty different colours of tile. It dispenses with the high modernist notion of the skyscraper as a pared-back, geometrical form, and its elliptical shape has a lot in common with Foster and Partners' Swiss Re building, which has a similarly striking presence in the skyline of London. The Swiss Re 'has all the hallmarks of the iconic building – the reduction to a striking image, a prime site, and a riot of visual connotations' (Jencks 2005: 185). However, as Jencks continues, such buildings are still highly functional, and allow for new configurations of internal space (allowing shafts of daylight between floors, for example), as well as providing an important relationship to the city around it.

The use of such architects to provide geometrically unconventional forms is a means by which places distinguish themselves in a global skyline market. Along

*Figure 6.3* Jean Nouvel's Torre Agbar, Barcelona.

with the new buildings going up in Dubai and the Gulf, we can see the same issues if we look at the skylines of booming cities such as Shanghai, Beijing and Hong Kong.

Much has been written about the re-emergence of Shanghai within both the Chinese polity and economy. The city has had a key role in post-reform economic policy, as the headquarters of China's trading activities, as an industrial powerhouse derived from its location on the Yangtse River Basin, and as a major employer within China (Olds 2001: 178; Wu 2000). As a means of achieving this, the central government established Pudong New Area Administration, one of several areas of China where approved forms of capitalist economic activity would be encouraged. Of the four sub-sectors of Pudong, the Lujiazui Central Finance District is undoubtedly the most significant, and is the location of many of the most emblematic skyscraper developments in contemporary China (Olds 2001: ch. 5). As Dawson (2005: 17) describes:

> As manmade cliffs and mountains Pudong is more impressive as a kaleido-scope of mosaic geometry, spooled past a car window, than as a hands-on experience. From afar, the towers seem to overlap. . . . The China Insurance Building is a pair of Siamese towers, swaddled in ribbon windows, and sporting two-spoked wheels pierced by hatpins. The Bank of China tower is a lipstick revolving out of its protective sheath and Shanghai Pudong Development Bank has four identical graph-paper facades. Any structure under forty floors is a dwarf in this assembly of royal egos, none of whom are capable of communicating with each other. After hours the lights go out and Pudong ceases to exist. The towers are dormant, the streets empty.

*Figure 6.4* Herzog and de Meuron's Olympic Stadium model, on public display in Beijing.

As described in Chapter 1 the prevalence of foreign architects within China has caused some controversy. On the one hand, many overseas architects have complained about being excluded from the building process after their initial provision of concept sketches or masterplans. As Kris Olds describes, the Richard Rogers Partnership saw its carefully elaborated masterplan dismembered in Shanghai's race to develop land (Olds 2001: ch. 5). A more powerful critique emerges from within China, however, over the perceived Westernisation of the country, and the stylistic retreat from traditional Chinese architectural design. For example, the awarding of a series of major public commissions in Beijing to European architects (most notably Herzog and de Meuron's Olympic stadium, and Paul Andreu's National Theatre), have been the subject of considerable delay (Hawthorne 2004; Lubow 2006).

Yet what would constitute a traditional Chinese design? For Rowe and Kuan (2004), architects over the years have adopted widely varying tactics in dealing with Chinese traditions. First, a number of firms completely ignored vernacular traditions, a trend most common in the foreign concessions such as Shanghai, Hong Kong and Nanjing. The most significant of these firms was Palmer and Turner, founded in Shanghai in 1868, whose major commissions such as the Hong Kong and Shanghai Banking Corporation headquarters were rendered in a Western neo-classical form. Second, in the early twentieth century North American architects such as Henry K. Murphy and Henry H. Hussey, as well as American-trained Chinese architects such as Lu Yanzhi, took an adaptive approach, which attempted to reconcile tradition and modernity, 'between *ti*, or essence, and *yong*, or application' (p. 61). A third perspective was offered in the 1920s and 1930s by returning Chinese architects who had been educated abroad. Yang Tingbao, for example, a student of the University of Pennsylvania who had studied with, among others, Louis Kahn, would bring Western methods to his public building commissions such as Nanjing Central Hospital, yet with Chinese detailing. Fourth, it is important to note the life-long commitment to conservation of existing vernacular architecture, found in the archival and archaeological work of Liang Sicheng (1901–72), who would 'as he mastered the complex grammar of various Chinese traditional constructive systems [become] critical of his contemporaries' use of traditional Chinese architecture in modern buildings' (p. 84).

Foreign architects have similarly adopted a wide range of approaches to building in China. They have often identified a particular motif, which could then be replicated in an expressive form. Herzog and de Meuron's stadium resembles a bird's nest, seen as being a harmonious natural object, and representing culinary esteem. Foster and Partner's new terminal at Beijing airport resembles a dragon, long celebrated within Chinese culture (Lubow 2006). Yet skyscraper designs have proven to be more challenging. The World Financial Center tower in Shanghai, developed by the Japanese Mori company and designed by Kohn Pedersen Fox, adopted a novel solution to relieve wind pressure at the top of the building, designing in a circular hole of 150 feet in diameter – which for some Chinese resembled the Japanese rising sun flag. Ultimately the hole was altered to a trapezoidal form (Lubow 2006).

In 1999, the Jin Mao Tower opened in Pudong as China's tallest building, designed by Adrian Smith of SOM's Chicago office. According to Blair Kamin, for many years the architectural critic on the *Chicago Tribune*, Smith had not visited Shanghai when he identified the form that his projected building would take. Instead, he visited the firm's in-house library to familiarise himself with Chinese design history, and became fascinated with the pagoda form, which he set about reinterpreting for a skyscraper. Kamin described how the pitch to the Chinese clients was based around a short film, which located the design within a vernacular lineage. The film began with footage of three, rurally located Chinese pagodas, before sweeping back into the stepped-back design of the Shanghai tower (Kamin 1994: 12). Smith based his octagonal floorplate design on the belief in eight as a lucky number in Chinese culture, further reflected in the decision to have 88 floors in the building.

Such deference to feng shui principles guides many Chinese skyscraper designs. In Hong Kong, for example, the design codes exhibited in Norman Foster's Hong Kong and Shanghai Bank, and the competing Bank of China design by I.M. Pei, were the subject of considerable debate, particularly as the two towers were constructed against the back-drop of Hong Kong's transition from British to Chinese rule. As Carter Wiseman has noted in his biography of I.M. Pei, the site of the Bank of China was that of a Japanese Second World War military police headquarters, where many prisoners had been tortured. As such, Hong Kong's feng shui masters (or geomancers) had advocated a site analysis to mitigate the malign effects of the site.

> The Bank of China people, representing an officially atheistic society, were steadfastly opposed to the practice and refused to have the traditional analysis done. Not surprisingly, freelance advice began to proliferate almost as soon as the design was made public. As if the unhappy history of the site was not curse enough, the local geomancers noted that the masts atop the tower could be interpreted either as chopsticks held vertically in an empty rice bowl (a symbol of poverty) or as the sticks of incense used to memorialise the dead. Far worse were the X's made by the crossbracing that was to be expressed on the facades. Local authorities noted immediately that, at best, the X's evoked the mark traditionally drawn on a failing student's exercise by a calligraphy instructor. At worst, they suggested the custom of hanging a name tag around a condemned man's neck and slashing an X through it to signify that he was 'finished'.
>
> (Wiseman 1990: 291)

The triangular shafts used by Pei had also been identified by local geomancers as daggers that hack into surrounding skyscrapers, and which had a malign influence on the British Government House during the handover of control to China (see also Abbas 1997: 79–90). However, as Wiseman records, the bank's officers were aware that the building was partially designed to symbolise the integration of China and Hong Kong, and allowed a private feng shui consultation. Pei accordingly altered the façade design to dress the cross-braces with glass, allowing them to appear as diamonds; the building's topping out was brought forward to the auspicious date of 8 August, 1988.

Thus all architects working in high profile locations have to take a position on how they, as foreigners, can locate their buildings within a perceived local context or cultural style. This often seems to be apologetic. For example, SOM – with its legacy of a pioneering International Style homogeneity – has been very conscious of losing its Bunshaftian 'Alaska and Munich' notoriety when working abroad. As the design director of its London office stated in 2002:

> [W]e noted recently that the SOM team working on a new development in the center of Lisbon was composed of architects of twelve different nationalities, almost all of them European. I can state emphatically that all of these talented young people were very conscious of the need to consider what it is that makes the Portuguese identity unique. This is not to say that the answers are easy to find. It is extremely hard work (perhaps even more so if you happen to be Portuguese), but we'll never get there if we believe the identity of the project should be about the architect.
>
> (Oltmanns 2002: 31–2)

Larry Oltmanns aims to reassure us about the sensitivity of SOM to local identities, but fails to do so. The assumption that there is a unified, essentialised, Portuguese national identity fails to recognise that nations are social constructions, built up over decades and centuries of conscious myth-making.

Such dilemmas have often been raised in the context of SOM's work, not least in the Middle East. Roger Duffy, talking about the Kuwait Police Academy, argues that it

> is shaped by pre-Islamic desert influences. We went back in history to the way that people built in that part of the world before the spread of Islam in the 5th century. There were thousands of years of history before Islam that dealt with issues of hotness and coolness, light and dark spaces, shade and shadow, the sound of water, and the strength of natural light.
>
> (in Bussel 2000: 11)

Similarly, finding a context for the Emaar-funded Burj Dubai would pose a challenge for Adrian Smith, the tower's architect. As Smith would explain, Burj Dubai:

is an interesting project because there is very little context for a building of this height to draw from in Dubai. . . . You know the onion dome shapes that you see in mosques and other buildings in Dubai, for example; we used these shapes but in plan, not in elevation. The onion dome shapes will only be seen when looking up from near the base at certain angles. . . . The other aspect that relates to Dubai is the desert flower – the shape of the desert flower has three major petals and three minor petals. This is seen in plan and is a central organizing force in the building . . .

(Emporis 2003)

These discourses which seize upon a motif before whittling it to produce a structural solution are, in some cases, post-hoc rationalisations which are part of the architect–client relationship.

However, there has been a stylistic counter-reaction from Western-educated Asian architects such as Ken Yeang (Malaysia), William Lim and Tay Kheng Soon (Singapore), and Sumet Jumsai (Thailand) who have *had to* develop new design strategies as a means of countering the market hold of the likes of major US architectural firms such as Pelli, Kohn Pedersen Fox or SOM (Kusno 2002: 131). The difficulty faced by these architects is in stepping beyond a nationalist imagining to a pan-Asian concept that gives them a competitive economy of scale in the region's construction markets, confronting 'the relative failure of the Modern Movement to even consider appropriate environmental solutions to the problem of the high-rise in the tropics' (Steele 1997: 383). Similarly, tall building design in earthquake-prone areas is a key factor in countries such as Japan and Taiwan, and many of the aforementioned 'critical regionalist' responses offered in Southeast Asia are centred around climatic concerns. In Yeang's case, the 'bioclimatic skyscraper' gives us a range of new forms driven by the need to capture winds and provide shading; Tay's interest in tropicality is driven by a clear-sighted avoidance of symbolic quotation and the need to adopt technological form to tropical climates, to harness Western-developed technology to specific climatic conditions (Kusno 2000, 2002; and the collection in Tzonis *et al.*, 2001).

Despite these critical regionalist responses, cosmopolitan theorists such as Sandercock (1998) see the high-rise building form and the modernist planning paradigm as a force of homogenisation, as a threat to the social diversity and multiculturalism of the contemporary city. For Jane Jacobs (2001), this is a misplaced critique, as it involves too close a reading of the symbolic pretensions of the tower at the expense of a focus on the specific social context of the developer. She illustrates this with two examples from Australia. The first, the Grollo Tower, was an attempt to build the world's highest building in Melbourne:

The discourse that this development proposal has generated rehearses much that is familiar: it is a phallus, it is simply the will to power, it is authoritarian.

In summary, it is the unwelcome manifestation of a globalised idea in a local place – a violence that is given a certain amplification by being the product of a race for the tallest building in the world. . . . Yet the certainty of this criticism has been unsettled by the fact that this developer is one Bruno Grollo, a migrant Australian, a representative case of a multicultural Australian success story. His place in the ideal of multicultural Australia is regularly confirmed in press reports that mention what migrant generation he belongs to, feature his extended family, and refer to this rich man's unusual residential loyalty to the once migrant suburb of Thornbury. The Grollo tower is one of those cases which bring the limits of cosmopolitanism into clear view. Grollo-the-migrant developer and his world's tallest building confound cosmopolitan intentions. It has drawn some of the most cosmopolite of critics into a position which has to deny one vector of difference (Grollo's position as the migrant success story) in order to protect another (the diversity of the urban fabric).

(Jacobs 2001: 24–5)

The second example Jacobs draws from Sydney's Chinatown. Writing in 2001, she refers to a proposed Draft City Plan which placed more stringent restrictions on the neighbourhood's floor space ratio than the adjacent CBD, in order to conserve the townscape of the heavily promoted 'ethnic' enclave. This was challenged as being discriminatory by local – Chinese – entrepreneurs. 'In this instance,' notes Jacobs, 'the highrise does not erase difference but is fully inhabited by the unpredictable politics of difference' (2001: 25).

We could add another, fascinating example. On 23 March 1999, the Bangladesh government issued a postage stamp in honour of Fazlur Khan, 'showing a picture of his face emerging from a brick façade in the background and with an image of the Sears Tower on his left' (Ali 2001: 217). Khan was born and educated to degree level in Bangladesh, but moved to the US on a Fulbright Award in 1952 to achieve Masters and doctoral awards in civil engineering. In 1955, he joined SOM, rising through the ranks to become a general partner in 1970 (the only engineer to have that status at that time). Khan was fundamental in developing the supertall skyscrapers that would become SOM's trademarks, John Hancock Tower and Sears Tower in Chicago. The ironies should be obvious: Khan, celebrated on a postage stamp in a Muslim country with an emblem of that icon of American capitalism as a back-drop. But it is another illustration of the 'small stories' of transnational mobility of personnel, and of how images of buildings travel in unpredictable ways.

## Conclusions

The skyscraper occupies complex connotative terrain: of bureaucratic rationalism, the ruthless march of corporate workplace 'organisation men'; of homogenisation, as the International Style at its most arrogant sought to erase cultural specificities; as metonymic of corporate 'secrets' and anonymity; of material dominance (the citadel metaphor); of financialisation (with its revenue envelopes of volumetric, lettable space, driven by the verticality of its floorplates as much as its height); and of an internalisation of city life, soaring above the messy vulgarity of the street. To understand the complexity of the skyscraper, it is necessary to go beyond its formal, overwhelming proportions, and to engage in a process of 'surface accounting': 'to bring into view how the coherent given-ness of this seemingly self-evident 'thing' is variously made or unmade' (Jacobs 2006: 3). For example, the book and documentary series 'Skyscraper' by Karl Sabbagh, broadcast on PBS in the US, followed perhaps the most influential current SOM practitioner (David Childs) as he designed Worldwide Plaza on Manhattan's Eighth Avenue. Childs disagrees with the developer over the colour of the building's bricks. 'Five hours of watching all these people struggle with one another may be too much process for anyone,' admits Paul Goldberger (1990), but it does bring the focus of analysis down from the skyline and onto a fleshy, street-level plane. Similarly, Meredith Clausen's (2005) biography of the Pan Am (now MetLife) Building in Manhattan pieces together a fascinating narrative of corporate decline and its relationship to the symbolic contours of headquarter buildings.

The growing trend in understanding urbanisation as a relational process requires a view of specific, material spaces – airports, skyscrapers – as being switching points or containers of people and technologies that are interconnected with other similar spaces many miles distant. Given the complexity and contingencies of these flows, it is ironic that many of the metaphors, adjectives and tropes used to represent and talk about the skyscraper emphasise fixity, solidity, rootedness and permanence. They are often central to debates about the changing nature of particular cities, and their place in the urban landscape and the city biography are worthy of fuller exploration. Yet this 'global' history of the skyscraper conceals a range of complex relational geographies, from a conventional locational geography (the distribution of tall buildings in the world's cities), to a mobile range of visual codes and corporeal movements, to debates over the nature of transnationalism, global–local relations, and ideals of a 'universal' building style popularised by the modernist movement. As Jacobs (2001) puts it:

> If we were to linger a little longer around the lobbies, corridors, undercrofts, parks, roof-tops and apartments of the highrise, would this experience simply confirm the homogenising vitality of a global architectural form? Or might it open out a space in which to contemplate the vital contours of a local zone of contact, a space in which it would be possible to see the radical hybridisations of the form, the creation of a mongrel highrise carved out of the contingencies of local governance and the tactics of everyday living.
>
> (p. 23)

This is a challenge for theorists of the commercial and residential high-rise alike. This could range from ethnographies of living in elevated territories (Barley and Ireson 2001), to considering the social and cultural geographies of the view (Griffin 2003). There are intriguing questions over the nature of skyscrapers and the visual (including the increasingly creative use of façade and interior lighting), which may perhaps be connected to debates over the privileging of visuality in the imagining of cities. There is growing evidence to suggest that tall buildings might be considered as code-space (to borrow Dodge and Kitchin's (2004) analysis of the modern air travel system), given the complex security, climate, and information systems used in regulating these structures (see Philip Kerr's (1996) novel *Gridiron* for an entertaining satire on this). And then there are the genuine outcasts, the 'smokers' huddling or solitary at the doorways of smoke-free offices, captured in Louise Dignand's photography (in Barley and Ireson 2001: 84–5), all the while engaging in an interesting and complex form of sociality.

# 7   The ethics of architectural practice

Senior staff at Foster & Partners wrestled with their consciences before deciding to design an ostentatious 'Palace of Peace' for a regime universally criticised for its poor human rights record. A pyramid taller than Nelson's Column, for President Nazarbayev of Kazakhstan, will go on site in the new capital of Astani next month, but Foster's deputy chairman David Nelson admitted it had been a difficult decision. 'We believe the nature of the project – it is about bringing together Jews and Muslims – is in itself a worthy thing to be doing at this point in time,' he said. 'You can change these things slowly by working in the country. You could boycott the place, but I don't think that would help. Norman [Foster] and I talked about it on many occasions.'

(*Building Design* 2005)

The pursuit of new commissions in an increasingly globalised architectural market poses serious dilemmas for firms. When the UK's leading architectural firm accepts a commission from the President of a country that has been criticised by numerous sources – including the UK government's Foreign Office – for its apparent harassment of political opponents and restrictions on democratic organisation, it is time to consider their rationale for doing so. Indeed, the decision to design such a building in Kazakhstan prompted *Building Design* magazine to run a theme issue asking architects just what commissions they would, and would not, consider. Ethically challenging commissions included issues concerning the function of the building itself, such as prisons or polluting factories. But the biggest challenge comes when working abroad for politically dubious regimes or clients, something that has certainly become an increasingly problematic area (Blackler 2005).

Foster and Partners are not alone in being presented with such challenges. It may not help to boycott the place, but as Deyan Sudjic has recently argued: 'Whatever the architect's intentions, in the end they find themselves being defined not by their own rhetoric, but by the impulses that have driven the rich and the powerful to employ architects, and to seek to shape the world' (Sudjic 2005b: 327). In this context, debates about architectural ethics become tangled up in wider issues concerning the private nature of the architectural firm, the geopolitical context in which it operates, and the complex dilemmas facing architects seeking to see their designs realised.

In Chapter one, I discussed how the motivations of architectural firms cannot be defined by market-driven rationality alone. To recap, the private nature of many firms (where share ownership is held tightly by a self-selected group of partners) means that to fulfil the imperative of firm growth or diversification, architects are compelled to consider a wide range of proposals by a wide range of clients. However, there is another layer of complexity. While many ethical issues are discussed at the level of individual conscience, architects operating within firms are immediately bundled into an ethical framework of shared responsibility (where legal recourse falls on to a firm's directors, for example). This is complicated for architects, who operate within two different ethical frameworks. As Kris Olds has argued, globally operative architects:

> inhabit the 'neo-worlds' of late capitalism. They easily negotiate the stretched out social spaces tied to both the *business* networks of architecture (the moneyed white collar property developers and senior state officials) and the *professional* networks of architecture (the intelligentsia-managed institutions that help define the discourse of Architecture).
>
> (Olds 2001: 154–5, emphasis in original)

Such architects are thus tied into distinct, if overlapping, social networks with their own ethical rules and responsibilities, and their own power relationships. Additionally, the 'stretched out' spaces within which they operate sometimes elude the regulatory frameworks of the nation state, and move into a less clearly defined area of global ethics.

The whole notion of an ethics of architecture as a set of moral principles, a means of assessing what forms of human conduct are 'right or wrong', is one that immediately raises problems of analysis. Even if one could smooth over the centuries of debate over the nature of ethics, one would then have to agree upon a stable definition of what might constitute *architecture*. Here, I work with a simple categorisation of architectural ethics, following Wasserman *et al.* (2000: 7): the architect as a professional, abiding to a certain code of professional ethics; the conduct of the architectural process, that set of client-driven, economic and social pressures that help define the design process; and the 'embedded ethics' of the building itself that may or may not be seen as distinct from the previous two categories.

This chapter looks at how issues of ethics and social responsibility have been faced by some leading architects. It explores the nature of political, environmental and ethical responsibility with reference to several recent high profile architectural commissions, by Rem Koolhaas/OMA, Foster and Partners, and others. It questions the degree to which architects are compromised in their ability to intervene in broader debates about urbanity and society.

## Going East: the geopolitics of architecture

> What attracts me about China is that there is still a state. There is something
> that can take the initiative of a scale and of a nature that almost no other
> body that we know of today could ever afford or even contemplate.
>
> (Koolhaas, in Leonard 2004)

Chinese State Television, the central broadcasting organ of the Chinese Communist Party, announced in 2001 that it was seeking to build a new headquarters
complex in Beijing. For OMA, troubled by the long series of setbacks that had
dogged its US work, the Chinese market offered both intellectual stimulus and
commercial promise. Working in tandem with the East China Architectural
Design Institute, OMA's striking design – a ziggurat groundscraper – would win
over the design judges, and the firm was awarded the commission in mid-2002.
Charles Jencks, who was on the jury that selected OMA ahead of other major
firms including SOM, KPF, Philip Johnson, Toyo Ito and some Chinese firms,
explained the building's appeal as follows:

> The most important idea in the brief was that the building should be a 'land-
> mark,' and the words clearly implied something approaching the status of
> Gehry's Bilbao. Koolhaas grasped the logic involved, and in his presentation
> stressed the fact that if the future central business district of Beijing were to
> have 300 skyscrapers, then the 301st would certainly be a faint echo, not the
> desired landmark ... I advocated the scheme for this reason and also because
> it was such a stunning iconic building...
>
> (Jencks 2005: 107)

However, problems quickly arose. Fearful of an overheating economy, Chinese
officials began to rein in some of the more extravagant aspects of its major public
projects. The CCTV project itself was challenged by some Chinese academics
who resented the excessively avant-gardist nature of the building, and the inva-
sion of China by foreign architects. Koolhaas flew to China to address one of the
most influential architectural schools at Tsinghua University, where he reputedly
wooed the crowds with a curious mix of cautious political subversion and a vigor-
ous anti-Americanism in architectural design (Zalewski 2005: 118–19). In
autumn 2003 the project was confirmed, and construction got underway.

The commission arose at two historical junctures. As I described in chapter
one, China emerged onto the world architecture stage in the early 2000s in direct
relationship to its sudden economic take-off, propelled by the growing potency
of its major cities. In contrast with the rigorous planning laws that had held back
some of OMA's American jobs, their Chinese client was more receptive to their
avant-garde leanings. As Daniel Zalewski puts it, 'All his life, he [Koolhaas] had

*Figure 7.1* Chinese State Television (CCTV) building, by OMA: model on public display in Beijing.

yearned for the creative anarchy of Jazz Age Manhattan. He had found it in Delirious Beijing' (p. 118). The second historical juncture was that of 9/11. The CCTV commission was announced in 2001, and suddenly the world's leading architects were faced with two, plum, commissions in the heart of the superpowers' major cities. Koolhaas made great play of refusing to participate in the Ground

Zero redesign. During a speech in 2003 at Columbia University, he argued that Daniel Libeskind had 'with remarkable efficiency ... succeeded in capturing the totalitarian moment' (in Risen 2003), by which he was referring to the upswell in American nationalism which came in the aftermath of the terrorist attacks, and which Libeskind had done little to dampen. As he noted in an interview:

> I just felt the conditions for the WTC were not right. Because, it was clear that in the American context you would have to make a monument, which would be dedicated to the WTC.... On the other hand, we felt that, ultimately, it was no different from the usual American way of business ... on the one hand, there's Libeskind, and on the other hand there were typical groups of Foster, Skidmore, etc. ready for it. We were not going to do that. We were simply not convinced by the integrity of that whole operation.
>
> (Koolhaas 2005)

Koolhaas thus cunningly linked this commentary on the 'American way' to his decision to turn his back on that symbol of Americana, the skyscraper. He thus simultaneously sought to justify his controversial structural form *and* his ethical stance on the commission.

OMA's success met with criticism outside China, however. While numerous Western architectural practices have set up offices and accepted commissions from various branches of the Chinese state, the CCTV contract was given added political sensitivity by its material role as the production site of highly controlled state news broadcast media. It was only a little over a decade since pro-democracy protests in Tiananmen Square had ended in mass killings of unarmed civilian protesters. At that time, the renowned Chinese American architect I.M. Pei had – in the midst of the construction of his Bank of China tower in Hong Kong – decried the events in an article in the *New York Times* (in Wiseman 1990: 293–4). In the following years, the harsh treatment of pro-democracy protesters had been well-documented, so it was the fact that Koolhaas had chosen the project with such precision that worried critics. Deyan Sudjic (2005b: 111), observed pointedly that

> It is unlikely that Mies van der Rohe would have had a very sympathetic hearing if he had won the 1933 competition for Hitler's Reichsbank in Berlin and advanced a similar argument about the bright future promised by the imminent economic transformation of Hitler's Germany...

For Ian Buruma, a well-known critic of the Chinese regime, the problem lay with the function of the specific building:

> Unless one takes the view that all business with China is evil, there is nothing reprehensible about building an opera house in Beijing, or indeed a hotel, a

hospital, a university or even a corporate headquarters. But state television is something else. CCTV is the voice of the party, the centre of state propaganda, the organ which tells a billion people what to think.

Buruma's argument is premised on the conviction that China is 'one of the most rightwing countries in the world today, more rightwing even than Chile under Pinochet, where there were still pockets of organised activity not under the junta's control' (Buruma 2002). The championing of the CCTV project is thus seen as being contemptuous towards the country's growing opposition movement. Unlike his colleagues designing the Beijing Olympic stadia, masterplans, tower blocks, office buildings, shopping malls and every other imaginable structure, Koolhaas is criticised for aestheticising the building's function. As Buruma continues, 'It is hard to imagine a cool European architect in the 1970s building a television station for General Pinochet without losing a great deal of street cred'.

Koolhaas defends the firm's intervention as follows:

> We are deeply aware that this is not an innocent project, and we have considered our own values very carefully. . . . We have chosen to participate in China now because we believe that the process of modernization needs pressure from within.
>
> (in Zalewski 2005: 118)

As the project leader Ole Scheeren put it:

> A young new generation in their early thirties and forties are in charge of the company and pushing forward the process of modernisation. The declared aim is to become the BBC of China, and the many publicly accessible functions of the new building program point towards a democratisation of the institution.
>
> (2005: 4)

Perhaps critics would have been kinder had Koolhaas not chosen to overextend the symbolism of the building itself, and OMA's role in shaping a new China. The analysis of the conditions in which his projects are conceived are often lacking a social dimension. As Buruma concludes: 'if he is serious about reinventing urban life, he will have to address political questions, as well as technological ones. Surfing is not always good enough' (Buruma 2003: 67–8).

## Environmental ethics

Architects have a vital role as advocates of sustainable solutions. But we also need more progressive developers and politicians with courage to set goals and incentives for society to follow. Some countries have given a lead:

Germany has long understood the need to reduce consumption and adopt renewable energy sources, and that is reflected in building codes. Others, in varying degrees, lag behind. There are no technological barriers to sustainable development, only ones of political will. If we are to avoid the environmental damage wrought by the unsustainable patterns of the past, then the established and emerging economies must act in unison and with urgency before it is too late.

(Foster 2005)

Norman Foster's stout advocacy of the centrality of architects in debates over ecological sustainability is no bad thing. Set against the agonisingly slow response to evidence of global warming among political leaders worldwide, the environmental movement needs as many allies as it can get. However, as Foster identifies, the issue is one of political will. Only strict central government controls or taxes on the full ecological footprints of new developments can compel the architect's client – the developer – to follow ecologically sustainable principles. Yet Foster could be accused of being disingenuous here. His firm's recent mixed-use masterplan for the 1.2 million square metres ex-steelworks site of Milan Santa Giulia uses the rhetoric of the garden city, with extensive parks surrounding the apartment blocks catering for the predicted 9,000 residents. However, in order to make the development *economically* sustainable, it is predicted that the district will be 'populated by 50,000–60,000 citizens' which includes those who visit the conference centre, the commercial facilities, the hotels, and the workplaces. While much is rightly made of the area's integration into the high-speed rail network, and the provision of a city centre tram link, the project also contains no fewer than 8,000 public and 13,000 private parking spaces both above and below ground (www.milanosantagiulia.com/, accessed 29 December 2005). More troubling still is the near total absence of any quantification of such a huge masterplan's ecological footprint in its broadest sense.

Architects certainly have an important part to play in finding technological solutions to issues of energy conservation and urban living. In a slightly tongue-in-cheek conclusion to a paper on building and environmental ethics, Craig Delancey argues that 'architecture can indeed save at least some of the world' (2004: 159). However, the basis for such claims has to be considered within a fuller assessment of the embedded ethics of the construction and design of buildings, and the construction of a so-called green building is one that has to be audited at a range of levels. First, the most common 'green' stance, is to design buildings as organisms that operate on sound principles of energy use and conservation, that are self-sustaining as far as possible. Here, the building's 'green' credentials are assessed on the basis of the operating methods of the building itself, as in its heating, cooling and insulating properties. Second, there is the trade-off between the materials used in such a building and the embodied costs of getting them on-site. Third, there is the extended use of the building by its users: if a new development has no car-parking spaces but is not a standard-bearer for 'green' materials or methods, is it a more environmentally ethical building? Fourth, the greenest building could, of course, be let to or bought by firms that directly prosper from explicit resource exploitation and depletion (Olds 2001). Fifth, there is the building's role as a mechanism for realising the surplus value of human capital. The 'new generation' of 'green' office buildings pioneered by architects are justified in their ability to make employees happier (through natural air supply, for example), and in turn more productive (see Melchert Saguas Presas (2005) for a fascinating discussion of how transnational corporations commission or tenant these buildings).

A further ethical challenge comes with the rash of commissions for airport design and development. These offer major rewards for leading firms, both in terms of fee income and professional and public recognition. For example, Renzo Piano enhanced his reputation with a stunning design for Kansai airport, near Osaka. Norman Foster can look to his projects at London Stansted and Hong Kong's Chep Lap Kok as contributing factors to the success of his practice. Richard Rogers Partnership (now Rogers Stirk Harbour + Partners) won the RIBA Stirling Prize for their design of a new terminal at Barajas airport in Madrid, in 2006, and are behind the design of London Heathrow Terminal Five, which opened in 2008.

However, while airport designs have a central place in the history of modern architecture, recent evidence about the contribution of aviation to global warming has given rise to widespread social concern about the rapid increase in flights occurring around the world. As the Intergovernmental Panel on Climate Change (IPCC) noted in 1999:

> Although improvements in aircraft and engine technology and in the efficiency of the air traffic system will bring environmental benefits, these will not fully offset the effects of the increased emissions resulting from the projected growth in aviation. Policy options to reduce emissions further include more stringent aircraft engine emissions regulations, removal of subsidies and incentives that have negative environmental consequences, market-based options such as environmental levies (charges and taxes) and emissions trading, voluntary agreements, research programs, and substitution of aviation by rail and coach. Most of these options would lead to increased airline costs and fares. Some of these approaches have not been fully investigated or tested in aviation and their outcomes are uncertain.
>
> (IPCC 1999: Section 6.4)

In other words, technological solutions may provide benefits but only if passenger numbers and air freight levels remain steady.

In *Cities for a Small Planet* (1997), Richard Rogers outlined his manifesto for addressing 'sustainable cities'. He drew attention to the impact of cars on the urban environment, arguing instead for compact, densely settled cities, with a strong emphasis on public transport, pedestrianism and cycling. Drawing on the lessons learnt in the practice's design for Shanghai's Lu Zia Sui financial district (1997: 41–9), he stressed the opportunity for compact neighbourhoods stitched into the rest of the city, rather than being isolated from them. In these cases, Rogers was making a bold, sensible case for adapting ecological principles to large-scale masterplanned projects. Yet Rogers makes no mention of airports in his book, despite their centrality to the economic and social fabric of cities. Both Heathrow Terminal Five and the Barajas project are unequivocally expansionary, catering for a projected increase in passengers from sixty-five million to ninety million a year, in the case of the former, and from forty-eight million to seventy million a year in the case of the latter. The Barajas development contains 9,000 car parking spaces, stylistically integrated through a curved, turfed roof (Glancey 2006a). Both certainly have a strong public vocation, by contrast with the machine-like passenger processing that has characterised conventional terminal design.

My argument here is not that architects should stop designing airports, or that limitless flying per se is morally wrong (though this is an ethical position that is beginning to gain credibility). It is simply to highlight an element of bad faith in the misleading badging of such developments as sustainable. They are not. The discourse associated with such airports – as civic-minded, and environmentally friendly – is true only if one operates with an incredibly restricted understanding of the embedded ethics of the building. As an envelope, yes, green airports are a possibility. But only if one ignores what is happening out on the runways and link roads and car parks that surround these light green structures. Indeed, turning these environmental disasters into things of beauty has a parallel with some of the debates over the use of architectural monuments to prop up unpopular political regimes. In the absence of firms publishing the estimated carbon footprint of their schemes, it is difficult to make a clear assessment of the role of architects in curbing environmental abuses.

## The architect and the city

> [D]evelopers and real estate interests, in their wildest dreams, could not have come up with such an intellectually credible screen for their activities, an intellectually and academically respectable and viable means of diverting attention away from the toughest issues in land development and the building process toward trivial matters of surface.
>
> (Ghirardo 1991: 15)

*Figure 7.2* Chicago skyline reflected in Anish Kapoor sculpture, Millennium Park.

Diane Ghirardo makes a pointed attack on the fusion of architecture with commerce in the urban development process. But how far are architectural firms implicated in the development politics of major cities? Here, I provide three brief examples where well-known architectural firms have played a central role in controversial urban redevelopment schemes.

First, and as we have seen, Skidmore, Owings & Merrill have had a strong presence in the downtowns of most US cities (Hartman 2002), but they have a particularly strong power base in Chicago. As well as a long history of design of key commercial buildings in the Loop, it has recently acted as master planners for the city's 2016 Olympic bid, and for its Millennium Park project (see Figure 7.2). Consider the following anecdote concerning SOM architect Bruce Graham, conjured up in Ross Miller's book on the redevelopment politics of a block of downtown Chicago, *Here's the Deal*:

> In the last days of 1980, a black limousine moved slowly through Chicago holiday traffic. Bruce Graham autocratically directed the limo from the back seat, all the time lecturing a younger man seated to his left. Graham's attentive partner was Lawrence F. Levy, a client for whom the architect was designing a new skyscraper. Bruce Graham told his new client fabulous

stories about how architecture was reshaping America. Levy couldn't get enough of the architect's spiel, although he thought he had heard some of the same stories before.

(Miller 1996: 94)

As Larson (1993: 128) perceptively notes, elite architects 'are somewhat ambivalent in talking about their relationship with developers' and leave 'ultimate value judgements to the political sphere'. Graham, an expert on the buildings and blocks of Chicago's downtown, was able to advise the developer of potential redevelopments permitted on each site. Graham himself has stated that this was deliberate, that 'we deliberately went out to do work with developers so that . . . bad architects wouldn't take over Chicago' (in Larson 1993: 131). However, considerable introspection has gone on within the firm as to the degree to which following a developer's agenda blunts the possibilities for creative expression, as Chuck Bassett (long-time head of SOM's San Francisco office) lamented in 1989, interviewed by Betty Blum:

> Much of SOM's work is with developmental organizations. Jerry Hines and his group would be an excellent example. They have a site, they develop exactly what they think they want in square footage and they know exactly how much money they're going to spend. There is a staff experienced in every stage of development – programming, supervision of the architectural and engineering effort and the construction process. They have standards that they've developed with other buildings that will apply to the one you're going to work on for them. They know right down to the last penny what the rental rates are going to be, and what kind of return they must have. . . . As an architect, you have to be experienced and able enough to buy into that arrangement and be able to satisfy them and still get a building that keeps you happy.

(p. 114)

Bassett goes on to describe how, during the 1950s and 1960s, cost-cutting developers had rigid commercial criteria for how an office block should be designed:

> They stripped everywhere except the lobby and elevator cabs to keep costs down and used assumptions in their financial calculations so conservative that they almost completely eliminated risk. The buildings were terrible and our cities are littered with them. We architects did our share, including SOM. The Equitable buildings in Chicago and New York are excellent examples . . .

> BLUM: Was this based on market research or their budget or what?
> BASSETT: Yes, and old-fashioned greed. The architectural profession fell right

into step. We all loved doing flat walled, elegant and largely featureless buildings. It was a fateful coincidence of clients with austere budgets and architects whose credo was austerity.

(Art Institute of Chicago 1989a: 116)

SOM has long had a close relationship to urban development politics within the leading American cities. In New York, for example, SOM pitched to Chase Manhattan bank that their research revealed that the bank could consolidate its sites to create a 'superblock' in the financial district, a move that would ultimately spearhead a redefinition of Manhattan zoning laws. The firm also successfully presented the proposal to an enthusiastic Mayor Wagner in City Hall. The resulting scheme – One Chase Plaza – was significant because 'it marked David Rockefeller's opening gambit towards reshaping Lower Manhattan and leveraging the value of his family's real estate holdings there' (Darton 1999: 15). One Chase Plaza itself 'proclaimed the bank's emergence at the forefront of a new, streamlined, globalized finance that leaped adroitly over the outmoded barrier of national frontiers' (Darton 1999: 15). Its replacement of sturdy stone by transparent glass as material of choice for the banking industry was an important stylistic change in commercial office building. The densely packed tower took up only 30 per cent of its site, and heralded the arrival of the high modernist skyscraper–public plaza that would sweep the world's business centres. This shift in the zoning laws would be the catalyst for the development of probably the most notorious skyscraper development in the world, Minoru Yamasaki's World Trade Center.

My second example of how leading architects can become embroiled in major redevelopment schemes concerns Frank Gehry. In late 2006, a New York State Oversight Board gave the green light to the Atlantic Yards project, a development of disused railyards not far from downtown Brooklyn, in between Prospect Heights and Fort Greene. The developers, Forest City Ratner Companies, an established Manhattan developer, seized upon the re-emergence of Brooklyn as one of the most desirable locations in an overheated New York housing market. With the plan centred around the relocation of the New Jersey Nets basketball franchise to Brooklyn, the developer had advertised the brand new stadium, 4,000 permanent new jobs, housing units, and tax revenues that would accrue to the borough. With a number of the plots of the site being amalgamated under eminent domain, the plan called for an elaborate fusion of sixteen new high-density towers with public space. Bruce Ratner, a developer long criticised for lacking an interest in the architectural qualities of his works, turned to Frank Gehry as his preferred candidate as designer.

A critical coalition of Brooklyn residents, including Steve Buscemi and Heath Ledger, had formed into a pressure group named Develop Don't Destroy Brooklyn. Aghast at the scale of the sixteen new tower blocks proposed, they protested against the overwhelming density and the traffic congestion that would surely occur (Bleyer 2006; Confessore 2006a, b; Ourossoff 2006). The centrepiece of Gehry's proposal was to be a 189 metre tower block that he nicknamed 'Miss Brooklyn', which the protestors argued would cause overshadowing and over-power the borough's iconic Williamsburg Savings Bank tower. They also protested about the role of the *New York Times* in its coverage of the project. The *Times*, it should be noted, had an interest in Forest City Ratner, who were part developers of their new headquarters building in Times Square (designed by Renzo Piano with Fox and Fowle). Norman Oder's critique of the *Times* coverage of the development makes fourteen complaints, among them the accusation that the paper's architectural critics, first Herbert Muschamp and then Nicolai Ourousoff, had acted as 'cheerleaders' for the project. Muschamp

> failed to disclose his own ties to FCR in his rapturous assessment of the Atlantic Yards proposal and failed to disclose the Times's ties to FCR. Current critic Nicolai Ourousoff has praised the project without considering its effects on the surrounding neighbourhoods. Neither has tried to assess FCR's much-criticized architectural record in Brooklyn.
>
> (in Oder 2006: vii)

Muschamp's early coverage of the scheme was certainly adulatory: 'I would say that the city's future needs urbanism of this caliber at least as much as this example of it requires the support of New York. Those who have been wonder-ing whether it will ever be possible to create another Rockefeller Center can stop waiting for the answer. Here it is' (Muschamp 2003). Ever since Bilbao, Muschamp had eulogised Gehry to a degree seen to be embarrassing by many critics (Stern *et al.*, 2006: 139).

The Gehry design was particularly controversial given the scale of the develop-ment, his artistry utilised as a means of camouflaging, beautifying, or otherwise legit-imising the comprehensive application of eminent domain, and a drastic shift in the social and economic profile of the neighbourhood. It is a clear example of how celebrity architects, as discussed in Chapter 3, can be used to help brand controver-sial developments. It also displays how architectural ethics, so often conceived as being determined by or embedded within a single building, become challenged when the design grows into a major piece of city building. This was not the first time that Gehry had been accused of a rather overbearing approach to city planning. Mike Davis's (1991) memorable book *City of Quartz* is probably best-known for the chapter 'Fortress LA' – a series of vignettes that appeared to resonate with many dis-gusted by the emerging social landscapes of 1990s California – and is crowned by his likening of Frank Gehry to 'Dirty Harry'. Here, Gehry – with his jagged, menacing buildings – was, for Davis, aestheticising and embedding the very harsh, defensive, sense of LA urbanism that those seeking a 'humanising' of the city sought to avoid.

A third example of the role of major firms in controversial urban redevelopments can be found in the long-running battle over Spitalfields Market, on the edge of London's historic financial district, in the mid-1990s. The appointment of Foster and Partners to redesign a fiercely defended piece of bohemia was a consciously strategic act on the behalf of the Spitalfields Development Group. Some likened the razing of half of Spitalfields Market to the destruction of Les Halles, the celebrated Parisian market hall that was put to the bulldozer blade in the late 1960s before the public had a chance to form a coherent opposition. While it was the case that a cash-strapped local authority had sanctioned the redevelopment, some critics were conscious that the leading design firms were only too happy to accept the brief and, hence, legitimate the project. As Deyan Sudjic writes: 'Of all Britain's architects, Foster has the clout to be able to urge his clients not to do the predictable thing and to persuade them in the case of the market to work with what is there, rather than destroy it' (Sudjic 2001). Of course, Sudjic knows that even the most liberal-minded of development firms – let alone property trusts – would refuse to sanction a design that significantly reduced the financial viability of a building. The architect's problem is that she enters a world where property – the raw material of the architect's trade – is an asset, a commodity. In the words of David Harvey (1994: 427), 'the rebuilding of urban space ... becomes, as it were, a "spatial fix" for capitalism's overaccumulated capital'.

However, there is a danger in going too far in the opposite direction, of scapegoating architects – usually out of sheer frustration – as a punishment for their sophistry in obscuring the workings of urban capitalism. Thus while David Harvey (1994) calls for a closer examination of the 'invisible political economy of architectural production', the architect's position in the local state and its complex intersection of political clientelism, developer politics and civic boosterism may at times be overplayed for reasons of sheer visibility. In this sense, the role of the major architectural firm in the city is often contested:

> For neighbourhood action groups, the architect is usually the servile, but also imperious handmaiden of capitalism willingly placing large structures where they don't belong, producing wind and shadow and appropriating views, while causing more noise, traffic, and other phenomena that are felt to diminish quality of life.... Within the architecture world itself, the architect is seen as a victim, pursuing dreams of a perfect world while fending off the desires of clients to do things cheaply and meanly, trying to communicate the importance of good design to an uncomprehending public, working countless hours in search of ever greater perfection, and refusing to build any easy solutions.
>
> (Betsky 2004: 26)

## Conclusions

At the start of this chapter, I argued that in discussions of the ethics of architectural practice the architect should be considered, first and foremost, by his or her status within a firm, which relies on all sorts of commissions to subsidise its research, to develop its design vocabulary, to realise its designs and, before all of these are met, to pay the rent, pay the staff, pay insurance and make a profit. To be sure, the ethical dilemmas presented here may only face some of the more prominent firms that may be invited to design sensitive projects. However, it is precisely because such firms, and their charismatic design leaders, have such influence over international architectural discourse that their intentions are worthy of study.

As with all ethical disputes, debate tends to divide around relativist versus absolutist understandings of ethics. The issue of relativism may also have something to do with the practice of architecture, of its long-standing claims to being *art*. As Maurice Lagueux (2004) has noted, the growth of bioethics as a discipline is an understandable response to the challenge of recent technological developments. Why, he asks,

> have we not witnessed the birth and rapid development of a new 'archit-ethics' devoted to the analysis and discussion of ethical problems raised by architecture? . . . One might think that the absence of such a development is due to the fact that architecture is an art rather than a science, the former being, by its very nature, committed to aesthetical rather than ethical values, as was repeatedly claimed by the advocates of art for art's sake.
>
> (p. 117)

Those who seek to defend the power of architecture along those lines run up against the argument that it is precisely this point that encourages the powerful to employ those skilled in aesthetics. Perhaps, to answer Lagueux, there is little interest in an architectural ethics precisely because of the self-referentiality of the architectural discipline and profession, and the scepticism of those outside it towards the intentions of architects. This is exacerbated by the contradictory sources of legitimacy that the architecture profession draws upon. As Crawford (1991: 29) notes:

> Unlike engineering and medicine, which draw authority from science, or law, which receives it from the state, the architect's professional authority rested on an inherently contradictory base: combining the inherited identity of architecture as artistic creativity (reinforced by the powerful influence of the French Beaux-Arts system) with a more recent ideal of technological rationality.

This returns us to the distinction between architecture as autonomous, existing in a self-defining professional and ethical framework, and architecture as heteronomous, which places it within a broader set of social conditions. For Karsten Harries, the 'autonomous' approach requires 'no other justification than the aesthetical pleasure they can provide' (in Lagueux 2004: 130). Ghirardo (1991), countering this standpoint, suggests that 'architecture's conceptual framework is set out in such a way as to define what is relevant to the discourse on architecture and to exclude that which is deemed irrelevant' (p. 10). In this sense, the architect is pure technician, or pure artist, depending on perspective, who is merely fulfilling the years of training and dedication in the creation of built form 'to realize his or her creative potential and thereby bring Beauty and Truth to the untutored spectator' (Ghirardo 1991: 11). Following this line of argument, it has been suggested that since 'architects themselves must solve ethical problems by virtue of their internal character, one should not expect from philosophy the keys to their solution' (Lagueux 2004: 133). Criticism of architects' ethics thus touches on a sensitive issue for a profession that is always looking nervously at its historically accumulated privileges. For Larson (1993: 129–30):

> The postmodern erosion of barriers between 'high' and 'mass' culture has allowed architects to present purely commercial buildings as potential works of art. Yesterday's 'gentlemen architects,' steeped in tight distinctions between 'culture' and 'commerce', would neither have argued nor conceded the point ... The ideology of art gives a further twist to experts' *generic* abdication of individual responsibility. Architects (like other experts) seem to agree tacitly that one individual cannot go against the whole structure of the division of labor – therefore, one individual's moral choices cannot count all that much. Yet artists' faith in their own genius requires them to believe that it would, indeed, make a difference if someone less talented was hired in their place.

In this chapter, I have tried to set out some of the issues facing architects – both as individuals and firms – in an increasingly complex ethical terrain. I have come to no conclusion as to what kind of ethical framework is needed, nor wish to claim the moral high ground over the practices that have designed the projects described (though I do wish to suggest that some of the practices mentioned may reconsider their occupation of that high ground). However, the refrain that could perhaps be faintly heard from the architect at various points in the chapter – 'if we didn't design it, someone else would' – only serves to highlight a worrying abdication of ethical responsibility by some of the world's leading design firms.

# Conclusions

Architects who operate abroad have to be mobile. They can move their bodies – and may be asked to move their bodies – according to the goals of their firm or their individual careers. The drawings and models and spoken instructions that facilitate the building process are certainly mobile, enhanced by a technological exoskeleton. And this all contributes in specific ways to a mobility of fame and reputation, be it through a conscious attempt at self-promotion, the strategies of marketing officers, or the esteem of peers – not least, those who are training to be the architects of the future – in elevating a small group to global recognition. To conclude this book, I want to summarise the three themes that have structured the narrative: architecture as a (global) business, where design practice is made effective by good firm organisation; the nature of fame and reputation, which drives the success of some architects over others; and the globalisation of urban form, which has allowed architects to practise in many corners of the world, but not always in conditions of their choosing.

## Architecture as a business: the structuring role of the firm

A pervasive theme has been the importance of the business of architecture, the fact that the architect's *firm* is fundamental to the successful production of architectural output. As with other producer services, such as law, banking or advertising, architectural firms often operate within a set of conditions determined by macroeconomic factors, the expansion strategies of transnational corporations, and demand in particular sectors (such as retail space or airports, both important growth areas in emerging economies). In a highly competitive market, firms must be agile in their ability to respond to job opportunities, and should also be proactive in making contacts and developing their social networks (Olds 2001). Success is driven not least in the ability of architects 'to achieve relational proximity through translation, travel, shared routines, talk, common passions, base standards, brokers, epistemic and community bonding, and the ordering and orientation provided by files, documents, codes, common software, and so on' (Amin and Cohendet 2004: 99). In turn, firms rely on the range of embodied skills carried around by sectoral specialists in fields such as airport, hotel, transport, or office design, or the marketing skills and business acumen held by particular partners, as well as the more traditionally valued design skills of concept sketching, site interpretation, and knowledge of materials (Goodbun and Jaschke 2005).

To address these challenges, architects are increasingly required to address issues of corporate organisation, even to the extent of selling off part of the firm to a private equity group, as we saw in the case of Foster and Partners. As Roberts (2003) has suggested, there is an 'art' to global strategic management, one propagated by the business management literature: 'Many works are devoted to assisting the global manager to become a successful member of the transnational cosmopolitan business elite – at home in different cultures and able to think globally and at the same time to appropriate locally' (p. 19). This has been an important tool for design managers, but also for the successful selling of the design to clients.

The growing power of the computer in such designs makes it apparent that the development of new urban architecture could take two forms: a relatively standardised mode of lowest common denominator architecture, and the development of original, avant-garde structures, where concept designs (on paper, with models of wood) are then realised or refined using the latest computer software. Regardless, it is important to consider the transmission of architectural design as being material, even when it is apparently virtual, or 'informational': '. . . newspapers, the pictures on the television at night, books in libraries, CD roms, maps, films, statistical tables, spreadsheets, musical scores, architect's drawings, engineering designs, all of these are information – but information in material form' (Law and Hetherington 2000: 35).

This is fundamental to any understanding of architecture as a creative or cultural industry, as 'economically valuable knowledge' (Faulconbridge 2006: 517). All firms 'may well face distinctive challenges, such as how to shape path dependencies and inertia based on accumulated knowledges, how to manage a system of distributed knowledge, and how to balance exploration of new knowledge with exploitation of existing knowledge' (Amin and Cohendet 2004: 99). Thus even after the macro-organisational strategies of firms are taken into account (in terms of geographical and sectoral markets, for example) the micro-management of the design process has to be resolved.

## Fame and foreigners

In 2005, thirty-five of Italy's architects presented an open letter to the Italian government, published in *Corriere della Sera*, protesting the growing amount of major public commissions being given to foreign signature architects. Richard

Meier, Rem Koolhaas, I.M. Pei, Arata Isozaki, Norman Foster and Zaha Hadid had all picked up significant commissions in Rome and Milan, particularly. Their complaints were reported in the British press sympathetically; *Building Design* editorialised that such 'kerosene architecture', seemingly designed in-flight as the chief partner dashes from city to city, airport to airport, was justified but was undermined by 'practices of far less rigour and flair who exploit the global market with bad versions of the masters' work' (Booth 2005: 13).

As I discussed in Chapter 3, the signature architect is a form of celebrity which extends into commercial, professional, and even general public recognition. There, I considered the sociological underpinning of architectural celebrity, and the growth of a star system bolstered by developers, arts critics, and the media. This was, I suggested, a function of a symbolic economy where restaurateurs, couturiers, footballers, and other purveyors of highly visual commodities become celebrated for their talents. Few of these individuals can be dissociated from the commodity they sell: the exquisitely prepared scallop, the ultimate black dress, the unique free kick. And so with architects. Here, the 'expressive landmark has challenged the previous tradition of the architectural monument', be it the cathedral, museum or railway station of early modern economies:

> There was a hierarchy of public worth, not perfectly agreed and finely graded to be sure, but akin to that of everyday dress and civil address. Decency and appropriateness were its watchwords; deference and conformity were its curse. But in a world marketplace competing for attention, decency and deference carry little weight and even attacks on iconic buildings fail to register. In fact the insults often add a welcome *frisson*, the desired element of controversy and column inches – publicity.
>
> (Jencks 2005: 7)

It should be considered that this is in fact a confluence of trends, including postmodernism in commercial building, the explosion in image distribution through digitisation and the growing ability to make economically calculable deconstructivist buildings. At the same time as this trend has affected architectural form so it has affected the status of architecture as a profession.

In Chapter 3, I also discussed one of the most stubborn myths of architectural production, that of the architect as a 'creative genius'. This – that a single, uniquely gifted individual is the identifiable author of a particular building – has been one of the most overplayed and least sustainable ideas about architectural practice (as Middleton 1967 and Prak 1984 have made clear). Yet it is a myth that has been maintained by a popular media desire to retain identifiable ownership of artistic outputs, as the cases of Daniel Libeskind and Norman Foster demonstrate. As with the actress or the author, the architect relies on a 'publicity industry', an interlocking network of marketing professionals, critics, publishers, and

news outlets who re-present them to the broader public. Architects seek different types of recognition – from their professional peers and students; from
clients, particularly those who seek commercially successful architects, and from
various strands of public opinion. Certain individuals are associated with particular visual styles to such an extent that their work, their *signature* can be recognised in cityscapes worldwide. However, 'artistic' authorship can be difficult to
sustain in a global practice. We have seen significant tensions erupt both between
and within firms, whether it be Libeskind's bitter spat with David Childs at
Ground Zero, or the parting of ways between Norman Foster and his leading
design partner, Ken Shuttleworth, in the mid-2000s.

However, while the cultural populism of media celebrity is important, professional recognition is fundamental:

> Nowadays, an architect's professional recognition is contaminated by the
> designer's 'media celebrity,' but its chief expression is still the standing it
> confers in the circles that follow the profession's discourse. Standing may be
> local, national, or international; it includes a good measure of client satisfac-
> tion, especially for strong-service firms; yet it depends primarily on publica-
> tions, awards, professional societies, rankings in important design
> competitions, lectures, nominations to juries in awards programs or elite
> schools, faculty appointment in a renowned school – in sum, the marks of
> recognition bestowed by esteemed fellow architects, educators, and archi-
> tectural critics.
>
> (Larson 1993: 101)

The Pritzker Prize provides an outlet for this. And yet, it serves to cement the
myth of the architect as artist, designing free from outside influences, secure in
an autonomous relationship with the site, and with an upper hand over the client.

Changing practices of tourism have become an important issue in the interpretation of contemporary architecture. Indeed, some critics have gone as far as to
suggest that architecture today exists in a landscape of distorted perception, as
fragments grasped in a backdrop to a television advert, seen from a tour bus, in a
travel brochure, and all too rarely in a contemplative state. As I discussed in
chapter 6, just as the Petronas Towers were globally projected and spliced in
ways that undermined the intention of their client, so the perception of such
buildings are contained with a 'a larger mediated viewing experience' (Schwarzer
2005: 33). As Larson (1993: 11) has pointed out:

> Important, innovative, or just fashionable designs are repeatedly published in
> practically all the professional journals of the world. Because of the unmove-
> able nature of architectural objects, illustrated journals and 'picture books'
> (even more than serious and long treatises) perform an essential discursive

function: They constitute what I would call, after André Malraux, the imaginary museum of world architecture. They provide tangible raw material for the canon, the system of interpretation and justification that consecrates buildings as architecture.

This is a bold statement, but one that highlights the significance of the mediation of urban form. While buildings can be appreciated through practices of tourism, and while we saw the Pritzker jurists jetting around Europe on site visits, the basic fact of the immobility of buildings remains. Fame, fashion and reputation is thus subject to the materiality of mobility. The air cargoes of architectural magazines that are distributed worldwide, the carefully constructed websites (themselves embodiments of skilled labour) that now present a firm's projects, and the 'picture books' that line the shelves of bookshops and libraries are fundamental generators of architectural fame, certainly on a global scale.

Rem Koolhaas has been one of the most successful exponents of this, and it is interesting that many of his most striking recent projects have been commissioned by 'virtual' sectors such as entertainment, marketing and retailing. The *Wired* special issue, his *Content* magazine, the European Union branding work, the Prada restyle, the establishment of AMO, have all been attempts to fuse the identity of the organisation client with the final built form and spatial envelope delivered by the architect. As Klingmann suggests in the context of the firm's work for Prada, 'By using architecture as a tool for marketing and experiential design, Koolhaas effectively creates a space that closes the schism between architecture as "art" and architecture as "business"' (2007: 117).

## Urban form: visibility

[It] is astonishing that in the past quarter century a vast landscape has been produced without the kind of buildings that architects consider 'architecture,' a landscape almost entirely uninformed by the critical agendas or ideas of the discipline.... However, because so much of this new building is generic in design, if not downright ugly, and because it is spread out at low densities or hidden from view in cul-de-sacs, this vast body of work rarely figures in discussions of contemporary architecture. The prevalent attitude in architectural discourse – and not without reason – is that malls, office park buildings, apartment complexes, and suburban houses are overwhelmingly formulaic, market-driven, unimaginative designs unworthy of the designation 'architecture'.

(Dunham-Jones 2006: 1–2)

Finally, it is important to recognise that the examples that I have considered in the book have tended to be in the category of spectacular architecture. By contrast, in recent years there has been a growing interest in these apparently fea-tureless landscapes of cities. The architects that work for volume builders – who provide in-house construction and design of standardised, commercially driven designs – collectively dominate the vast majority of new construction in cities. The resulting landscape of urban sprawl is devoid of the carefully honed skills of place-making.

What does this mean for the discussion I have presented in the last seven chap-ters? Certainly, one of the key synonyms associated with 'global' is that of 'vision'. As Sue Roberts has argued, global management is often associated with a particular 'world-view'. Vision

> implies an ability to see, to envision global space. It also connotes an ability to see far ahead into the future ... Vision also has associations with being visionary: the idea of being able to see something that most people cannot – some sort of supernatural experience only a few have access to.
>
> (2003: 25)

So, precisely because of the difficulty of its reach, the global is as much about the unknowable, of what can't be seen, as what is visible. And so the buildings and architects that I have discussed here – even those of the apparently faceless megapractice, even those skyscrapers that contain so many 'little stories' (Jacobs 2006) – are but a tiny fraction of built form worldwide. So there is a question mark here that floats over all discussions on architecture – is it, as Dunham-Jones asks above, worthy of the name?

Certainly, an obsession with visibility – or attention-seeking – has been a feature of a lot of recent architectural commissions. As Charles Jencks (2005) has pointed out, there has been a turn to the 'enigmatic signifier' in building design. As with Disney's 'imagineers', architects provide a corporate client with an expressive structural dimension at a large material scale. We saw that the Guggenheim 'effect' demonstrated the fusion of three separate brands – Basque place, New York art foundation, Gehry as architect – into one incredibly suc-cessful (or at least, much-copied) package. What was unusual about the Guggen-heim was the willingness of their director – Thomas Krens – to openly speak the language of business, rather than the language of art. For this, he has found himself in trouble with his own trustees. This is perhaps because, as Twitchell remarks,

> the story – the home brand, if you will, of the nonprofits – is that the one thing they are is *not corporate*. The market, ugh, how vulgar ... [most museums] claim to have a higher calling than competing for market share. They are not soiled by the workaday world. They don't sell a product.
>
> (2004: 193)

However, while churches, museums and universities have sought out signature architects to design instant icons, critics have argued that this hinders a deeper architectural response to form and function. In the words of Michael Sorkin: 'The advocacy of branding is a sell-out in architecture, reducing its meanings to mere advertising, a fine obliviousness to the larger social implications of architectural practice' (2002: 4).

Of course, it is worth considering what these larger social implications are. Almost all such buildings involve an opportunity cost: that the money spent on the architecture could have been spent elsewhere, either on grassroots cultural initiatives, educational facilities, or some other policy priority. Architectural critics often assess the building without a consideration of its budget, and the budgets quoted for such public works are notoriously difficult to access and decode. As such projects often involve expensive remediation of brownfield land, site preparation, materials costs, transport and other infrastructural costs, the actual price of the building itself can be difficult to disentangle from the overall project costs. Indeed, media coverage of events often adopt unhelpful 'headline' figures exaggerating cost blow-outs.

Nonetheless, the clients who are so hungry for these iconic structures are often engaged in imaginatively remapping their place in the world. We saw in chapters 4 and 6 the importance of such reimagining in the Basque Country, in Malaysia and in Dubai. The Gulf – with its artificial islands in the shape of the world – is a current hotspot for such designs. One of the most intriguing recent developments has been the engagement of Thomas Krens to advise on a masterplan for a new cultural quarter in Abu Dhabi. The oil-rich Gulf emirate, rivalrous with its near-neighbour Dubai, saw itself as recreating a post-Baghdad, post-Beirut model of Middle Eastern cultural cosmopolitanism. Krens worked with Skidmore, Owings & Merrill to draw up a masterplan, using the canal-side grounds of the Venice Biennale as a model. A familiar roll-call of architects were commissioned to design individual buildings. Jean Nouvel – noted for his Institute of the Arab World in Paris – contributed a neo-Venetian vision of a water-based building incorporating a geodesic dome, allowing for a series of courtyards and alleyways. Zaha Hadid contributed a performing arts centre, and Tadao Ando designed a maritime museum. Most interestingly, however, came the 'civic' brands: rumours emerged of a Yale University art school outpost; the Louvre signed off on a deal to allow Abu Dhabi to use its name for thirty years, at a cost of $520 million; and Krens engaged Gehry to design a Guggenheim, derived from the nearest vernacular reference point, the medieval wind towers and Bedouin tents that act as a visual cliché for pre-modern Gulf urbanism (Ouroussoff 2007; Riding 2007).

As I described in the chapter on Rem Koolhaas, his work in Lagos, China and now the Gulf (Koolhaas and AMO 2007) raises pressing ethical issues. Koolhaas can perhaps be seen to be pushing the boundaries of architectural professionalism in an age of increasing globalisation, but the ethical terrain on which architects compete and build remains to be charted. Koolhaas is fascinated with the overnight buildings of the Pearl River Delta, and the apparent uselessness of architectural professionalism in these contexts. Yet his practice still turns out one-of-a-kind, agenda-setting pieces. And even his team's visual rendering of the everyday comes in highly stylised, beautifully arranged colour tomes. So in envisioning the globe, perhaps the subject matter of study is always going to be the remarkable, however generic it may appear. In a similar way, global architects operate in a situation where, with every flood, fire or civic crisis, the inequalities of urban life can be seen. Many architects have heeded these issues. Movements such as Global Studio, Architecture 2030, or Architects Without Frontiers, have sought to connect architectural practice with contemporary situations of under-development or environmental impact. Fuelled by a general understanding of the inequities of global capitalism, such groups mirror the more general debates in society about the ethics of urban development. The ethical dimensions to architectural practice that I addressed in Chapter 7 are still to be developed, and are still discussed in ways that reflect an unwillingness to really engage with the politics of building for the state in China, or Kazakhstan. As in any relational, heteronomous or process-based reading of architecture, the cause and effects of a building (why it was built, how it was financed and given planning permission, and the social and functional impact it makes) are in many ways more interesting than the formal properties of the building itself.

# Notes

## 1 The globalisation of architectural practice

1 I am grateful to Ralph Courtenay, then of HOK, and James Calder, then of DEGW, for discussing this with me in separate interviews in 2003.
2 Personal interview. See also Powell (2003).
3 Personal interviews with Roger Duffy and Gene Schnair of SOM.
4 Interview with Keith Griffiths; a history of Aedas can be found in Sinclair (2005).
5 www.fosterandpartners.com/News/2007.aspx.
6 For career biographies, see www.fosterandpartners.com.

## 2 Designing at distance

1 Similarly, Farrelly (2003) argues that the commissioning of Foster and Partners to work on a separate Sydney residential scheme (Regent Place) in 2003 by a different development company was sufficient to allow them to bypass a development application requirement that any building should have a FSR (floor-space ratio) of 14:1, the approved design having a FSR of 16.5:1. Furthermore, on a site with a complicated planning history (it was formerly a theatre), the Foster scheme dispensed with the stipulation of having cinemas built into the base of the towers (which lower the yield relative to residential or retail).
2 See Sato (1992) for an account of some of the cultural encounters between Foster Associates and the Obayashi Corporation in the construction of Century Tower, Tokyo.

## 3 Architectural celebrity and the cult of the individual

1 I am grateful to Chris Waggett, 126 Phillip Street Project Director August 1998 until October 2003 for this information.

## 4 The 'Bilbao effect'

1 http://en.wikipedia.org/wiki/List_of_guest_stars_on_The_Simpsons, accessed 13 January 2007.
2 http://en.wikipedia.org/wiki/The_Seven-Beer_Snitch, accessed 13 January 2007; screenshots on http://archidose.blogspot.com/2005/07/gehry-goes-2d.html.

# 5  Rem Koolhaas and global capitalism

1  The full-length book *Lagos: How it Works* was not published at the time of writing this (authored by Rem Koolhaas and Edgar Cleijne, edited by Ademide Adelusi-Adeluyi, published by Lars Müller Publishers).

# References

Abbas, A. (1997) *Hong Kong: Culture and the Politics of Disappearance*. Minneapolis: University of Minnesota Press.

Abel, C. (2000) 'A building for the Pacific century', in D. Jenkins (ed.), *On Foster ... Foster On*. Munich: Prestel, pp. 133–7. (First published 1986.)

Acland, C. (2003) *Screen Traffic: Movies, Multiplexes and Global Culture*. Durham, NC: Duke University Press.

Adams, N. (2007) *Skidmore, Owings & Merrill: SOM since 1936*. London: Phaidon.

*Aedas 2006–7 Annual Review*, www.aedas.com/2007_aedas_review.pdf, accessed 2 November 2007.

Akao, K. (2000) 'A client's view', in D. Jenkins (ed.), *On Foster ... Foster On*. Munich: Prestel, pp. 284–7.

Ali, M.M. (2001) *Art of the Skyscraper: the Genius of Fazlur Khan*. New York: Rizzoli.

Allenby, G. (2000) 'Piano wants music', *Sydney Morning Herald*, 10 February, p. 8. (www.smh.com.au)

Amin, A. and Cohendet, P. (2004) *Architectures of Knowledge: Firms, Capabilities and Communities*. Oxford: Oxford University Press.

AMO/OMA (2004) *Content*. Cologne: Taschen.

Appadurai, A. (1990) 'Disjuncture and difference in the global cultural economy', *Theory, Culture and Society* 7: 295–310.

Arnold, D. (2004) 'Does this man want your job?' *Building Design*, 21 May. www.world-architecture.com, accessed 7 July 2004.

Art Institute of Chicago (1989a) Chicago Architects Oral History project, Chicago Art Institute. Charles Bassett interviewed by Betty J. Blum, January 30, 31, February 1 1989. www.artic.edu/aic/libraries/caohp/bassett.html, accessed 20 November 2007.

—— (1989b) Chicago Architects Oral History project, Chicago Art Institute. Gordon Bunshaft interviewed by Betty J. Blum, April 4, 5, 6, 7 1989. www.artic.edu/aic/libraries/caohp/bunshaft.html, accessed 20 November 2007.

—— (1989c) Chicago Architects Oral History project, Chicago Art Institute. William Hartmann interviewed by Betty J. Blum, October 30, 31, November 1, 2 1989. www.artic.edu/aic/libraries/caohp/hartmann.html, accessed 30 November 2007.

—— (1997) Chicago Architects Oral History project, Chicago Art Institute. Bruce Graham interviewed by Betty J. Blum, May 25–8 1997. Quotation from transcript pp. 302–6, www.artic.edu/aic/libraries/caohp/graham.html, accessed 15 May 2006.

Bacon, M. (2001) *Le Corbusier in America: Travels in the Land of the Timid*. Cambridge MA: MIT Press.

Barley, N. and Ireson, A. (eds) (2001) *City Levels*. Berlin: Birkhäuser.

Barnes, T.J. (2002) 'Performing economic geography: two men, two books, and a cast of thousands', *Environment and Planning A* 34: 487–512.

Bathelt, H., Malmberg, A. and Maskell, P. (2004) 'Clusters and knowledge: local buzz, global pipelines, and the process of knowledge creation', *Progress in Human Geography* 28(1): 31–56.

Beaverstock, J., Taylor, P.J. and Smith, R.G. (1999) 'The long arm of the law: London's law firms in a globalising world economy', *Environment and Planning A* 31(4): 1857–76.

Beaverstock, J.V. (2002) 'Transnational elites in global cities: British expatriates in Singapore's financial district', *Geoforum* 33: 525–38.

Berens, J. (2001) 'A Passion for Taschen', *Observer*, 4 November 2001. http://books.guardian.co.uk/departments/artsandentertainment/story/0,6000,587153,00.html, accessed 21 February 2005.

Bernstein, F. (2002) 'Uninspired? A blue chip firm looks inward', *New York Times*, 29 September, p. 37. accessed via www.factiva.com, 29 April 2005.

Betsky, A. (2004) 'Rem Koolhaas: the fire of Manhattanism inside the iceberg of modernism', in *What is OMA/AMO?* Rotterdam: OMA/AMO, pp. 25–39.

Bielefeld, B. and Rusch, L-P. (eds) 2006) *Building Projects in China: a Manual for Architects and Engineers*. Basel: Birkhäuser.

Blackler, Z. (2005) 'A time for scruples', *Building Design*, 4 March. www.bdonline.co.uk/storyprint.asp?storycode=3047759&featureCode=&storyType=80, accessed 16 June 2005.

Blau, J. (1987) *Architects and Firms: A Sociological Perspective on Architectural Practice*. Cambridge MA: MIT Press.

Bleyer, J. (2006) 'On the block', *New York Times*, 22 October 2006. www.nytimes.com, accessed 26 January 2007.

Boden, D. and Molotch, H. (1994) 'The compulsion to proximity', in R. Friedland and D. Boden, *Nowhere: Space, Time and Modernity*. Berkeley: University of California Press, pp. 257–86.

Bohlen, C. (2002) 'Chairman gives the Guggenheim an ultimatum, then $12m', *New York Times*, 4 December. www.nytimes.com, accessed 9 November 2007.

Booth, R. (2005) 'Italy clips the wings of UK jet-set crew', *Building Design*, 16 September, p. 13.

Booth, R. (2007) 'Foster's staff force inquiry into trust fund', *The Sunday Times*, 27 May. www.timesonline.co.uk/tol/news/uk/article1845235.ece, accessed 6 November 2007.

Booth, R. and Blackler, Z. (2004) 'Waiting for the sun', *Building Design,* 3 December. www.bdonline.co.uk, accessed 21 February 2005.

Bradley, K. (1997) 'The deal of the century', *Art in America,* July, 85(7): 48–55; 105.

Bryson, J., Daniels, P. and Warf, B. (2003) *Service Worlds: People, Organizations and Technologies*. London: Routledge.

*Building* (2003) 'Business 160', from *Building 160 Supplement* www.world-architecture.com, accessed 14 July 2003.

*Building Design* (2004) 'Fosters partners hand over', *Building Design*, 3 December. www.bdonline.co.uk, accessed 21 February 2005.

—— (2005) 'Fosters peace mission', *Building* Design, 25 February. www.bdonline.co.

uk/story.asp?storyType=80&sectioncode=426&storyCode=3047353, accessed 16 June 2005.

Bunnell, T. (1999) 'Views from above and below: the Petronas Twin Towers and/in contesting visions of development in contemporary Malaysia', *Singapore Journal of Tropical Geography* 20(1): 1–23.

—— (2004a) *Malaysia, Modernity and the Multimedia Super Corridor: a Critical Geography of Intelligent Landscapes.* London: Routledge.

—— (2004b) Re-viewing the *Entrapment* controversy: Megaprojection, (mis)representation and postcolonial performance, *GeoJournal* 59(4): 297–305.

Buntrock, D. (2001) *Japanese Architecture as a Collaborative Process.* London: Spon.

Burns, T. (1998) 'Tourism – fresh perspectives taking root', *Financial Times*, 9 July. Survey – Basque Country, p. 4.

Buruma, I. (2002) 'Don't be fooled – China is not squeaky clean', *Guardian*, 30 July. www.guardian.co.uk/g2/story/0,3604,765315,00.html, accessed 20 February 2004.

—— (2003) 'The sky's the limit', in *Considering Rem Koolhaas and the Office for Metropolitan Architecture.* Rotterdam: NAi Publishers, pp. 53–72.

Bush-Brown, A. (1984) 'Introduction', *Skidmore, Owings and Merrill: Architecture and Urbanism 1973–1983.* London: Thames and Hudson, pp. 11–23.

Bussel, A. (2000) *SOM Evolutions: Recent Work of Skidmore, Owings and Merrill.* Basel: Birkhäuser.

Byles, J. (2000) 'The Bilbao effect', *The Village Voice*, 2–8 August. www.villagevoice.com/arts/0031,byles,16897,12.html, accessed 2 April 2007.

'Cashing in . . . Bilbao Guggenheim one year on' (1999) *World Architecture* 73, February: 45.

Castle, H. (2001) 'Editorial', in J. Chance and T. Schmiedeknecht (eds), *Fame and Architecture. Architectural Design* 71(4): 4.

Cembalest, R. (1992) 'The Guggenheim's high-stakes gamble', *ARTnews*, May: 84–92.

—— (1997) 'First we take Bilbao', *Artforum International*, September: 63–4.

Chance, J. (2001a) 'Fame versus celebrity', interview with Charles Jencks, in J. Chance and T. Schmiedeknecht (eds), *Fame and Architecture. Architectural Design.* 71(4): 12–17.

—— (2001b) 'The face of Jacques Herzog', in J. Chance and T. Schmiedeknecht (eds), *Fame and Architecture. Architectural Design.* 71(4): 48–53.

Chance. J. and T. Schmiedeknecht (2001) 'Introduction', in J. Chance and T. Schmiedeknecht (eds), *Fame and Architecture. Architectural Design.* 71(4): 5.

Cheng, M.B.C. (1997) 'Resurgent Chinese power in postmodern disguise: the new Bank of China buildings in Hong Kong and Macau', in G. Evans and M. Tam (eds), *Hong Kong: the Anthropology of a Chinese Metropolis.* Richmond, UK: Curzon, pp. 102–23.

Chung, C.J. (ed.) (2002) *The Harvard Design School Guide to Shopping.* Cologne: Taschen.

Chung, C.J., Inaba, J., Koolhaas, R. and Leong, S.T. (eds) (2001) *Great Leap Forward.* Cologne: Taschen.

City of Sydney Council (1998) Minutes of Planning Committee meeting, 17 December, Item 4. Accessed at City of Sydney Council archives, Town Hall, Sydney.

Clafton, S. (1998) 'Champion of lightness sets out to save us from ugly immersion', *Business Review Weekly*, 26 November: 98. (www.smh.com.au)

Clausen, M.L. (2005) *The Pan Am Building and the Shattering of the Modernist Dream.* Cambridge MA: MIT Press.

Cody, J.W. (2003) *Exporting American Architecture, 1870–2000.* London: Routledge.

Cohen, H. (2004) 'The Bilbao effect', *Business Report*, 23 April. www.businessreport.com/newsDetail.cfm?aid=4704, accessed 2 April 2007.

Cohen, J.-L. (1995) *Scenes of the World to Come: European Architecture and the American Challenge, 1893–1960*. Paris: Flammarion.

Confessore, N. (2006a) 'Developer defends Atlantic Yards, saying towers won't corrupt the feel of Brooklyn', *New York Times*, 12 May 2006. www.nytimes.com, accessed 26 January 2007.

—— (2006b) 'State approves major complex for Brooklyn', *New York Times*, 21 December. www.nytimes.com, accessed 26 January 2007.

Conversi, D. (1997) *The Basques, The Catalans, and Spain: Alternative Routes to Nationalist Mobilisation*. London: Hurst.

Crawford, M. (1991) 'Can architects be socially responsible?', in D. Ghirardo (ed.), *Out of Site: A Social Criticism of Architecture*. Seattle: Bay Press, pp. 27–45.

Crickhowell, N. (1997) *Opera House Lottery: Zaha Hadid and the Cardiff Bay Project*. Cardiff: University of Wales Press.

Crinson, M. (2003) *Modern Architecture and the End of Empire*. Aldershot: Ashgate.

Cuff, D. (1992) *Architecture: the Story of Practice*. Cambridge, MIT Press.

—— (2000) 'Epilogue: Still Practicing', in S. Kostof (ed.), *The Architect: Chapters in the history of the profession*. Berkeley/Los Angeles: University of California Press, pp. 345–57.

Davis, M. (1991) *City of Quartz: Excavating the Future in Los Angeles*. London: Verso.

—— (2006) 'Fear and money in Dubai', *New Left Review* 41, Sept–Oct: 47–68.

Darton, E. (1999) *Divided We Stand: A Biography of New York's World Trade Center*. New York: Basic Books.

Dawson, L. (2005) *China's New Dawn*. Munich: Prestel.

Day, M. (2000) 'Life at the leading edge'. Interview with Iain Godwin. *Cadserver* www.cadserver.co.uk/common/viewer/archive/2000/Dec/11/feature4.phtm, accessed 7 February 2005.

De Graaf, R. and Koolhaas, R. (2004a) 'E-conography', in AMO/OMA, *Content*: 376–89.

—— (2004b) 'Spiegel*ein* Spiegel*ein* an der Wand/Mirror Mirror on the Wall', in AMO/OMA, *Content*: 390–2.

Delancey, C. (2004) 'Architecture can save the world: building and environmental ethics', *The Philosophical Forum* XXXV(2): 147–59.

Delargy, M. (2001) 'HOK alliance to woo global clients', *Building*, 16 March. www.-world-architecture.com, accessed 23 October 2003.

Dodge, M. and Kitchin, R. (2004) 'Flying through code/space: the real virtuality of air travel', *Environment and Planning D: Society and Space* 36: 195–211.

Dovey, K. (1992) 'Corporate towers and symbolic capital', *Environment and Planning B* 19: 173–88.

Drexler, A. (1974) 'Introduction', in *Architecture of Skidmore, Owings & Merrill, 1963–1973*. London: The Architectural Press, pp. 8–38.

Dunham-Jones, E. (2006) 'Seventy-five per cent: the next big architectural project', in W.S. Saunders (ed.), *Sprawl and Suburbia*. Minneapolis: University of Minnesota Press, pp. 1–20.

Dunlap, D.W. (1999) 'The delicate matter of passing the torch', *New York Times*, 21 November. accessed via www.nytimes.com, 20 June 2004.

Dyckhoff, T. (2004) 'What's my line?', *Times*, 24 February, section 2, p. 16. www.global.factiva.com, accessed 5 April 2005.

Dyer, R. (1998) *Stars*. London: British Film Institute.

Easterling, K. (2005) *Enduring Innocence: Global Architecture and its Political Masquerades*. Cambridge MA: MIT Press.

Edensor, T. (1997) 'National identity and the politics of memory: remembering Bruce and Wallace in symbolic space', *Environment and Planning D: Society and Space* 29: 175–94.

Eerme, L. and Kinross, R. (2002) 'The architects of the book', *Domus* 847, April. www.hyphenpress.co.uk/journal/2002/05/22/architects_of_the_book    extended, accessed 11 March 2008.

English, J.F. (2005) *The Economy of Prestige: Prizes, Awards, and the Circulation of Cultural Value*. Cambridge MA: Harvard University Press.

Enwezor, O. (2004) 'Terminal modernity: Rem Koolhaas's Discourse on entropy', *What is OMA? Considering Rem Koolhaas and the Office for Metropolitan Architecture*. Rotterdam: NAi publishers, pp. 103–19.

Erner, G. (2005) *Victimas de la Moda: Cómo se crea, por qué la seguimos*. Barcelona: Gustavo Gili. (First published 2004 as *Victimes de la Mode? Comment en la crée, pourquoi on la suit*. Paris: La Découverte).

Emporis (2003) Adrian Smith, interviewed by Tom Finnegan, November 2003. www.emporis.com/en/cd/iv/as/, accessed 11 April 2007.

European Commission (2001) *Brussels, Capital of Europe: Final Report*. http://europa.eu.int/comm/dgs/policy_advisers/publications/docs/brussels_capital. pdf, accessed 28 February 2005.

Fairs, M. (2000) 'The outsider', *Building*, 46. www.world-architecture.com, accessed 23 October 2003.

—— (2003a) 'Ken Shuttleworth' [interview]. *Building*, 17 January. www.world-architecture.com.

—— (2003b) 'Ken the Pen', *The Guardian*, 22 January. http://arts.guardian.co.uk/features/story/0,,879565,00.html, accessed 11 March 2998.

—— (2004) 'Rem Koolhaas' Content', *Icon*. www.icon-magazine.co.uk/issues/011/content.htm, accessed 6 January 2007.

Farrelly, E.M. (2001) 'How one architect raised the bar', *Sydney Morning Herald*, 23 January, p. 14. (www.smh.com.au)

—— (2003) 'To foster goodwill, shortcuts and all', *Sydney Morning Herald*, 29 April, p. 15.

Faulconbridge, J.R. (2006) 'Stretching tacit knowledge beyond a local fix? Global spaces of learning in advertising professional service firm', *Journal of Economic Geography* 6: 517–40.

Fein, S. (2007) 'Condo cool', *Harvard Design Magazine* 26, Spring/Summer. www.gsd.harvard.edu/research/publications/hdm//back/26_Fein.html, accessed 23 November 2007.

Filler, M. (1990) 'Hierarchies for hire: the impact of the big firms since 1976', in K.M. Hays and C. Burns (eds), *Thinking the Present: Recent American Architecture*. New York: Princeton Architectural Press, pp. 23–44.

—— (1999) 'Eyes on the prize', *The New Republic*, 26 April/3 May, pp. 86–94.

—— (2005) 'Filling the hole', *The New York Review of Books* 52(3), 24 February www.nybooks.com/articles/17751, accessed 5 August 2006.

—— (2006) 'The master builder', *New York Times*, 17 March. nytimes.com, accessed 9 April 2007.

—— (2007) *Makers of Modern Architecture: From Frank Lloyd Wright to Frank Gehry*. New York: New York Review Books.

Findlay, K. (2004) 'In the company of property giants', *Building Design*, 19 March, p. 4. www.factiva.com, accessed 15 April 2005.

Foster and Partners (2001) *Foster Catalogue 2001*. London: Foster and Partners/Munich: Prestel.

—— (2007) 'Foster + Partners announces plans for its future'. www.fosterandpartners.com/News/293/Default.aspx, accessed 5 November 2007.

Foster, N. (2000) *Rebuilding the Reichstag*. London: Weidenfeld and Nicolson.

—— (2005) 'Building a sustainable future', CNN.com, 16 May. www.cnn.com/2005/WORLD/europe/05/11/foster.visionary/index.html, accessed 16 June 2005.

Frampton, K. (2000) 'On Norman Foster', in D. Jenkins (ed.), *On Foster . . . Foster On*. Munich: Prestel, pp.385–403.

—— (2005) 'The work of architecture in the age of commodification', in W.S. Saunders (ed.), *Commodification and Spectacle in Architecture*. Minneapolis: University of Minnesota Press, pp. ix–xviii.

Frank, T. (2000) *One Market Under God: Extreme Capitalism, Market Populism, and the End of Economic Democracy*. New York: Anchor.

—— (2005) 'Rocking for the clampdown: creativity, corporations, and the crazy curvilinear cacophony of the Experience Music Project', in W.S. Saunders (ed.), *Commodification and Spectacle in Architecture*. Minneapolis: University of Minnesota Press, pp. 60–77.

Frow, J. (2002) 'Signature and brand', in J. Collins (ed.), *High-Pop: Making Culture into Popular Entertainment*. Malden MA: Blackwell, pp. 56–74.

Gamson, J. (1994) *Claims to Fame: Celebrity in Contemporary America*. Berkeley: University of California Press.

Gandy, M. (2005) 'Learning from Lagos', *New Left Review* 33: 37–52.

Gargiani, R. (2006) *Rem Koolhaas/OMA*. Roma-Bari: Laterza.

Ghirardo, D. (1991) 'Introduction', in D. Ghirardo (ed.), *Out of Site: A Social Criticism of Architecture*. Seattle: Bay Press, pp. 9–16.

—— (2006, ed) *SOM Journal 4*. Ostfildern-Ruit: Hatje Cantz Verlag.

Glancey, J. (2006a) 'Jumbo portions', *The Guardian*, 13 February. www.guardian.co.uk, accessed 3 December 2007.

—— (2006b) 'Naked ambitions', *The Guardian*, G2 24 April, pp. 12–15.

Goetz, N. (2006) 'Von Gerkan, Marg and Partners – gmp', in B. Bielefeld and L-P. Rusch (eds), *Building Projects in China: a Manual for Architects and Engineers*. Basel: Birkhäuser, pp. 125–37.

Goldberger, P. (1990) 'How do you build a skyscraper? With frustration', *New York Times*, 7 May. www.nytimes.com, accessed 23 October 2005.

—— (2004) *Up From Zero: Politics, Architecture and the Rebuilding of New York*. New York: Random House.

Gómez, M.V. (1998) 'Reflective images: the case of urban regeneration in Glasgow and Bilbao', *International Journal of Urban and Regional Research* 22: 106–21.

Goodbun, J. and Jaschke, K. (2005) 'Fame and the changing role of drawing', in P. Davies and T. Schmiedeknecht (eds), *An Architect's Guide to Fame*. Amsterdam: Elsevier/Architectural Press, pp. 51–63.

Graham, H. and Sánchez, A. (1995) 'The politics of 1992', in H. Graham and J. Labanyi (eds), *Spanish Cultural Studies: An Introduction*. Oxford: Oxford University Press, pp. 406–18.

Graham, S. and Marvin, S. (2001) *Splintering Urbanism: Networked Infrastructures, Technological Mobilities and the Urban Condition*. London: Routledge.

Griffin, G. (2003) 'Beyond the beach and into the blue', *Cultural Studies Review* 9(1): 124–38.

Gutman, R. (1988) *Architectural Practice: a Critical View*. New York: Princeton Architectural Press.

Haigh, G. (2004) *Bad Company: the Strange Cult of the CEO*. London: Aurum.

Hardy, E. (2004) 'Kool and the gang', *Spike Magazine* www.spikemagazine.com/ 1104remkoolhaas.php, accessed 6 January 2007.

Harley, R. (1997) 'Renzo Piano: Building a vision', *Australian Financial Review*, 28 November, magazine, p. 10. (www.smh.com.au).

Hartman, C. (2002) (with S. Carnochan), *City for Sale: the Transformation of San Francisco*. Berkeley: University of California Press. Revised and updated edition.

Harvard Design Magazine (2004) 'Stocktaking 2004: Nine questions about the present and future of design', *Harvard Design Magazine*, Spring/Summer 2004: 4–52.

Harvey, D. (1989) 'From managerialism to entrepreneurialism: the transformation of governance in late capitalism', *Geografiska Annaler* 71B: 3–17.

—— (1994) 'The invisible political economy of architectural production', in O. Bouman and R. Van Toorn (eds), *The Invisible in Architecture*. London: Academy, pp. 420–7.

Harvie, C. (1994) *The Rise of Regional Europe*. Routledge: London.

Hawthorne, C. (2004) 'China pulls up the drawbridge', *New York Times*, 19 September. www.nytimes.com, accessed 28 October 2004.

Hay, G. (2004) 'King Richard the last?', *Building* 27. www.world-architecture.com, accessed 11 July 2004.

Hill, J. (2003) 'Hunting the shadow – immaterial architecture', *The Journal of Architecture* 8: 165–78.

Holman, O. (1996) *Integrating Southern Europe: EC Expansion and the Transnationalisation of Spain*. London: Routledge.

Holyrood Inquiry Transcript (2004) from Monday 29 March 2004 (Morning Session). www.holyroodinquiry.org/transcripts_documents/29–03–2004-am/transcript29–03 –2004-am.htm, accessed 8 April 2006.

Höweler, E. (2003) *Skyscraper: Designs of the Recent Past and of the Near Future*. London: Thames and Hudson.

Huxtable, A.L. (1984) *The Tall Building Artistically Reconsidered*. New York: Pantheon.

—— (1989) 'On awarding the prize', essay to accompany the Pritzker Prize to Frank Gehry. www.pritzkerprize.com/full_new_site/gehry_huxtableessay.htm, accessed 21 November 2007.

Hyatt Foundation (1999) *The Pritzker Architectural Prize 1999: Sir Norman Foster*. www.pritzkerprize.com.

Illoniemi, L. (2004) *Is it All About Image?* London: Wiley-Academy.

Imrie, R. (2003) 'Architects' conceptions of the human body', *Environment and Planning D: Society and Space* 21: 47–65.

Inaba, J. (2004) 'Maybe', in AMO/OMA, *Content*. Cologne: Taschen, pp. 256–7.

Inside the Minds (2004) *Inside the Minds: the Business of Architecture*. Boston MA: Aspatore Books.

IPCC/Intergovernmental Panel on Climate Change (1999) *Aviation and the Global Atmosphere. Summary for Policy-Makers*. www.ipcc.ch/ipccreports/sres/aviation/index.htm, 3 December 2007.

Ivy, R. (2003) 'From the field: Chinese business blitz', *Architectural Record* 2003: 114–19.

Jackson, P. (1999) 'Commodity cultures: the traffic in things', *Transactions of the Institute of British Geographers* 24: 95–108.

Jacobs, J.M. (1994) 'Negotiating the heart: heritage, development and identity in postimperial London', *Environment and Planning D: Society and Space* 12: 751–72.

—— (2001) 'Hybrid highrises', in J. Barrett and C. Butler-Bowden (eds), *Debating the City: an Anthology*. Sydney: Historic Houses Trust of New South Wales/University of Western Sydney, pp. 13–27.

—— (2006) 'A geography of big things', *Cultural Geographies* 13(1): 1–27.

Jameson, F. (2003) 'Future City', *New Left Review* 21: 65–79.

Jencks, C. (2000) 'Branding – signs, symbols or something else', Charles Jencks in conversation with Rem Koolhaas. *Fashion and Architecture/Architectural Design* 70(6): 34–41.

—— (2001) 'Functional icons: Charles Jencks in conversation with Norman Foster', in J. Chance and T. Schmiedeknecht (eds), *Fame and Architecture. Architectural Design* 71(6): 24–33.

—— (2002) *The New Paradigm in Architecture: the Language of Post-Modernism*. Newhaven: Yale University Press.

—— (2005) *The Iconic Building*. London: Frances Lincoln Publishers.

Jenkins, D. (ed.) (2000) *On Foster ... Foster On*. Munich: Prestel.

—— (2004) *Norman Foster: Works. Volume 4*. Munich: Prestel.

Jones, A. (2005) 'Truly global corporations? Theorizing "organisational globalization" in advanced business-services', *Journal of Economic Geography* 5: 177–200.

Jones, K.B. (2001) 'Unpacking the suitcase: travel as process and paradigm in constructing architectural knowledge', in A. Piotrowski and J.W. Robinson (eds), *The Discipline of Architecture*. Minneapolis: University of Minnesota Press, pp. 127–57.

Kamin, B. (1994) 'Duel in the sky', *Chicago Tribune*, 6 February, p. 12.

—— (1997) 'Door opens on Skidmore's inner workings', *Chicago Tribune*, 29 November, p. 1. www.chicagotribune.com, accessed 18 February 2005.

Kerr, P. (1996) *Gridiron*. London: Vintage.

Kimmelman, M. (1998) 'The global straddler of the art world', *New York Times*, 19 April. www.nytimes.com, accessed 7 April 2007.

King, A.D. (2004) *Spaces of Global Cultures: Architecture, Urbanism, Identity*. London: Spon.

Kirwan-Taylor, H. (2004) 'Hands off my gherkin', *Evening Standard Magazine*, 26 November, pp. 27–30.

Klingmann, A. (2007) *Brandscapes: Architecture in the Experience Economy*. Cambridge MA: MIT Press.

Kloosterman, R. and Stegmeijer, E. (2005) 'Delirious Rotterdam? The formation of an innovative cluster of architectural firms', in R.A. Boschma and R.C. Kloosterman (eds), *Learning from Clusters: A Critical Assessment from an Economic–Geographical Perspective*. Dordrecht: Springer/Geojournal Library.

Knox, P.L. (1987) 'The social production of the built environment: architects, architecture and the post-modern city', *Progress in Human Geography* 11: 354–77.

Knox, P.L. and Taylor, P.J. (2005) 'Toward a geography of the globalization of architecture office networks', *Journal of Architectural Education* 58(3): 23–32.

Knutt, E. (2001) 'The king is dead, long live the king', *World Architecture*, May 2001. www.world-architecture.com, accessed 1 August 2003.

Kohn, A.E. (2004) 'Running the architectural marathon', in *Inside the Minds: the Business of Architecture*. Boston MA: Aspatore Books, pp. 9–31.

Koolhaas, R. (1996) 'Architecture and Globalization', in W.S. Saunders *et al.* (eds), *Reflections on Architectural Practices in the Nineties*. New York: Princeton Architectural Press, pp. 232–9.

—— (2002a) 'Junkspace', *October* 100, Spring: 175–90.

—— (2002b) 'Junkspace', in Chung, C.J. (ed.) *The Harvard Design School Guide to Shopping*. Cologne: Taschen, pp. 408–21.

—— (2003) Guest editorial, *Wired* 11 (6) June. www.wired.com/wired/archive/11.06/newworld_pr.html, accessed 29 January 2006.

—— (2004) 'Junkspace', in AMO/OMA, *Content*. Cologne: Taschen, pp. 162–71.

—— (2005) 'Interview with Rem Koolhaas' by Ma Weidong. *A + U (Architecture and Urbanism): CCTV by OMA* (Special Issue), July: 10–18.

Koolhaas, R. and AMO (2007) *The Gulf*. Baden: Lars Müller.

Koolhaas, R., and Harvard Project on the City (2001) 'Lagos', in R. Koolhaas and Harvard Project on the City, S. Boeri and Multiplicity, S. Kwinter, N. Tazi and H.U. Obrist, *Mutations*. Bordeaux: Arc en rêve centre d'architecture, Barcelona: ACTAR, pp. 650–720.

Kusno, A. (2000) *Behind the Postcolonial: Architecture, urban space and political cultures in Indonesia*. London: Routledge.

—— (2002) 'Architecture after nationalism: political imaginings of Southeast Asian architects', in T. Bunnell, L. Drummond and K.C. Ho (eds), *Critical Reflections on Cities in Southeast Asia*. Tokyo: Brill, pp. 124–49.

Lacy, B.N. (1999) 'The Pritzker Architecture Prize: the First Twenty Years', in M. Thorne (ed.), *The Pritzker Architecture Prize: the First Twenty Years*. Chicago: Art Institute of Chicago/New York: Harry N. Abrams, pp. 20–5.

Lagueux, M. (2004) 'Ethics versus aesthetics in architecture', *The Philosophical Forum* XXXV(2): 117–33.

Larson, M.S. (1993) *Behind the Postmodern Façade: Architectural Change in Late Twentieth-Century America*. Berkeley: University of California Press.

Latour, B. (1987) *Science in Action: How to Follow Scientists and Engineers Through Society*. Cambridge MA: Harvard University Press.

Law, J. and Hetherington, K. (2000) 'Materialities, spatialities, globalities', in J.R. Bryson, P.W. Daniels, N. Henry and J. Pollard (eds), *Knowledge, Space, Economy*. London: Routledge, pp. 34–49.

Leftly, M. (2002) 'Aedas staff doubles after merger', *Building* 27. accessed via www.-world-architecture.com, 23 October, 2003.

Leonard, M. (2004) 'Power housing', *Financial Times*, 3 March. www.factiva.com, accessed 5 April 2005.

Levine, M.P., Miller, K. and Taylor, W. (2004) 'Introduction: Ethics and Architecture', *The Philosophical Forum* XXXV(2): 103–15.

Levinson, N. (2004) 'Future present: a new generation of Chinese architects is changing the rules of the game', *Architectural Record* 3: 74–6.

Li Yao (2005) 'Collaboration', *A + U (Architecture and Urbanism): CCTV by OMA*. (Special Issue) July: 194.

Libeskind, D. (2001) *Daniel Libeskind: the Space of Encounter*. New York: Universe Publishing.

—— (2004) *Breaking Ground: An Immigrant's Journey from Poland to Ground Zero*. New York: Riverhead.

Lin, N. (2001) 'Architecture: Shenzhen', in C.J. Chung, J. Inaba, R. Koolhaas, and S.T. Leong (eds), *Great Leap Forward: Harvard Design School Project on the City*, pp. 156–263.

Loeffler, J.C. (1998) *The Architecture of Diplomacy: Building America's Embassies*. New York: Princeton Architectural Press.

Lowendahl, B. (2000) *Strategic management of Professional Service Firms*. Copenhagen: Copenhagen Business School Press.

Lubow, A. (2000) 'Rem Koolhaas builds', *New York Times Magazine*, 9 July. www.nytimes.com, accessed 15 April 2004.

—— (2006) 'The China Syndrome', *New York Times Magazine*, 21 May. www.nytimes.com, accessed 9 November 2007.

Luna, I. (2006) 'Structural contradictions', in I. Luna with T. Tsang (eds), *On the Edge: Ten Architects from China*. New York: Rizzoli, pp. 27–34.

Lury, C. (2005) '"Contemplating a self-portrait as a pharmacist": a Trade Mark Style of Doing Art and Science', *Theory, Culture and Society* 22(1): 93–110.

Luscombe, B. (1996) 'Making a splash', *Time*, 8 April. www.time.com, accessed 17 December 2006.

McDonald, P. (2005) *The Star System: Hollywood's Production of Popular Identities*. London: Wallflower Press.

McGetrick, B. (2004) 'Editor's letter', in AMO/OMA, *Content*. Cologne: Taschen, p. 16.

McKee, B. (1996) 'SOM retrenches', *Architectural Record* 85 (5), 1 May. www.factiva.com, accessed 29 April 2005.

McMahon, B. (2005) 'Italy's architects in revolt against superstar invaders', *The Guardian*, 8 September, p. 11.

McNeill, D. (2005) 'In search of the global architect: the case of Norman Foster (and Partners)', *International Journal of Urban and Regional Research* 29(3): 501–15.

—— (2007) 'Office buildings and the signature architect: Piano and Foster in Sydney', *Environment and Planning A* 39: 487–501.

*Marketer* (2002) Eugene Kohn interviewed by Sally Handley (newsletter of the Society for Marketing Professional Services) 21(2) April 2002: 4–7, 16.

Malkin, E. (2007) 'A tower fight, but just what borough is this?', *New York Times*, 20 September. www.nytimes.com, accessed 9 November 2007.

Mattelart, A. (1979) *Multinational Corporations and the Control of Culture*. Brighton: Harvester Press.

Melchert Saguas Presas, L. (2005) *Transnational Buildings in Local Environments*. Aldershot: Ashgate.

Melvin, J. (2001) 'High-tech knights', in J. Chance and T. Schmiedeknecht (eds), *Fame and Architecture. Architectural Design*. 71(4): 38–41.

Metcalf, A. and Van der Wal, M. (2001) *Aurora Place Renzo Piano Sydney*. Sydney: Watermark.

Middleton, M. (1967) *Group Practice in Design*. New York: George Braziller.

Miller, R. (1996) *Here's the Deal: the Buying and Selling of a Great American City*. New York: Knopf.

Mitchell, W.J. (2003) *Me++: The Cyborg Self and the Networked City*. Cambridge MA: MIT Press.

Moneo, R. (2004) *Theoretical Anxiety and Design Strategies in the Work of Eight Contemporary Architects*. Cambridge MA: MIT Press.

Moore, R. (2002) 'Norman's conquest', *Prospect*, March: 52–6.

Mornement, A. (2000) 'The world architects', *World Architecture*, June 2000. www.world-architecture.com.

Murray, P. (2004) *The Saga of Sydney Opera House*. London: Spon.

Muschamp, H. (1997) 'The miracle in Bilbao', *New York Times*, 7 September. http://query.nytimes.com/gst/fullpage.html?res=9E07E6D61630F934A3575AC0A9 61958260, accessed 9 November 2007.

—— (2003) 'Courtside seats in an urban garden', *New York Times*, 11 December, nytimes.com, accessed 27 January 2007.

NAi (2003) *What is OMA? Considering Rem Koolhaas and the Office for Metropolitan Architecture*. Rotterdam: NAi Publishers.

Nance, K. (2006) 'Building on tradition', *Chicago Sun-Times*, 24 September. www.suntimes.com/entertainment/nance/68465,SHO-Sunday-som24.article, accessed 23 November 2007.

Nasar, J.L. (1999) *Design by Competition: Making Design Competition Work*. Cambridge: Cambridge University Press.

Nasr, J. and Volait, M. (eds) (2003) *Urbanism: Imported or Exported? Native aspirations and foreign plans*. Chichester: Wiley-Academy.

*New York Times* (2006a) 'Dubai: workers riot at tallest skyscraper project', *New York Times*, 23 March. www.nytimes.com.

—— (2006b) 'In Dubai, an outcry from Asians for workplace rights', *New York Times*, 26 March. www.nytimes.com.

—— (2006c) 'US sets up a perch in Dubai to keep an eye on Iran', *New York Times*, 20 November. www.nytimes.com.

Niesewand, N. (2008) 'Grand designs', *Vogue (UK)* January: 138–45, 176.

Nimmo, A. (2004) 'Foster and Partners come to the Antipodes', Interview with David Nelson. *Architecture Australia* July/August. www.archmedia.com.au/aa/aaprintissue. php?issueid=200407&article=17, accessed 7 February 2005.

Nobel, P. (2003) 'The house that Bilbao didn't build', *New York Times*, 20 April www.nytimes.com, accessed 9 November 2007.

—— (2005) *Sixteen Acres: the Rebuilding of the World Trade Center Site*. London: Granta.

Nussaume, Y. and Mosiniak, M. (2005) *Construire en Chine*. Paris: Moniteur.

Nye, D.E. (1996) *American Technological Sublime*. Cambridge MA: MIT Press.

O'Neill, P. and Gibson-Graham, J.K. (1999) 'Enterprise discourse and executive talk: stories that destabilize the company', *Transactions of the Institute of British Geographers* 24: 11–22.

O'Neill, P. and McGuirk, P. (2003) 'Reconfiguring the CBD: work and discourses of design in Sydney's office space', *Urban Studies*. 40(9): 1751–67.

Ockman, J. (1995) 'SOM 1984–1994', in S. Dobney (ed.), *SOM: Selected and Current Works*. Mulgrave: Images, second edition, pp. 9–15.

—— (2001) 'Midtown Manhattan at Midcentury: Lever House and the International Style in the City', in P. Madsen and R. Plunz (eds), *The Urban Lifeworld: Formation, Perception, Representation*. London: Routledge, pp. 177–203.

—— (2004) 'New politics of the spectacle: "Bilbao" and the global imagination', in D.M. Lasansky and B. McLaren (eds), *Architecture and Tourism: Perception, Performance and Place*. Oxford: Berg, pp. 227–39.

—— (2005) 'Bestrode the world like a colossus: the architect as tourist', in J. Ockman and S. Frausto (eds), *Architourism: Authentic, Escapist, Exotic, Spectacular*. Munich: Prestel, pp. 158–85.

Ockman, J. and S. Frausto (2005) *Architourism: Authentic, Escapist, Exotic, Spectacular*. Munich: Prestel.

Oder, N. (2006) '*The New York Times* and Forest City Ratner's Atlantic Yards: High-rises and low standards'. http://dddb.net/documents/times/TimesReport.pdf, accessed 26 January 2007.

Olds, K. (2001) *Globalization and Urban Change: Capital, Culture, and Pacific Rim Mega-Projects*. Oxford: Oxford University Press.

Oltmanns, L. (2002) Interview, in *A + U (Tokyo)* 11(386): 31–2.

OMA, Koolhaas, R. and Mau, B. (1995) *S, M, L, XL*. Cologne: Taschen.

Ourossoff, N. (2006) 'Skyline for sale', *New York Times*, 4 June. www.nytimes.com, accessed 26 January 2007.

—— (2007) 'A vision in the desert', *New York Times*, 4 February. www.nytimes.com, accessed 5 April 2007.

Owings, N.A. (1973) *The Spaces in Between: An Architect's Journey*. Boston, MA: Houghton Mifflin.

Pascoe, D. (2001) *Airspaces*. London: Reaktion.

Pearman, H. (2002) *Contemporary World Architecture*. London: Phaidon.

Pearson, A. (2003) 'Good morning, Vietnam', *Building* 35. www.world-architecture.com, accessed 17 November 2003.

Peck, J. (2005) 'Struggling with the creative class', *International Journal of Urban and Regional Research* 29(4): 740–70.

Pells, R. (1997) *Not Like Us: How Europeans Have Loved, Hated and Transformed American Culture Since World War II*. New York: Basic Books.

Pfeifer, S. (2007) 'Foster buys out employees prior to sale', *Sunday Telegraph*, 19 March. www.telegraph.co.uk, accessed 6 November 2007.

Piano, R. (1997) *The Renzo Piano Logbook*. London: Thames and Hudson.

—— (2004) *On Tour with Renzo Piano*. London: Phaidon.

Plaza, B. (1999) 'The Guggenheim-Bilbao museum effect: a reply to María V. Gómez's "Reflective images: the case of urban regeneration in Glasgow and Bilbao"'. *International Journal of Urban and Regional Research*, 23: 589–92.

—— (2006) 'The return on investment of the Guggenheim Museum Bilbao', *International Journal of Urban and Regional Research* 30(2): 452–67.

Pogrebin, R. (2006) 'Joshua Prince-Ramus leaving Koolhaas's OMA to start new architecture firm', *New York Times*, 14 May. www.nytimes.com, accessed 9 November 2007.

Powell, K. (2000) 'Norman Foster's triumph', in D. Jenkins (ed.), *On Foster ... Foster On*. Munich: Prestel, pp. 439–48.

—— (2003) *KPF: Vision and Process: Europe 1990–2002*. Basel: Birkhäuser.

Prak, N.L. (1984) *Architects: the Noted and the Ignored*. Chichester: John Wiley.

Pridmore, J. (2007) 'A new order', *chicagomag.com*, February. www.chicagomag.com, accessed 25 March 2007.

Quantrill, M. (1999) *The Norman Foster Studio: Consistency Through Diversity*. London: Spon.

Rattenbury, K. (2004) 'Architecture books', *Icon*, September. www.icon-magazine.co.uk/issues/015/essay_text.htm, accessed 28 February 2005.

Rayner, J. (2006) 'How the world's top chefs went global', *Observer Food Magazine*, May, pp. 41–7.

*Real Estate Weekly* (2002) 'Eugene Kohn appointed executive fellow of university program', 31 July. www.allbusiness.com/periodicals/article/232856–1.html, accessed 3 June 2006.

Rein, I., Kotler, P. and Stoller, M. (1997) *High Visibility: the Making and Marketing of Professionals into Celebrities*. Lincolnwood (Chicago): NTC Business Books.

Riding, A. (2007) 'The industry of art goes global', *New York Times*, 28 March. www.nytimes.com, accessed 5 April 2007.

Rimmer, P.J. (1991) 'The global intelligence corps and world cities: engineering consultancies on the move', in P.W. Daniels (ed.), *Services and Metropolitan Development: International Perspectives*. London: Routledge, pp. 66–106.

Risen, C. (2003) 'Still delirious: has Koolhaas abandoned city?', *New York Observer*, 7 September. www.observer.com/node/48013, accessed 9 November 2007.

Ritzer, G. (1996) *The McDonaldization of Society*. Revised edition. Thousand Oaks, CA: Pine Forge.

Roberts, S. (2003) 'Global strategic vision: managing the world', in R.W. Perry and B. Maurer (eds), *Globalization under Construction: Governmentality, Law and Identity*. Minneapolis: University of Minnesota Press, pp. 1–37.

Robinson, J. (2002) 'Global and world cities: a view from off the map', *International Journal of Urban and Regional Research* 26(3): 531–54.

Rogers, R. (1997) *Cities for a Small Planet*. P. Gumuchdjian (ed.) London: Faber and Faber.

Rose, S. (2002) 'The man who would be king', *The Guardian* http://education.guardian.co.uk, accessed 4 March 2003.

Ross, C. (1996) 'The politics of identity: party competition in the Basque Country', *International Journal of Iberian Studies* 9: 98–109.

—— (1997) *Contemporary Spain: A Handbook*. London: Arnold.

Rowe, P.G. (1996) 'Design in an increasingly small world', in W.S. Saunders *et al.* (eds), *Reflections on Architectural Practices in the Nineties*. New York: Princeton Architectural Press, pp. 220–30.

Rowe, P.G. and Seng Kuan (2004) *Architectural Encounters with Essence and Form in Modern China*. Cambridge MA: MIT Press.

Ryan, N. (2007) 'Prada and the art of patronage', *Fashion Theory* 11(1): 7–24.

Sabbagh, K. (1991) *Skyscraper: the Making of a Building*. London: Penguin.

—— (2001) *Power into Art: the Making of Tate Modern*. London: Penguin.

Saint, A. (1983) *The Image of the Architect*. New Haven: Yale University Press.

Sandercock, L. (1998) *Towards Cosmopolis: Planning for Multicultural Cities*. Hoboken, NJ: John Wiley & Sons.

Sato, C. (1992) 'Working with Foster Associates', in C. Davies and I. Lambot (eds), *Century Tower: Foster Associates Build in Japan*. Chiddingfold, Surrey: Watermark, 133–5.

Saunders, W.S. (ed., 1996) *Reflections on Architectural Practices in the Nineties*. New York: Princeton Architectural Press.

Scheeren, O. (2003) 'A question of position' (interview, 20 September 2003), in European Association of Architectural Eduction, 'News Sheet' 68, February 2004, pp. 19–28. www.eaae.be/eaae2/documents/news%20sheets/Ns_February_2004.pdf, accessed 16 February 2006.

—— (2005) 'Made in China', *A + U (Architecture and Urbanism): CCTV by OMA*. (Special Issue) July: 4–5.

Schiller, H.I. (1976) *Communications and Cultural Domination*. New York: M.E. Sharpe.

Schnair, G. (2004) 'New work in China: A Work in Progress', *Urban Land Asia* December: 22–5, 39.

Schwarzer, M. (2005) 'Architecture and mass tourism', in J. Ockman and S. Frausto (eds), *Architourism: Authentic, Escapist, Exotic, Spectacular*. Munich: Prestel, pp. 12–33.

Scott Brown, D. (1989) 'Room at the top? Sexism and the star system in architecture', in E.P. Berkeley (ed.), *Architecture: a Place for Women*. Washington: Smithsonian Institute Press, pp. 237–46.

Seddon, E. (2001) 'Meet our man in London, Paris, New York...', *Building* 12. www.world-architecture.com, accessed 17 November 2003.

Seidler, H. (2003) *The Grand Tour: Travelling the World with an Architect's Eye*. Cologne: Taschen.

Sherwood, S. (2005) 'The Oz of the Middle East', *New York Times*, 8 May, www.nytimes.com.

Shore, C. (2000) *Building Europe: the Cultural Politics of European Integration*. London: Routledge.

Shuttleworth, K. (2003) 'The tip of an iceberg', letter to *Building* 5 (2003). www.world-architecture.com.

Sigler, J. (2000) Interview with Rem Koolhaas (RK) conducted by Jennifer Sigler (JS). www.indexmagazine.com/interviews/rem_koolhaas.shtml, accessed 17 February 2006.

Sinclair, K. (2005) *Making Connections: Aedas architects in Asia.* Published by Aedas.

Sincoff, J. (1998) Interviewed by Lee Slade, *Marketer* 18(2): 4–7, 13, 16. www.smps.org/marketer/marketerarch/498mrkter.pdf, accessed 4 December 2007.

Sklair, L. (2005) 'The transnational capitalist class and contemporary architecture in globalizing cities', *International Journal of Urban and Regional Research* 29(3): 485–500.

Somol, R.E. (1999) 'Dummy text, or the diagrammatic basis of contemporary architecture', in P. Eisenman (ed.), *Diagram Diaries.* New York.

Sorkin, M. (1994) 'SOM Story' (article first published in 1984), in *Exquisite Corpse: Writings on Buildings.* London: Verso, pp. 80–1.

—— (2002) 'Brand aid', *Harvard Design Magazine* 17: 4–9.

Spring, M. (2007) ' "Why would I stop" ', *Building* 16 November: 46–9.

Steele, J. (1997) *Architecture Today.* London: Phaidon.

Stephens, S. (2006) 'Crowding the marquee', *Architectural Record* 6: 98–104.

Stern, R.M., Fishman, D. and Tilove, J. (2006) *New York 2000: Architecture and Urbanism between the Bicentennial and the Millennium.* New York: Monacelli Press.

Studwell, J. (2003) *The China Dream: The Elusive Quest for the Greatest Untapped Market on Earth.* London: Profile.

Sudjic, D. (2001) 'Save Spitalfields from market forces', *Observer*, 15 July. www.factiva.com, accessed 27 June, 2005.

—— (2004) 'Actually, that was my gherkin...', *The Observer*, 1 February. www.arts.guardian.co.uk/features/story/0,,1137137,00.html, accessed 11 March 2008.

—— (2005a) text box in feature article 'On Criticism', *The Architect's Newspaper*, 16 November: 20.

—— (2005b) *The Edifice Complex: How the Rich and Powerful Shape the World.* London: Allen Lane.

Tellitu, A., Esteban, I. and González Carrera, J.A. (1997) *El Milagro Guggenheim: Una Ilusión de Alto Riesgo.* Bilbao: Diario El Correo.

Thorncroft, T. (1998) 'The art of making money', *Financial Times*, 6 June, p. 7.

Thrift, N. (2005) *Knowing Capitalism.* London: Sage.

Thrift, N. and French, S. (2002) 'The automatic production of space', *Transactions of the Institute of British Geographers* 27: 309–35.

Till, K. (2005) *The New Berlin: Memory, Politics, Place.* Minneapolis: University of Minnesota Press.

Timmons, H. (2006) 'Oil's a means, not an end, at Dubai Inc.', *New York Times*, 17 February 2006. www.nytimes.com, accessed 9 December 2007.

Tombesi, P., Dave, B. and Scriver, P. (2003) 'Routine production or symbolic analysis? India and the globalisation of architectural services', *The Journal of Architecture* 8: 63–94.

Twitchell, J.B. (2004) *Branded Nation: the Making of Megachurch, College Inc., and Museumworld.* New York: Simon and Schuster.

Tzonis, A., Lefaivre, L. and Stagno, B. (eds) (2001) *Tropical Architecture: Critical Regionalism in the Age of Globalization.* Chichester: Wiley-Academy.

Urry, J. (2002) 'Mobility and proximity', *Sociology* 36(2): 255–74.

—— (2003) 'Social networks, travel and talk', *British Journal of Sociology* 54(2): 155–75.

—— (2004) 'Connections', *Environment and Planning D: Society and Space* 22: 27–37.

Vidler, A. (2000) 'Diagrams of diagrams: architectural abstraction and modern representation', *Representations* 72: 1–20.

Vogel, C. (2005) 'Guggenheim loses top donor in rift on spending and vision', *New York Times*, 20 January. www.nytimes.com, accessed 9 November 2007.

Wang, W. (2001) *SOM Journal 1*. Ostfildern-Ruit: Hatje Cantz Verlag.
—— (2003) *SOM Journal 2*. Ostfildern-Ruit: Hatje Cantz Verlag.
—— (2004) *SOM Journal 3*. Ostfildern-Ruit: Hatje Cantz Verlag.
Ward, J. (2001) 'The outsider', *Architecture* 90 (4), 1 April: 60. www.factiva.com, accessed 15 April 2005.
Wasserman, B., Sullivan, P. and Palermo, G. (2000) *Ethics and the Practice of Architecture*. New York: Wiley.
Webster, J. (1998) 'My fault is that I am an independent artist, not a carpet', *Independent on Sunday*, 16 August, culture supplement, p. 3.
Williams, J.J. (2006) 'Academostars: name recognition', in P.D. Marshall (ed.), *The Celebrity Culture Reader*. New York: Routledge, pp. 371–88. [First published in *The Minnesota Review* 52–4, fall 2001.].
Williams, S. (1989) *Hongkong Bank: the Building of Norman Foster's Masterpiece*. London: Jonathan Cape.
Wiseman, C. (1990) *I.M. Pei: a Profile in American Architecture*. New York: Harry N. Abrams.
*World Architecture* (1999) 'Ch-ch-ch-ch-changes', July–August. www.world-architecture.com, accessed 23 October 2003.
Wu, F. (2000) 'The global and local dimensions of place-making: remaking Shanghai as a world city', *Urban Studies* 37(8): 1359–77.
—— (2004) 'Transplanting cityscapes: the use of imagined globalisation in housing commodification in Beijing', *Area* 36(3): 227–34.
Xue, C.Q.L. (2006) *Building a Revolution: Chinese Architecture since 1980*. Hong Kong: Hong Kong University Press.
Yang, A. (2004) 'The new, true spirit', *The Architect's Newspaper*, 19 October, p. 17. www.archpaper.com/feature_articles/true_new_spirit.html, accessed 21 November 2007.
Young, E. (2003) 'Corporate culture change', *RIBA Journal*, June. www.world-architecture.com.
Zalewski, D. (2005) 'Intelligent design: Can Rem Koolhaas kill the skyscraper?', *The New Yorker*, 14 March, pp. 110–25.
Zucker, G. (2006) 'Interview with FOA's Alejandro Zaera-Polo', *32*. www.32bny.org/past/issue_fivesix/articles/zaerapolo.html, accessed 23 May 2006.
Zukin, S. (1991) *Landscapes of Power: From Detroit to Disney World*. Berkeley: University of California Press.
Zulaika, J. (1997) *Crónica de una Seducción: El Museo Guggenheim Bilbao*. Madrid: Nerea.

# Index